Abortion Regret

Abortion Regret

The New Attack on Reproductive Freedom

J. Shoshanna Ehrlich and Alesha E. Doan

PRAEGER™

An Imprint of ABC-CLIO, LLC
Santa Barbara, California • Denver, Colorado

Library of Congress Cataloging in Publication Control Number: 2018054241 (print)

ISBN: 978-1-4408-3984-9 (print)
    978-1-4408-3985-6 (ebook)

23 22 21 20 19   1 2 3 4 5

This book is also available as an eBook.

Praeger
An Imprint of ABC-CLIO, LLC

ABC-CLIO, LLC
147 Castilian Drive
Santa Barbara, California 93117
www.abc-clio.com

This book is printed on acid-free paper ∞

Manufactured in the United States of America

For Liliana Monique
May you grow up in a world where we
learn to value two simultaneous truths—
the intrinsic beauty of choice and life.
A. E. D.

For Alan and Emma and my parents—
my heart and center always.
J. S. E.

Contents

Preface and Acknowledgments

When we made the decision to coauthor this book, we realized that we were taking a huge chance as we had never met one another face-to-face. Through a series of conversations and email communications regarding a shared research interest, we realized that we were both investigating the phenomena of abortion regret from different perspectives, drawing upon our backgrounds in law, policy, gender studies, and political science. Since committing to this undertaking, we have worked seamlessly together as fully coequal authors bringing our shared knowledge, perspectives, and deep feminist commitments to our investigation of how the abortion regret framing has not only been deployed to limit access to abortion but has also been used to reinscribe conventional gender norms culturally and institutionally.

Although a growing number of scholars are writing about the emergence of the abortion regret narrative onto the antiabortion stage, we believed that the time had come for an interdisciplinary book on the subject given its growing prominence in the antiabortion movement. As we pooled the research we had each already done, we came to understand the full spectra of abortion regret, which, as this book demonstrates, encompasses far more than the latest rhetorical turn used to flame the conflict over abortion. Our research led us to conceptualize abortion regret as a unifying strategy for the antiabortion movement, which it has adeptly wielded to help usher in restrictive legislation while raising the level of stigma that continues to surround women's reproductive decision making, most acutely around pregnancy termination. Throughout this book, we trace the development of the abortion regret narrative from its 19th-century roots through its strategic deployment in the political and legal arenas. In tandem, we deconstruct the narrow construction of gender and abortion experiences that are embedded within this expansive narrative, and challenge the positioning of it as an uncontested worldview that has been institutionally legitimized through hundreds of antiabortion policies.

The trajectory of the book moves from the 19th century to the present. In tracing the arc of the regret narrative, we seek to show that efforts to regulate or ban abortion have never simply been about protecting unborn life. Rather, they have also been aimed at managing women's bodies ostensibly for their own good while preserving the state's power to encode gender and racialized norms into law. We argue that these socially constructed composites of women have carried 19th-century proscriptive norms forward into the contemporary regret narrative. These initially surfaced in the sanctified space of the nation's crisis pregnancy centers (CPCs) and have now become embedded in hundreds of laws that restrict access to abortion. To tell this story, we draw on several sources of data, including in-depth interviews, textual analysis of primary sources, and content analyses, all of which are detailed in the methods appendix.

We also want to highlight a few important considerations that directly reflect the complexity of our topic. First, the book makes liberal use of interviews with people working or volunteering in CPCs, and it also draws upon a variety of other sources in which women narrate their abortion regret stories. We do not seek to discredit their individual experiences of postabortion pain, or the certitude or sincerity of their beliefs. In particular, the book is not intended to challenge the religious convictions of those who believe that abortion disrupts God's gendered order of creation and thus leads inevitably to regret. Rather, our concern is with the concerted effort of abortion opponents to elevate a culturally relative belief structure into an objective and universalizing statement of truth and to encode this highly personal view into law to manage women's reproductive bodies. In short, our intent here is to investigate how women's experiential knowledge of abortion regret has been cultivated into a political strategy that seeks to limit access to abortion by purportedly speaking on behalf of all women, regardless of the accuracy of this story. Accordingly, our deconstruction and critique of the abortion regret narrative takes aim at its strategic elevation into a universal truth tilled from women who are predisposed to opposing abortion.

We also wish to note our use of language—as the choice of words when talking about abortion is often highly freighted. First, when discussing groups or individuals who are opposed to abortion, our preferred term is *antiabortion;* however, at times, we do use the term *pro-life* to clearly and accurately convey expressed ideas and beliefs. Second, although we recognize that not all people seeking abortions are or identify as women, and that this can add significant obstacles when seeking to access reproductive health services, we do use the term *woman/women* throughout most of the book. Our intent is not to discount these well-documented barriers. Rather, it is to highlight the ways in which the regret narrative is deeply gendered and grounded in a binary construction of gender roles and norms. As we argue in this book, its emergence onto the larger social, political, and legal arenas is in fact meant to reinscribe traditional gender norms, particularly those that narrowly define women as mothers. Within this context, abortion is viewed as an inherently dangerous act precisely because it dismantles the core of female identity—namely, motherhood.

In closing, we want to acknowledge that this book draws upon material that has been previously published as follows: Alesha E. Doan and J. Shoshanna Ehrlich, "'Teaching Morality by Teaching Science': Religiosity and Abortion Regret," in *Reproductive Ethics: New Challenges and Conversations,* edited by Lisa Campo-Engelstein and Paul Burcher (New York: Springer International, 2017), 117–35; J. Shoshanna Ehrlich, "'Like a Withered Tree Stripped of Its Branches': What the *Roe* Court Missed and Why It Matters," *Columbia Journal of Gender & Law* 35 no. 2 (2018): 175–227; Alesha E. Doan, Carolina Costa Candal, and Steven Sylvester, "'We Are the Visible Proof': Legitimizing Abortion Regret Misinformation through Activists' Experiential Knowledge," *Law & Policy,* 2018 40 no. 1 (2018): 33–56.

We also want to express our gratitude to the many people who helped to bring this book to fruition. We start with Catherine M. Lafuente from Praeger, who enthusiastically supported this project from start to finish. Her patience, sense of humor, and ever quick responses to our many inquiries are greatly appreciated.

We are also indebted to an outstanding group of undergraduate and graduate students from the University of Kansas and the University of Massachusetts Boston, and we note with pleasure that several have graduated into colleagues over the course of this project. Elise Higgins rises to the top of our gratitude list. We are immensely indebted to her for the time, effort, and unfailing optimism she brought to this project. We also want to thank Destina Agar, Carolina Costa Candal, Hui Chen, Gabby Fiore, Hella Dijsselbloem Giron, Julieth Jaramillo-Rodriguez, Theresa Kelleher-Palmarin, Jacob Longaker, Yeon Joo Kim, Tom Ringenberg, Benjamin Rogers, and Steven Sylvester for the time and effort they spent collecting data and literature for this project. The book has greatly benefitted from their collective contributions.

On a personal note, we would like to thank our families. Tom Farrell and Spencer Doan—you have been (and always will be) the best part of my day. And to Alan Stoskopf and Emma Stoskopf-Ehrlich—there are no words big enough to capture my love and my gratitude.

ONE

"Making Their Bodies Dens of Murder": The Physicians' 19th-Century Campaign to Criminalize Abortion

In 1839, in the opening lecture to medical students at the University of Pennsylvania, Dr. Hugh L. Hodge, a professor of obstetrics, instructed his audience that as the *"physical guardians* of women and their offspring,"[1] medical men had a duty to prevent women from "voluntarily destroy[ing] their progeny," whom, he declared, were *"living beings"* from the moment of conception forward.[2] He accordingly called upon the members of his audience to "wage a war of extermination" against this evil practice.[3] Similarly, in the 1855 opening lecture at Harvard Medical School, Dr. David C. Humphreys Storer, a professor of obstetrics and medical jurisprudence, blamed the increase in uterine diseases on the "fearful influence" of *"unnatural causes"* by which he meant women's growing reliance upon abortion as a means of limiting their number of offspring—an act that he regarded as the moral equivalent of infanticide.[4] He accordingly urged the "upright men of the profession" to "feel and act as one man" to halt the "virtuous mother" from intentionally destroying her offspring.[5]*

---

* When Storer's Introductory Lecture was first published, the section relating to abortion was omitted due to the objections of at least one prominent member of the Harvard faculty. It was subsequently published 17 years later in the *Journal of the Gynecological*

Deploying a highly gendered narrative, both Hodge and Storer made clear that this masculine project of repair was necessary to halt women from engaging in a practice that they deemed to be "in violation of every *natural* sentiment, and in opposition to the laws of God and man" (italics added).[6] For both men, this natural sentiment—as divinely enjoined—was firmly linked to woman's innate maternalism. Storer thus castigated women who sought to violate God's dictates, which he proclaimed cannot be "broken with impunity" as the "Lawgiver is inexorable," by deliberately avoiding maternity.[7] Exemplifying his disdain for the abortion-minded woman, he reproached the "fashionable young bride" who wished "still to enjoy the immunities of unmarried life—to be as free, as unshackled as ever" and the mother who had learned from others that "woman was born for higher and nobler purposes than the propagation of the species."[8]

Adding gloss to this understanding of woman's true nature, Hodge characterized her as "'the last, best gift of Heaven'" to man.[9] Although couched in the language of praise, Hodge explained that this "admirable arrangement of Providence" fixed woman's subordinate place in the domestic firmament by placing her under the "superintendence" of her "nominal lord" in order that she might properly realize the obligations imposed upon her on account of "the peculiarity of her anatomical and physiological developments."[10]

These early lectures by elite male physicians inspired Dr. David Storer's son, Dr. Horatio Robinson Storer ("Storer"), to launch a national campaign to criminalize abortion. As the younger Storer took up the cause, in addition to reiterating the view that personhood begins at conception, thus making abortion at all stages of pregnancy the equivalent of murder, he also elaborated on these initial claims that women who aborted subverted their maternal nature. He further asserted that as the "physical guardians" of women, the nation's "regular" physicians (meaning those who had been formally educated in the medical arts) had a moral and professional duty to prevent them from interfering with the "holiest duty of [their] sex to bring forth living children."[11] By doing so, doctors would accordingly be able to claim that in seeking to criminalize abortion, they were also engaged in the critical practice of stabilizing the domestic order and protecting women from potential physical and mental ruin—a claim that, as we will see in

---

Society of Boston, which was founded and edited by his son Dr. Horatio Robinson Storer, who launched the physicians' antiabortion crusade (Dyer 2005, 5–6 & 29).

Chapter Four, would be picked up again by the 20th-century proponents of the "pro-woman/pro-life" antiabortion position.

In addition to reflecting a deeply gendered and divinely rooted understanding of women's place in society, the physicians' arguments for why the state needed to step in and manage their bodies were also laced with racialized and nativist sentiments. As they repeatedly and fearfully explained, abortion was becoming increasingly common among the "better-sort" of married woman, while those at the lower end of the social and economic strata were continuing to procreate at seemingly alarming rates. As Reva Siegel succinctly put it, "the doctors who advocated criminalizing abortion quite openly argued that regulating women's reproductive conduct was necessary, not merely to protect fetal life, but also to ensure women's performance of marital and maternal obligations and to preserve the ethnic character of the nation."[12] To this end, the physicians seamlessly interwove assertions regarding the need to rescue the nation from imminent decline if not outright disintegration into their woman-protective claims.

This chapter tells the story of the physicians' campaign to criminalize abortion. To understand the significance of their undertaking, we begin with an overview of the legal and social status of abortion prior to the inception of their activism on this issue. From there, we trace the mobilizing efforts of Horatio Storer as he engaged the newly emergent American Medical Association in a national effort to persuade both state lawmakers and the public that ending the scourge of abortion was an urgent public project— as well as one that served to enhance the status of elite doctors. Although woman's rights activists of the time did not directly challenge the physicians' legal position on abortion, they actively deployed a counternarrative that located the need for abortion in the social realities of women's marital lives—a reality that demanded submission to the sexual wants of their husbands.

ABORTION IN 19TH-CENTURY AMERICA

Prior to 1821, when the state of Connecticut enacted a law making it a crime to provide a woman who was "quick with child" with a "deadly poison" to induce a miscarriage, no American legislative body had addressed the issue of abortion.[13] Rather, the legal status of abortion was based on English common-law principles.

Under the common law, an abortion that was performed prior to "quickening," which is when a pregnant woman first feels fetal movement (typically sometime between the fourth and six month of pregnancy), was not considered to be a crime. Until then, the fetus was not thought to have an identity that was separate and apart from the pregnant woman. After quickening, abortion could be punished as a crime. However, it was not considered to be the equivalent of murder and was punishable as a misdemeanor rather than as a more serious felony offense.† Only the person performing the abortion could be indicted under the common law—the pregnant woman was not considered a party to the crime.

When Connecticut passed the nation's first criminal abortion law, the measure was part of an omnibus criminal reform statute that was inserted between a provision governing the "intent to kill or rob" and one addressing the "secret delivery of a bastard child."[14] As James C. Mohr explains, the Connecticut law and other similar measures that were passed in a number of states between 1821 and 1841 were not enacted in response to a "substantial public outcry for anti-abortion activity" and no "legislator took a political stand on abortion . . . [or] cast a recorded vote for or against abortion as a question by itself."[15] Rather, as he explains, these laws were aimed at regulating the *practice* of abortion, as the methods used to induce a miscarriage, such as toxic poisons, often killed the pregnant woman along with the fetus. In short, they were aimed at "regulating the activities of apothecaries and physicians" rather than at "dissuading women from seeking abortions."[16]

Reinforcing Mohr's position, in an early report aimed at mobilizing his colleagues to push for laws banning abortion, Storer excoriated the weakness of the current legal regime, which he argued did nothing to protect fetal life. As he explains: *"By the Common Law and many of our State Codes, foetal life, per se, is almost wholly ignored and its destruction unpunished;* abortion in every case being considered an offense mainly against the mother, and as such, unless fatal to her, a mere misdemeanor, or wholly disregarded."[17] He thus concluded "[i]n a word, then, in the sight of the common law, and in most cases of the statutory law, the crime of abortion, properly considered does not exist."[18]

At this historic juncture, abortion was generally associated with the errant behavior of unmarried women seeking to restore their virtue through erasure of the deed, rather than with, as would soon be the case,

---

† As explained by the Supreme Court in the landmark case of *Roe v. Wade* (see Chapter Two), the historical evidence is not entirely clear regarding the status of post-quickening abortions, and it is possible that abortion at any stage was never "firmly established as a common-law crime." *Roe v. Wade,* 410 U.S. 113, 137 (1973).

gender-subversive matrons who were seeking to avoid their maternal destiny. As Hodge bluntly put it, these unfortunates resorted to abortion to "destroy the fruits of illicit pleasure, under the vain hope of preserving their reputation by this unnatural and guilty sacrifice."[19] Given its association with illicit behavior, as Mohr explains, abortion was generally regarded as a "fundamentally marginal practice" that did not attract much attention unless a woman died or was seriously injured.[20]

By mid-century, however, the abortion rate had started to rise, and regular physicians began reporting on this trend with growing alarm. For example, an influential committee of the American Medical Association reported in 1859 that the decrease in the size of families could only be explained by the "fearfully extended crime" of abortion,[21] while Dr. Andrew Nebinger remarked in an address to the Philadelphia County Medical Society that, "to say to you that criminal abortion is now and has been for a long series of years on the increase . . . is only to express that, which is familiar to everyone who has paid thoughtful attention to the subject . . . So broad and vastly extended is the practice . . . that it may be said to be now . . . prevailing as a great immoral, body and soul defiling epidemic."[22]

Most alarming, however, to the regular physicians who would soon rally to the antiabortion cause, was the fact that the rates were rising among married women who were purposefully seeking to limit the size of their families. Capturing the clear distinction that most physicians drew between the errant maiden and the married woman, in his annual address to the San Francisco Medical Society, Dr. Henry Gibbons explained that "[w]e can appreciate the motives that lead to feticide in females who have slipped from the path of virtue—unjustified and criminal as the act still is. But that married women should follow in the path of the harlot admits not the shade of an excuse or palliation."[23] Or, as Dr. August K. Gardner put it, "for the married shirk, who disregards her divinely-ordained duty, we have nothing but contempt . . . If glittering gems adorn her person, within there is foulness and squalor."[24] Compounding, or perhaps at the root of the horror they felt over the fact that married women were adopting the behavior of the "harlot" who had "slipped from the path of virtue," was the fact that they tended to be "white, Protestant, native-born . . . and of the middle or upper class."[25] In short, the married women who were seeking to control their fertility were from the same social strata as the regular doctors, while women of "inferior" status were continuing to fulfill their maternal obligations. As Mohr bluntly puts it, in mobilizing against abortion "the doctors both used and were influenced by blatant nativism."[26]

THE PHYSICIANS' ANTIABORTION CAMPAIGN

At the 1857 meeting of the Suffolk District Medical Society, Dr. Horatio Storer alerted the Boston physicians in the audience to the alarming frequency of induced abortions among respectable married Protestant women in the city as he observed in his medical practice. Seeking to mobilize his peers to end what he would soon characterize as the "slaughter of countless children now perpetrated in our midst,"[27] he persuaded both the local society and the recently founded American Medical Association (AMA) to establish committees for the purpose of investigating the matter of criminal abortion with a view "toward its general suppression."[28]

At its 1859 annual meeting, the AMA's appointed Committee on Criminal Abortion presented its report (which Storer authored) condemning the "wanton and murderous destruction" of the unborn. In a series of unanimously adopted resolutions, the AMA formally declared it the duty of its members "as physicians, and as good and true men" to "publicly . . . enter an earnest and solemn protest against such unwarrantable destruction of human life" and to "present this subject to the attention of the . . . legislative assemblies . . . with the prayer that the laws by which the crime of procuring abortion . . . may be revised."[29]

Moving forward, the AMA remained firmly committed to the antiabortion cause, and as Mohr writes, "the vigorous efforts of America's regular physicians would prove in the long run to be the single most important factor in altering the legal policies toward abortion in this country."[30] Reflecting their determination, by the end of the century all states had criminalized abortion from the inception of pregnancy, unless a doctor certified that the procedure was necessary to save the life of a pregnant woman.

The logical question, of course, is: What compelled Storer and his colleagues to take up the antiabortion cause? According to Mohr and Luker, authors of classic works on the subject, a key motivating factor was the desire of physicians to upgrade their professional status. In large measure, this concern was prompted by the proliferation of lay healers in the early decades of the 19th century. These included, by way of example, botanic practitioners, natural bonesetters, and homeopaths. Not only did these "irregular healers" increase the competition for patients, but rooted in the democratic and antimonopolistic spirit of the Jacksonian era, they also regarded "the medical profession as a bulwark of privilege, and . . . adopted a position hostile to both its therapeutic tenets and its social aspirations."[31] With some success, they accordingly appealed to state lawmakers to repeal the medical licensing laws that were currently on the books, which they viewed as "an expression of favor rather than competence."[32]

Dispirited by both the challenge to their position and the competition for clients, regular physicians mobilized to consolidate the status of the medical profession on higher and more certain ground. To this end, as Mohr writes, they both sought to "recapture what they considered to be their ancient and rightful place among society's policy makers and servants,"[33] as well as to persuade lawmakers that they were deserving of licensing laws aimed at driving the irregulars out from the practice of medicine. Notably, in this regard, the AMA was founded in 1847 to help spearhead the effort by regular physicians to "improve, professionalize, and ultimately control the practice of medicine in the United States."[34]

According to Luker, the drive for professionalization required that the regular physicians find a way to "distinguish themselves both scientifically and socially from competing practitioners," and they seized upon abortion as the perfect tool for this task.[35] Laying claim to their superior medical training, they denounced quickening as a "mistaken and exploded" marker of the origins of life,[36] and asserted that scientific principles firmly established that "life is manifest as soon as the ovum is impregnated."[37] As Luker explains, the focus on abortion enabled elite doctors to "claim both *moral stature* (as a high-minded, self-regulating group of professionals) and *technical expertise* (derived from their superior training)."[38] In this spirit, as Mohr writes, the antiabortion campaign accordingly offered the medical profession a promising opportunity by which it might "recapture some of the luster of its golden past."[39]

Although Storer and his colleagues may have seized onto antiabortion activism as the ideal platform from which to launch their drive for licensing laws, their objections to the practice were also deep and far-ranging. In addition to their expressed concern for the urgent need to protect prenatal life, they also regarded abortion as a profoundly subversive act. Described by Mohr as among "the most defensive groups in the country on the subject of changing sex roles"[40] and as also actuated by a "blatant nativism,"[41] the antiabortion physicians discursively constructed aborting matrons as threats to established gender and racialized hierarchies.

Laying claim to a manly sense of purpose, they accordingly drew upon normative understandings of woman's divinely ordained place in the universe—as shaped by racial, class, religious, and ethnic considerations—to argue that the abortion decision should be entrusted to their expertise. Their template for reform was thus forged in a paternalistic and racialized code of male moral authority over women's reproductive bodies for their own purported good, the good of the family, and the good of the nation. We now turn to a consideration of the gendered tropes that were woven into their antiabortion arguments, followed by a discussion of the racial and nativist motifs.

A Bold and Manly Appeal: Eradicating The "Fearful Extent of the Evil That Exists in Our Home"

As David C. Reardon, the chief architect of the pro-woman/pro-life anti-abortion strategy would do more than a century later, Storer drew upon his experientially derived knowledge of abortion's purported adverse impact on women to inspire his colleagues to take up the antiabortion cause. Starting with the manly nature of this call to action, their efforts were grounded in a firm belief in the importance of asserting male moral authority over abortion-minded women who forsook their maternal obligations based either on ignorance or more likely on selfish considerations.

Storer characterized the physicians' consultation rooms as confessionals "wherein under the implied pledge of secrecy and inviolate confidence, the most weighty and at times astounding revelations are daily made."[42] In his role as intimate confidant (a role that, as discussed in Chapter Four, Reardon would subsequently also lay claim to), he was a self-described witness to the fearful reality that induced abortion interfered with "all the elements of domestic happiness and . . . the matron's own self-respect," and transforms the marital relationship from a "spiritual union" into a "sensual" one, thus making it akin to "legalized prostitution."[43]

Grounded in this "truth" based on their firsthand knowledge of women's experiences, Storer and his colleagues proclaimed it their duty to rescue errant matrons from their untoward anti-maternalist impulses. As framed, this was not simply a struggle between physicians who happened to be men and their patients who happened to be women; rather, it was a contest born out of a deeply gendered understanding of the social role and place of each in the natural order. Fused together as mutually reinforcing strands, these physicians effectively deployed a binary model of female transgression and male moral responsibility as a catalyst for reform. Expressing the twining of these elemental assumptions, after impressing the importance of the physicians' duty to inform their patients that abortion is "the destruction of human life" upon the members of the Philadelphia County Medical Society, Dr. Andrew Nebinger explained to his colleagues that if "after being properly instructed, they still persevere in importuning us . . . they are not only inviting us to step far, far down from our high position as physicians, . . . *they are offering an indignity to our manhood . . .*" (italics added).[44]

According to the 1859 AMA Report on Criminal Abortion, a doctor's duty toward his female patients was derived from the fact that he was entrusted with the "physical guardianship" of women. Although delineated by the use of the term *physical* to matters of the body, as the following legal definition of the term *guardian* makes clear, guardianships are intrinsically inegalitarian relationships: "[a] guardian is a person lawfully invested with the power, and charged with the duty, of taking care of the person and managing the property and rights of another person, who, for some peculiarity of status, or defect of age, understanding, or self-control, is considered incapable of administering his own affairs."[45]

Reinforcing the conflation of woman's physical body with her mental incapacity, Storer stressed that it was a woman's physiological makeup that rendered her incapable of self-governance: "[i]f each woman were allowed to judge for herself in this matter, her decision upon the abstract question would be too sure to be warped by personal considerations, and those of the moment. Woman's mind is prone to depression, and, indeed, to temporary actual derangement. . . . During the state of gestation the woman is therefore liable to thoughts, convictions even, that at other times she would turn from in disgust or dismay."[46] Anchored in the decisional incompetence associated with pregnancy, Storer thus "reasoned from the body," to use Siegel's evocative language,[47] to justify the physicians' claim that the law should invest them with statutory authority over women's reproductive decisions.

This hierarchal relationship was rooted in mutually reinforcing gender norms. Not only did it reflect the physicians' distrust of women's decisional capacity, it was also infused with their own sense of masculine vigor and purpose. Embodying the manliness of their efforts, in his 1855 speech to the entering class of Harvard Medical School, the senior Storer expressed the unmet hope that "one of the *strong men* of the profession . . . would have spoken . . . against [the] existing and universally acknowledged evil" of abortion. However, having waited in vain for this wall of silence to be breached, he felt compelled to urge his audience to speak out as "one man" against the evil that "stalks at midday through the length and width of the land" because a "*true man* fears, can fear, nothing" (italics added).[48]

Buttressing the potential power and authority of a united manhood, his son, Horatio Storer, subsequently advised his colleagues that a "bold and manly appeal" would be more effective than the "scattered influence of honorable practitioners alone" in ending the evils of abortion.[49] He accordingly decreed that a "bold and *manly* utterance of the truth . . . should be made by the members of the profession on every occasion [emphasis added]."[50] Echoing these sentiments, in a lecture to medical students, A. E. Small implored that "[b]y all that is human, all that is noble and grand in the attributes of *true manhood* . . . every physician should set up his face against this practice and hold it up as murder in public and private [emphasis added]."[51]

Although clearly aimed at restricting women's autonomy, doctors framed this distinctly masculine project as one of direct benefit to women. Waxing eloquent, Dr. Hodge proclaimed it was "the absolute necessity of the science of obstetrics to . . . protect and preserve a being so wonderfully constructed, so interesting, so moral, so intellectual, and so influential for good over the best interests of man, and over the destinies of nations."[52] Accordingly, as Storer and his activist colleagues urged, it was incumbent upon them to persuade lawmakers of the necessity of erecting "better and more effective safeguards . . . about *our* women to 'protect them from themselves [emphasis added]' "[53]—a motif that would be taken up more than a century later by the proponents of the pro-woman/pro-life antiabortion position.

Poetically capturing the deep paternalism of this "pro-woman" sense of mission, Dr. Nebinger explained: "[i]n this work, I desire to be regarded as the friend of woman. . . . So far from being pleased to behold her stained and spotted with crime . . . I would have her as pure and as white, because of her freedom from vice, as was Eve, when she, in full exemption from sin, dwelt in perfect purity and surpassing beauty in the garden of Eden."[54] As they sought to restore women to their dwelling place of "perfect purity and surpassing beauty," antiabortion physicians vacillated between themes of female ignorance and transgression to justify their assertion of authority over women's pregnant bodies.

Rescuing Women from Their Dense Ignorance Regarding the Origins of Life

Arguably the most generous explanation given by some antiabortion doctors as to why a married woman might abort was that she did not understand that a pre-quickened fetus was fully human. As Hodge explained, even "[e]ducated, refined, and fashionable women—yea in many instances, women whose moral character is, in other respects without reproach . . . are perfectly indifferent respecting the foetus in utero. They seem not to realize that the being within them is indeed *animate*—that it is, in verity, a *human being*."[55] Similarly, Storer elucidated that although all women realized that an abortion involves the "premature expulsion of the product of conception," it was less well known "that this product of conception is in reality endowed with vitality from the moment of conception itself."[56] Notably, the 1859 AMA Report on Criminal Abortion adopted this conciliatory explanation for why women engaged in the "wanton and murderous destruction" of their children.[57] However, views soon hardened, and, in the 1871 AMA Report on Criminal Abortion, the aborting woman was chastised for being "unmindful of the course marked out for her by Providence" and blamed for diminishing the "strictly American" proportion of the population.[58]

The attribution of women's actions to their ignorance enabled doctors to avoid confronting the fact that they, particularly those "educated, refined, and fashionable women" of their social strata, might, in fact, be motivated by a far more troubling consideration—namely, the avoidance of their maternal obligations. In short, by blaming the horror of abortion on "the completeness of [women's] ignorance,"[59] doctors could cast them as *"inadvertent* murderesses, persons led astray because they believed in the doctrine of quickening," thus enabling them to "condemn the 'sin' without the necessity of condemning the 'sinner.'"[60] In turn, this framing offered upright matrons the hope of retaining their mantle of respectability.

The stress upon women's ignorance reinforced the masculine nature of the physicians' mission. Seeking to rescue them from the "relic[s] of a barbarous physiology,"[61] the burden fell to them "as good and true men" to "enlighten this ignorance."[62] Dramatically capturing the pressing nature of this mission, having called upon his colleagues to devise a "blessed plan" through which "women may be promptly and fully instructed in all that regards the life of the being in her womb . . . and as to the murderous nature of the offense of destroying it," Dr. Andrew Nebinger implored them to take immediate action. Seeking to rouse them, he exhorted: "'Why stand we here idle?' [W]hy sleep we like an unworthy and never watchful sentinel, when the citadel of woman's purity is being daily and hourly assailed, and not sound the alarm that 'all is not well with her?'"[63]

By teaching abortion-minded women that the destruction of their unborn children was the moral equivalent of infanticide, doctors could claim that they were saving "these wretched women . . . [from] murdering their children through ignorance."[64] In turn, this allowed them to take credit for restoring domestic order, as once so enlightened, what virtuous woman "would be accessory to so foul a deed as the destruction of her offspring, nestling in the sanctuary assigned it by creative wisdom and benevolence."[65]

Although some antiabortion physicians may have genuinely assumed that women were careless in their attitude toward abortion because they mistakenly believed that the being within them was not fully human, and that once set straight, they would no longer "be accessory to so foul a deed," a suspicious strand flowed beneath this stream. As Storer remarked, "I have already stated *that in many instances* it is alleged by the mother that she is ignorant of the true character of the act of willful abortion, and in *some cases* I am satisfied that the excuse is sincerely given"; casting doubt, however, upon the veracity of even those whose "excuse is sincerely given," he continues on to state that "in these days of the general diffusion of a certain amount of physiological knowledge, *such ignorance would seem incredible*" (italics added).[66]‡ Echoing this view of the untrustworthy woman, Dr. D. Meredith Reese likewise suggested in his report on infant mortality in New York that "even the married, to postpone the cares of a family, the perils of parturition, the privations and duties of maternity" may persuade themselves "into the *vulgar fallacy* that there is no life before quickening, and that early abortionism is therefore less than murder" (italics added).[67] Meanwhile, Dr. William M. Pritchett commented on women's sometimes "pretended surprise" at hearing from their medical attendant that abortion was tantamount to cold-blooded murder.[68]

This vacillation regarding the sincerity of married women's belief that their unborn children were not yet fully human and that abortion was therefore of little consequence reveals an uncertainty over whether they were indeed hapless victims of their own ignorance or instead the callous murderesses of unborn children—a tension that, as we will see, would reemerge in the 20th-century antiabortion movement. Certainly, attributing the abortion decision to female ignorance rather than to a desire to avoid maternity was a far more benign explanation for their reproductive behavior, which allowed the doctors to cast themselves as morally superior guards standing ready to halt the assault on the "citadel of woman's purity" by enlightening their ignorance. However, as the following discussion makes clear, this was

---

‡ This fits with Luker's assertion that at the time the physicians launched their crusade, "[w]omen (and the general public) knew that pregnancy was "a *biologically* continuous process from beginning to end" (Luker 1985, p. 25, italics in original).

not the dominant view of women's behavior. Far more commonly, aborting women were cast as domestic subversives whose behavior threatened natural hierarchies—a view that allowed doctors to position themselves as stalwart defenders of both the family and the nation.

The "Wicked Freak of a Married Woman"

Although the antiabortion physicians exhibited some solicitude toward married women who aborted out of ignorance regarding the facts of fetal life, they had little compassion for the "wicked freak of a married woman" who was "perfectly indifferent concerning the foetus in utero."[69] Storer made clear that "no language of condemnation can be too strong" for such women.[70] In a similar vein, Dr. William Pritchett exclaimed that the profession had "nothing but contempt" for the "married woman who disregards her divinely-ordained duty because she "'does not want to be bothered with any more brats,' 'Can hardly take care of those she has,' 'is going to Europe in the spring,' etc."[71] Similarly, after characterizing abortion with its "soul-destroying wickedness" as the "most horrid social enormity of the age," Dr. Augustus Gardner proceeded to denounce the married woman who destroyed her unborn child as a "pitiful, God-forsaken wretch" whom "all true humanity despises . . . and hoots at."[72]

But what accounts for the harshness of their views? Why did the physicians who led the antiabortion campaign lack compassion for married women who wished to avoid or postpone the obligations of motherhood? In answering these questions, we come face-to-face with the strength of their conviction that abortion was, as Reva Siegel succinctly puts it, "a rebellious, incipiently political act,"[73] which had to be vigorously suppressed if the gendered domestic and social order that they held dear was to remain intact. Although proponents of the contemporary pro-woman/pro-life antiabortion position similarly regard abortion as disruptive of the gendered ordering of creation, as we will see, in contrast to the physicians, they instead cast aborting women as victims who must be protected, rather than as gender rebels who must be managed.

Repeatedly in the articles they wrote for medical journals and in the speeches they gave before their colleagues, antiabortion physicians characterized abortion as contrary to "nature and all natural instinct."[74] As Storer proclaimed, "Is there no alternative but for women, when married and prone to conception, to occasionally bear children? This . . . is the end for which they are physiologically constituted and for which they are destined by nature."[75] Accordingly, he opined that, "Were women intended as a mere plaything, for the gratification of her own or her husband's desire, there would have been no need for her of neither uterus nor ovaries."[76]

As would again be the case with the modern proponents of the pro-woman/pro-life frame, the antiabortion physicians' concept of nature was inextricably linked with the divine. Storer thus declared it women's "holiest duty . . . to bring forth living children,"[77] while Pritchett cast it as their "divinely-ordained duty."[78] Directly linking this sacred duty to physiology, Dr. Nathan Allen declared that "the organization of woman . . . demonstrate[s] that married life and the production of children are one of the primary objects of her creation . . . *it is a law which God has made applicable* to all races and nations" (italics added).[79]

The phrase "physiological sin," which Dr. H. S. Pomeroy used to express his opposition to all acts, including abortion, that interfered with "[n]ature so that she cannot accomplish the production of healthy human beings,"[80] neatly encapsulates this infusion of divine belief into the domain of science. As Reva Siegel writes, the concept "enfolded old authority into new, using religion and science to define the obligations of marriage in reproductive terms."[81] In short, not only did the antiabortion doctors derive "a wife's duty from facts about her body,"[82] they also imbued these facts with sacred meaning, thus impressing the stamp of the divine upon women's corporeal being.

In addition to drawing a direct causal link between the subversive nature of abortion and its proclaimed negative impact on the overall physical and emotional well-being of women, Storer and others also specifically warned of the adverse consequences of interfering with the divine. In this spirit, the 1871 report of the AMA Committee on Criminal Abortion warned that the woman who "becomes unmindful of the course marked out for her by *Providence*," (italics added) and "yields to the pleasures but shirk[s] from the pains and responsibilities of maternity," no longer "merit[s] the respect of a virtuous husband."[83] Looking to the future, she can therefore expect to sink "into old age like a withered tree, stripped of its foliage; with the stain of blood upon her soul," and to die "without the hand of affection to smooth her pillow"—a bleak fate that she has brought upon herself as "[s]uch was not the plan of *the Deity* with regard to woman; such is not the character of her high destiny" (italics added).[84] Equally dismal, Dr. Henry Gibbons, in the annual address before the San Francisco Medical Society, forewarned that the married woman who subverts the "holy instinct" is a monster who, through her "satanic perversion of nature," destroys the "Divine image in [her] heart."[85]

Grounded in their view that woman's divinely ordained duty was to bring forth living children, not surprisingly, the antiabortion physicians were dismissive of the reasons why a married woman might want to terminate a pregnancy, such as, for instance, the "fear of labor" or worries about the "care, the expense, or the trouble of children"—considerations that Dr. Pritchett dismissed as "trifling and degrading."[86] Likewise, capturing their sense of contempt for the concerns of women considering abortion, an editorial in the *Medical and Surgical Reporter* explained that the "only reason given by [married women] for killing their own offspring, and making their bodies dens of murder is the *inconvenience* of having children . . . and not to be prevented by fulfilling maternal destiny, from running about town, visiting friends, dressing finely, and attending parties, theaters, and the like."[87] The author thus concluded that married women were "carrying the law of convenience as far as the devil could wish."[88] In a similar vein, Dr. J. M. Toner admonished his colleagues not to "pander to the depraved sentiments, or to succumb, for the love of gain, to the unnatural demands . . . [of] the fashionable [wife]" who "does not wish to have her family increased, or attend to the wants of her offspring, and thereby forego the pleasures and freedoms of society" as her "sole happiness seems to depend upon [her] being seen upon the public promenade, and participants in the desultory pleasure of ballroom excitement."[89]

The doctors also mocked women's vanity. As one doctor put it, in considering abortion, many married women were seeking to "immolate themselves on the altar of fashion or pleasure."[90] Similarly dismissive, Dr. Edwin M. Hale opined that women aborted because they wished to avoid the fate of those whom "before they became mothers, were as beautiful and attractive as themselves, but [were] now faded and perhaps worn by care and disease."[91]

Running beneath the surface of these varied explanations for why women were engaged in behavior that openly flouted the "holiest duty of [their] sex," one can plainly glimpse the antiabortion physicians' palpable fear that respectable middle-class matrons were being influenced to reject motherhood by the woman's rights movement. Formally launched in 1848 in Seneca Falls New York by a small, dedicated group of activists, the movement's founding document, the Declaration of Sentiments and Resolutions (modeled after the Declaration of Independence) boldly proclaims that "the history of mankind is a history of repeated injuries and usurpations on the part of man toward woman, having in direct object the establishment of an absolute tyranny over her" and that it was women's duty to "throw off such government" in favor of the "equal station to which they are entitled."[92]

Perhaps most directly relevant in the present context, the declaration boldly proclaimed that "woman has too long rested satisfied in the circumscribed limits which corrupt customs and a *perverted application of the Scriptures* have marked out for her, and that it is time she should move in the enlarged sphere which *the Creator* has assigned her" (italics added).[93] As expressly stated, this enlarged sphere included the *"sacred* right to the elective franchise" (italics added)—a right that had long been seen as incompatible with woman's refined nature and her domestic duties.[94]§ Doubly threatening, not only did these (and other similar) demands directly challenge the doctors' view that bearing children was woman's holiest obligation and identifying an expanded sphere of action as divinely ordained, the declaration further directly repudiated the physicians' understanding of God's created order as a "perverted application of the Scripture."

The doctors sounded the alarm that feminist agitation for an expanded realm of female activity had incited women to look upon "the carrying into effect the noblest purposes of their being as alike a disaster and disgrace."[95] Echoing these sentiments, in a letter to the *Medical Record,* Dr. E. T. Milligan scoffed that "[m]ost American wives look on pregnancy as a domestic calamity and no amount of advice on the enormity of their sin or on their responsibility to Almighty God will deter them from what they believe to be the exercise of woman's rights."[96] Likewise, expressing disdain for the era's "weak-minded and fashionable wives" who "sneer at a neighbor because of her large family" and look "upon maternity as a disgrace," Dr. Hale bemoaned the fact that maternity was no longer "considered a crown of honor" and a woman was no longer "revered in proportion to the number of her children."[97]

---

§ For further detail on the 19th-century woman's rights movement, see Lois W. Banner, *Elizabeth Cady Stanton: A Radical for Women's Rights* (2000); Ellen Carol DuBois, *Feminism and Suffrage: The Emergence of an Independent Women's Movement* (1999); Eleanor Flexner, *Century of Struggle: The Woman's Rights Movement in the United States* (1996); Kathryn Kish Sklar, *Women's Rights Emerges within the Anti-Slavery Movement 1830–1870* (2000).

The doctors' animosity toward the "'new woman' [who] seems to think that having children is one those disagreeable incidents which must be avoided"[98] reflected their apprehension that the gendered order of creation was at risk of being dismantled by those who foolishly believed that "woman was born for higher and nobler purposes than the propagation of the species."[99] As Dr. Montrose Pallen explained, "[w]oman's rights and woman's sphere are, as understood by the American public, quite different from that understood by us as Physicians . . ."[100] Elaborating, he went on to state that, "[w]oman's rights" now are understood to be, that she should be a man, and that her physical organism, which is constituted by Nature to bear and rear offspring, should be left in abeyance, and that her ministrations in the formation of character as a mother should be abandoned for the sterner rights of voting and law making."[101] He thus decried the fact that "the whole country is in an abnormal state" on account of recent attempts to "force women into men's places."[102]

Similarly, Dr. H. S. Pomeroy chided those who sought to lead women astray, observing that "[t]here are apostles of woman's rights who, in their well-meaning but misdirected efforts to arouse women to claim privileges now denied them, encourage their sisters to feel ashamed of the first and highest right which is theirs by the very idea of nature."[103] With a sigh of relief, however, he predicted that, "[w]hen we become thoroughly civilized we shall hear very little about woman's rights because then woman will be in the full enjoyment of the one right which embraces all others. . . . When that time comes . . . women will not hesitate between maternity and a 'career.'"[104]

The antiabortion physicians accordingly implored married women to embrace their maternal obligations. For example, Dr. Gardner urged them to "accept the noble office you are called upon to perform" by "fold[ing] your children into your own selves."[105] In so doing, he promised that the "true woman" would come to realize that her desire for "dress and fashion" was meaningless beside these "pure joys."[106] And although he claimed to "feel sympathy with nearly every effort that has been put forth by earnest and true women for the advancement of their sisters," Dr. Pomeroy nonetheless went on to blame the woman's rights movement for the fact that "there has grown to be a feeling among many women—some of them good and true ones, too—that the duties of maternity are a sort of low-grade drudgery which properly may be left to those who lack the will and the ability necessary to carry them into a higher sphere."[107] His expressed hope was that women would come to appreciate the fact that "nations are made or unmade according to the love and care bestowed upon children before their birth, and the influence they receive in the nursery"; only then, he prophesied "will woman learn the dignity and blessedness of maternity, and . . . redouble her endeavors to acquire and use her every right and to drink more deeply at the fountain of knowledge—not that she may fill a sphere higher than maternity, but prepare to fill that sphere so well that her descendants may be of earth's noblest and best."[108]

The obvious question that arises in this regard is how did 19th-century woman's rights activists respond to these charges of domestic subversion? Critically, did they counter the doctors' demand for criminalization with a counterpush to preserve (or expand) a woman's legal authority over her reproductive body? The simple answer is that they did not directly engage with them on the issue of the criminalization of abortion. This answer may come as a surprise to readers given the close link between contemporary feminism and the demand for access to legalized abortion. However, it is important to recognize that their approach to the issue reflected the social and economic realities of a particular time and place.

The general reluctance of 19th-century feminists to publicly take on the antiabortion physicians, despite their compassion for women who turned to abortion to control their family size, reflects a myriad of factors. One concern was that overt activism on this issue might well have subjected them to the charge that they endorsed radical "free love" principles, thus further marginalizing the woman's rights cause.[109]** More importantly, however, as Linda Gordon explains in her classic work on the subject, they feared that the separation of intercourse from reproduction would have "increased men's freedom to indulge in extra-marital sex without increasing women's freedom to do so," thus diluting male commitment to the marital family unit that middle-class women were dependent upon for their economic survival.[110] Moreover, although activists called for the enlargement of women's sphere and the loosening of men's patriarchal control in the domestic realm, they did not seek to minimize the importance of motherhood in women's lives; rather, as Gordon writes, they "commonly used the presumed special motherly nature and sexual purity of women as an argument for increasing their freedom and status."[111]

Although 19th-century feminists may not have publicly advocated for women's right to abortion, they nonetheless turned the physicians'

** Free lovers espoused a sexual morality based on an open, equal, and freely chosen commitment, rather than one premised upon legally sanctioned conjugal bonds.

explanation of why women aborted on its head. Rather than blaming a married woman's recourse to abortion on the "apostles of woman's rights" who sought to persuade her that "she was born for higher and nobler purposes than the propagation of her species," they instead insisted that it was the *lack* of rights, particularly when it came to a wife's obligation to submit to her husband's sexual demands, that compelled women in this direction. Capturing this view, Mohr cites an article in the *Women's Advocate* of Dayton, Ohio, asserting that, "[t]ill men learn to check their sensualism, and leave their wives free to choose their periods of maternity, let us hear no more invectives against women for the destruction of prospective unwelcome children, whose dispositions, made miserable by unhappy ante-natal conditions, would only make their lives a curse to themselves and others."[112] In short, woman's rights activists crafted a counternarrative that, although not directly challenging the physicians' position on abortion, defied their depiction of the morally depraved wife who subverted God's gendered order of creation by rejecting motherhood.

Flowing directly from their attribution of blame to husbands who could not control their lust, woman's rights activists forcefully argued that women could not take their rightful place in society as the equals of men until they had sovereignty over their own person. Quoting a private letter of Elizabeth Cady Stanton, Tracy A. Thomas highlights the point that the ability to control one's body, particularly with respect to sexuality and reproduction was "the battleground where our independence must be fought and won."[113]

Given the disinclination of 19th-century feminists to separate marital intercourse from procreation, which they believed would encourage men to stray, they instead insisted that women had the right to control access to their bodies based upon when they were open to the possibility of pregnancy—a position they fought for under the banner of "voluntary motherhood."[114] Although this concept may sound quaint to modern ears, it is important to recognize that it was a radical rejoinder to both the prevailing legal and social understanding of male marital privilege and the antiabortion physicians' belief that woman's "holiest duty was to bring forth living children."

Marking Her Uterus with the "Stamp of Derangement"

Having cast abortion as a "violation of all law, human and divine, of all instinct [and] all reason,"[115] not unexpectedly, the medical literature was full of stern warnings regarding the parade of horribles that awaited a woman who dared to "arrogate to [herself] a right to decide as to the morality of taking or destroying the life of an unborn child."[116] Reflecting the senior

Storer's caution that the laws of nature "cannot be broken with impunity" because the "lawgiver is inexorable,"[117] the harms that awaited an aborting woman were frequently presented as punishment for her unnatural "breach of nature's law."[118] As Hale put it, "[p]regnancy is a natural condition which cannot be arrested without the most calamitous results not only to the local condition of the reproductive organs, but to the general physiological functions of the whole system"[119]—results that Dr. G. Maxwell Christine characterized as the "evident punishment" that an "[o]utraged nature" unfailingly "inflicts upon the culprit."[120]

The range of predicted negative physical outcomes ran the gamut from the "decay of womanly beauty"[121] to "chronic weakness, disease and disarrangement of her organs, and, possibly . . . the forfeiture of her life."[122] Storer also warned about the risk of death; invoking the punishment motif, he declared the loss of life a "penalty of unwarrantably interfering with nature, being occasioned by syncope, by excess of pain or by moral shock from the thought of the crime."[123]

Storer also made clear that the potential risks of trifling with nature were not limited in time, and that although a woman "may seem to herself and to others to successfully have escaped [the] dangers" associated with abortion, she might well succumb to its punishing consequences upon reaching the "critical turn of life . . . when the fountains of youth dry up" and she "ceases from the periodical discharges, which in health and with care are the secret of her beauty, her attraction, her charm."[124] Accordingly, once the "stamp of derangement" had been impressed upon the womb, there was little comfort for the woman who had "had her own way against the dictates of her conscience" because, in addition to the immediate dangers, she faced the further burden of "looking forward through all the rest of her life to possible disease, invalidism or death as the direct consequence of her folly."[125]

Particularly relevant to present purposes, in addition to stern warnings about the physical risks of abortion, the antiabortion physicians also warned of the likely emotional consequences—a theme that drives today's pro-woman/pro-life antiabortion position. Dr. Hale thus declared that remorse was the inevitable and predicable outcome of an act that he characterized as the "sin of child-murder."[126] In a similar vein, Storer counseled that:

> there is probably always a certain measure of compunction for the deed in the woman's heart—a touch of pity for the little being about to be sacrificed—a trace of regret for the child that, if born, would have proved so dear—a trace of shame at casting from her the pledge

of a husband's or a lover's affection—a trace of remorse for what she knows to be wrong, no matter to what small extent, or justifiable, it may seem to herself.[127]

Although Storer's language appears to be somewhat gentle as he speaks simply of a "touch of pity" or "a trace of regret," the theme of punishment is nonetheless apparent in his suggestion that a woman should expect to suffer from the commission of what she knows to be the wrongful act of "sacrificing" the "little being . . . that, if born, would have proved so dear."

Storer, however, also paints a far grimmer picture of the likely emotional impact of abortion. Again, drawing upon the exacting demands of the laws of nature, he remarks that their infringement "must necessarily cause derangement, disaster, or ruin."[128] Elaborating, he goes on to explain that "the thought of the crime, coming upon the mind at a time when the physical system is weak and prostrated, is sufficient to occasion death. The same tremendous idea, so laden with the consciousness of guilt against God, humanity, and even mere natural instinct, is undoubtedly able, where not affecting life, to produce insanity."[129] Moreover, these consequences may be immediate or descend later in life, brought on "by those long and unavailing regrets, that remorse, if conscience exists, is sure to bring."[130] In short, plagued by guilt-driven remorse, women who terminated a pregnancy risked death or madness, with the former, according to Storer, being the preferred outcome, presumably because it would bring about an end to abortion-induced suffering.

Although perhaps the most outspoken in this regard, Storer was not alone in linking mental derangement to abortion. For instance, the superintendent of the Michigan State Asylum spoke of remorse-induced insanity in women who, once having born a child, came to realize the "priceless value of the gift [they] previously refused to accept."[131] In a similar vein, Dr. John P. Gray, superintendent of the State Lunatic Asylum, remarked that for many years he had "received and treated patients whose insanity was directly traceable to this crime, through its moral and physical effects."[132]

It is worth pausing to note that even if the claims these physicians made about the adverse physical and emotional consequences of abortion were scientifically accurate, rather than reflecting an ideological bias, pregnancy and childbirth during this time period were hardly the proverbial walk in the park. Referring to the "physical dangers associated with childbirth" as the "shadow of maternity," Judith Walzer Leavitt explains in her classic work on the subject that "[m]ost married women, and some unmarried women, had to face the physical and psychological effects of recurring pregnancies, confinements, and postpartum recoveries, which all took their toll on their time, their energy, their dreams, and on their bodies. The biological act of maternity, with all its risks, thus significantly marked women's lives as they made their way from birth to death."[133] Significantly, they faced the risk of serious injuries such as torn cervixes and prolapsed uteri at a time when "gynecological practice was still relatively primitive and pregnancy every few years common."[134] Childbirth also frequently resulted in maternal death. As Leavitt starkly puts it—"[n]ine months of gestation could mean nine months to prepare for death. A possible death sentence came with every pregnancy."[135]

According to Leavitt, the very real and palpable risks of pregnancy and childbirth exacted a heavy emotional toll on women. Accordingly, not only did they "spend considerable time worrying and preparing for the possibility of not surviving their confinements," they were also generally well aware "that if procreation did not kill them, it could maim them for life."[136] Given the potential seriousness of postpartum injuries, which might confine a woman to bed for the remainder of her life, as Storer similarly noted with regard to abortion, "the fears of future debility were more disturbing [to some] than fears of death."[137]

Nonetheless, Storer and other antiabortion physicians regularly insisted that the emotional and physical tolls of abortion were significantly greater than those associated with childbirth. However, in light of their view that the aborting woman was a gender outlaw whose criminal conduct ineluctably marked her uterus with a "stamp of derangement," it seems rather self-evident that their view of the comparative risks was shaped by a priori beliefs regarding the intrinsic evils of abortion in direct contrast to the sacred nature of motherhood.

Supporting this view, 19th-century doctors themselves remarked on the serious dangers of pregnancy and childbirth. For example, Dr. Charlotte B. Brown commented that repeated cycles of pregnancy and childbirth might well "cause women to be invalids, with special diseases."[138] Dr. W. W. Johnson intoned that "[c]onfirmed ill health is so common after the establishment of the marriage relations and after childbirth among American women that any observation bearing upon this point will be of interest."[139] He continued on to explain that in many cases, "the health is never regained . . . [and the] principal manifestations of this persistent ill health are chronic anemia, with malnutrition, and impaired or altered function in all the organs, especially in those of the nervous system."[140]

Elaborating on the "altered functions of the nervous system," and thus making clear that doctors regarded childbirth as an emotionally risky proposition, neurologist George M. Beard asserted in his book on nervousness in America that the "simple act of giving birth opens the door to unnumbered woes . . . ending by a life-long slavery to sleeplessness, hysteria, or insanity."[141][††] Of particular note, doctors generally believed puerperal insanity to be responsible for at least 10 percent of female asylum admissions.[142]

According to Dr. William Montgomery, it was not uncommon for women to feel "depressed or dispirited with gloomy forebodings"[143] in the early months of pregnancy; although, as he observed, these feelings typically lifted as gestation progressed toward childbirth. However, he also made clear that on occasion this depression did not lift, but instead assumed "a more serious aspect, and the woman is constantly under the influence of a settled and gloomy anticipation of evil, sometimes accompanied with that sort of apathetic indifference which makes her careless of every object that ought naturally to awaken an interest in her feelings."[144] Continuing on, he explained that in the event a pregnancy followed this course, it was typically "accompanied by very evident derangements in bodily health."[145]

Deploying an intersectional lens, a number of scholars have documented the racialized understandings of the body that shaped these medical narratives of female reproductive suffering. Grounded in "biologically essentialized"[146] understandings of racial difference, including claims about the specific characteristics of the "negro pelvis,"[147] many physicians asserted that although "savage women of the dark races gave birth painlessly, civilized white women suffered greatly in childbearing."[148] Reflecting interlocking assumptions regarding race and gender, Miriam Rich explains that this "highly racialized [and exclusive] understanding of femininity" was yoked to the view that "civilized women: white, native-born, middle or upper-class ladies" exhibited "a high degree of sensitivity to suffering" that black (and other) women were immune from due to their position on the bottom rungs

---

†† See Laura Briggs (2000) regarding the deeply racialized and class-specific significance of the 19th-century "epidemic" of nervous disorders in women.

of the evolutionary scale.[149]‡‡ Significantly, she argues that with the demise of slavery, which had previously functioned to "stabilize racial differences," these "ascendant medico-scientific studies of race were deployed to protect the "integrity of racial boundaries by embedding them in the measurements of the body and the conformation of the bones."[150]

It is hopefully apparent that a deeply troubling irony is at work here. Specifically, physicians directed their antiabortion campaign toward the very same class of women they believed were most likely to suffer from the travails of pregnancy and childbirth. This observation complicates our existing gendered analysis of the antiabortion campaign and makes clear that this singular lens does not adequately capture the animating sentiments that drove the doctors to fight for the criminalization of abortion. We can catch a glimpse of the racial and nativist themes that populated the campaign in Dr. W. W. McFarlane's tongue-in-cheek proposal to end the "slaughter of innocents . . . practiced by *our* society women," by sending "Chinese women Missionaries on Nobb Hill to teach *our* aristocratic ladies the sacredness of motherhood and the wrong of murder" (italics added).[151] Revealed here in this deliberate reversal of the traditional missionary relationship, one can sense the doctors' palpable fear that "their" women had become ignorant of their maternal duties while the lowly "other" fully embraced it—a fear that led them to characterize abortion as a wrong against the nation.

"An Offence of National and Political Character"

As we have seen, in seeking to criminalize abortion, Storer and his colleagues pushed back against woman's rights activists whom they charged with inciting women to abandon their maternal duties in favor of "the sterner right of voting and law making."[152] Significantly, however, as Nicola Beisel and Tamara Kay stress, "the critical political context for the anti-abortion movement was not simply the suffragists' claims for women's rights, but also the massive immigration that undermined Anglo-Saxon political power and social hegemony."[153] Grounded in the articulated fear that immigrants would soon outnumber the native-born population, antiabortion physicians

---

‡‡ See Briggs (2000) for a chilling discussion of how this racialized construct of pain was thought to render "the ostensibly insensate 'savage' woman fit material for medical experimentation, including the conduction of gynecological surgery on slave women without anesthesia, particularly those entailing considerable risk" (pp. 262–65).

accordingly also deployed racialized arguments to persuade their colleagues and the public at large that abortion by "their" women "threatened the Anglo-Saxon race."[154] In this regard, as Beisel and Kay explain, that although today we do not typically put the terms *race* and *Anglo-Saxon* together, and instead note that, quoting Johnson, we typically "see only subtly varying shades of a mostly undifferentiated whiteness," this was not the case in the 19th century.[155] As immigration rates rose, native Anglo-Saxons increasingly regarded "the Irish and Germans, and later the Jews, Italians and Slavs . . . *as members of inferior races* who were unfit for self-government and a threat to the republic" (italics added).[156]

By linking "reproductive politics" to "racial politics," antiabortion physicians hoped to prevent the nation from being overrun by immigrants they viewed as "bearers and propagators of alien values that would ultimately destroy American culture."[157] Building outward from the domestic realm, not only did they claim, as Storer put it, that "all the elements of domestic happiness" and the preservation of marriage as a "spiritual union"[158] depended upon married women's fulfillment of their procreative duties, they also asserted that the future character of the nation hinged upon the willingness of native-born wives to reproduce and replenish their kind.

In his influential mid-century study, which a number of antiabortion physicians as well as the AMA Committee on Criminal Abortion in the preparation of their 1871 report relied upon, Dr. Nathan Allen worriedly concluded based upon his analysis of census data that "all or nearly all" of the increases in population in New England were attributable to those of "foreign descent."[159] Similarly, in accordance with his "most careful analysis of the births and deaths" in Massachusetts, Dr. Jesse Chickering gloomily described the growing population imbalance:

> In many school districts of country towns, where the population is made up wholly or principally of American stock, you can hardly find new children enough to make in numbers a respectable school, where once these same neighborhoods thronged with children. On the other hand, in large towns and villages, where the foreign population abounds, we now find an abundance of children. . . . To such an extent has this foreign element increased that in some of the large towns and cities of the State it actually comprises full one-half of the all the schoolchildren.[160]

Capturing these demographic concerns, Storer thus observed that "the population of our older States" to the extent that it "depends upon the

American and native element . . . is stationary or decreasing"[161]—an observation that clearly marked immigrants and their offspring as other than American.

This was hardly a neutral recitation of the changing composition of the nation. Decrying the plummeting birthrate of the native Puritans, whom he described as once "a prolific people," Dr. Allen dolefully predicted that "if the average amount of children among the Americans to each marriage should continue to decrease . . . the best stock that the world ever saw, under what would be considered the best family training, the highest order of educational influences, and the purest religious instruction" was likely to "run out" and be replaced by "a people of foreign origin, with far less intelligence and a religion entirely different."[162] In a similarly desultory fashion, Dr. James S. Whitmore reported that "we are fast losing our national characteristics, and slowly merging into those of our foreign population" due to the abortion practices of native-born women.[163]

In addition to fearing the loss of the "national character," doctors also expressed their apprehension about the dilution of Anglo-Saxon political power. Gesturing to the future, Dr. Chickering pondered how long it would take if "a majority of all the youth and children under fifteen years of age in a place is made up from those of a foreign parentage" before "such a power will be felt in the management, if not in the control, of the municipal government of those towns and cities."[164] Indeed, as the observations of Dr. Joseph Taber Johnson subsequently made clear, by the turn of the century, these fears had been realized as represented by the fact that "cultured" Boston—"the proud city of the puritans" had "become almost, if not quite an Irish and a Catholic city, rejoicing in the possession of a Mayor by the classic name of O'Brien."[165]

This demographic shift invited a worrisome comparison with the Roman Empire. Attributing the collapse of the empire to "'Infanticide,' 'Aversion to marriage,' and 'The general reluctance to rear families,'" Dr. Allen, quoting, Seeley of Oxford University, apocryphally inquired as to whether "the purely native population of our country especially of New England [shall] follow in the footsteps of the Roman empire, and meet with a similar fate."[166] Tracking this concern, Dr. Francis H. Milligan noted that "[i]mperial Rome, with all her grandeur and greatness, fell" due to the "luxury and immorality of her citizens," thus implicitly suggesting that our great nation was likewise headed for a fall due to the fact that among "certain classes of American women childbearing has become vulgar and unpopular. Their lives are too much devoted to the calls of society. Fashion, to them, is everything, and in these glorious days of the Republic it is not considered fashionable to bear children, even in honorable wedlock."[167]

Predicting that "it [would] not be many years before the Americans left on American soil, will be few and far between" on account of the fact that it was "only among the foreign population, that the births are in excess," Hale declared abortion "an offence of a national and political character," and he called upon the national government to "interpose some check to its alarming increase."[168] Similarly decrying the fact that "in so far as depends upon the American and native element . . . the population of our older States . . . is stationary or declining," Storer likewise proclaimed that abortion was not merely a crime "against the life of the child and the health of its mother . . . but that it strikes a blow at the very foundation of society itself."[169] Looking to the "great territories of the West, just opening to civilization and the fertile savannas of the South," which stood ready to "offer homes for countless millions yet unborn," Storer thus pondered whether they were to "be filled by our *own* children or by those of aliens? This is a question that our *own* women must answer; upon *their* loins depends the future destiny of the nation" (italics added).[170]

In short, in addition to their duty to stabilize the domestic order by embracing their holiest obligation, middle-class married matrons were accordingly also tasked with a special responsibility to reproduce for the good of the nation. Standing as bulwarks against depopulation, their procreative capacity was accordingly not theirs alone to manage; rather, it was something they owed to "an intelligent Christianity, and to an intelligent and safe civilization, and to the State and Nation . . . to the great American idea of free schools and a free Protestant religion."[171]

CONCLUSION

In the later part of the 19th century, regular physicians launched an impassioned crusade calling for the replacement of the flexible common-law approach to abortion with a strict statutory regime. Although they certainly argued that this change was necessary to halt the "unwarrantable destruction" of the unborn, they also forcefully argued that the state needed to step in and manage the reproductive behavior of aborting women to protect the domestic and national order from their subversive conduct. To this end, the rhetoric of these physicians was laced with naturalized assumptions regarding women's holiest duties and the superiority of the "native-born."

Owing largely to the effectiveness of their campaign, by the end of the 19th century all states had laws making abortion a strict statutory crime, unless a doctor certified that the procedure was necessary to save the life of a pregnant woman. Of critical importance, this statutory antiabortion regime was never simply about protecting fetal life. As discussed, it was also put in place for the purpose of managing the behavior of a certain class of women based upon a set of interlocking beliefs regarding the immutability and advantageousness of existing gendered and racialized hierarchies.

As a matter of formal legal policy, these laws controlled the options available to pregnant women until well into the 20th century. As we will see in the next chapter, starting at about the midpoint of this century, the tide slowly began to turn against this strict state management of women's bodies. This shift helped to set the stage for the Supreme Court's landmark decision in *Roe v. Wade,* which constitutionalized the right to abortion—in turn, this result triggered a significant upsurge in antiabortion activism.

TWO

The Evolving Legal Status of Abortion

During the second half of the 19th century, elite physicians launched a successful campaign to make abortion a crime unless a doctor determined that it was necessary to save the life of a pregnant woman. Due largely to their efforts, by the end of the century, the quickening standard—which had previously marked the boundary between permissible and impermissible abortions—had been replaced by a strict statutory regime. With some liberalization, this approach remained largely in place until 1973, when the Supreme Court held in the landmark case of *Roe v. Wade* that women have a fundamental constitutional right to abortion.

The *Roe* decision is the first topic that we turn to in this chapter. Following a discussion of the court's constitutional reasoning that led to the invalidation of the nation's criminal abortion laws, we take a critical look at its crimped reading of the physicians' antiabortion campaign that elides its gendered and racialized tropes in favor of a narrow focus on the protection of fetal life. As we contend, the court's failure to confront this history has contributed to a masking of the deeply paternalistic nature of the contemporary pro-woman/pro-life antiabortion argument.

Following the discussion of *Roe*, we turn to the powerful counterreaction that the decision unleashed; although as we will see, the antiabortion movement has roots in the pre-*Roe* era. From here, we look at key Supreme Court abortion decisions in the two decades following *Roe*, with particular attention paid to its 1992 decision in *Planned Parenthood of*

Southeastern Pennsylvania v. Casey—a case that sits at the apex of this jurisprudential arc.

Before turning to the court's decision in *Roe,* it is important to recognize that the success of the physicians' 19th-century campaign to criminalize abortion did not mean that women stopped having abortions; rather, it meant that they did so "within a context of illegality."[1] Critically in this regard, the existing criminal laws did not delineate the contours of the therapeutic lifesaving exception, and there was considerable disagreement among doctors about precisely when an abortion was "necessary" to save a woman's life. Some doctors interpreted this therapeutic exception narrowly to only permit abortions when needed to prevent the imminent physical death of a pregnant woman, whereas others read it more broadly to take account of the burdens that an unplanned pregnancy might impose on the quality of a woman's life. Capturing this interpretive tension, Leslie Reagan writes that the indeterminacy of the law provided ". . . a space in which doctors and women could negotiate. . . . They could, whether in conscious collusion or unconscious sympathy, use the legal loophole to provide wanted abortions. The medical indications for this procedure left room for social reasons and personal judgment as well as for 'real' reasons."[2]

This indeterminacy resulted in an increased rate of abortion during the economically bleak years of the Great Depression when some doctors, who were moved by the suffering around them, became increasingly willing to read the therapeutic exception more broadly or to refer their patients to a practitioner who was willing to do so.[3] As a result, although they practiced in a legal gray area, most cities "had several physicians who 'specialized' in abortion, and many small towns had at least one physician-abortionist."[4] This liberalizing trend, however, came to a halt in the 1940s, when the Cold War era ushered in a period of deep conservatism that located female ambition and fulfillment squarely within the domestic realm. As during the physicians' campaign, abortion was again associated with disorder as it represented a woman's rejection of her feminine nature.

Reflecting this conservative ethos, hospitals began establishing therapeutic abortion committees (TACs) to rein in doctors who interpreted the lifesaving exception liberally. Responsible for determining when an abortion was "necessary" within the existing criminal framework, TAC results were wildly unpredictable. The process was also onerous and intrusive as women were compelled to offer up intimate details of their lives for scrutiny by a typically all-male committee. This system for parsing out legal abortions had a disproportionate impact on low-income women and women of color who were far less likely than more economically privileged white women to have an ongoing relationship with a trusted physician who could guide them through the process, which might well include a referral to a psychiatrist who was willing to state that suicide would be the likely outcome of compelled maternity.[5]

Capturing the inequity of the TAC system, one study showed that between 1951 and 1962, 88 percent of all legally performed therapeutic abortions in a private New York hospital were for patients of private physicians, rather than "ward" patients who received their care from hospital staff, resulting in a "clear racial disparity . . . in the data of mortality."[6] Highlighting the starkness of this gap, in the early 1960s, "one in four childbirth-related deaths among white women was due to abortion; in comparison, abortion accounted for one in two childbirth-related deaths among nonwhite and Puerto Rican women" in New York City.[7]

ROE v. WADE: THE CONSTITUTIONAL FRAMEWORK

In the landmark case of *Roe v. Wade (Roe)* the United States Supreme Court considered a constitutional challenge to a criminal abortion statute from the state of Texas, which made it a crime to "procure or perform an abortion" unless a physician determined it was "for the purpose of saving the life of the mother."[8] Like the laws that were still in effect in a majority of the states, the Texas statute reflected its 19th-century origins.

It should, however, be noted that by the time the Supreme Court handed down its decision in *Roe,* about one-third of the states had already relaxed their strict 19th-century criminal regime.[9] Most of these states simply expanded the boundaries of the existing therapeutic exception to include, for example, situations of rape or incest or where a woman's health was at risk, while a few took the far bolder step of actually repealing their criminal antiabortion law up until a designated point in pregnancy. As we will see, this growing push for liberalization also gave rise to a nascent antiabortion movement.

The initial push for the liberalization of the existing criminal abortion laws came primarily from physicians and public health officials. Notably, in the early 1950s, doctors became aware of a tremendous variability among these laws with respect to, as noted previously, when they considered an abortion to fit within the narrow lifesaving therapeutic exception. Accordingly, the more liberal-minded among them who, for example, might be willing to perform an abortion based upon economic exigencies or serious mental health indications, recognized that their approach put them at risk of prosecution or professional sanction if they performed an abortion for reasons other than literally saving a pregnant woman from impending death.[10]

Making clear that this was no idle concern, in 1964, the California Board of Medical Examiners brought charges of unprofessional conduct against nine doctors who had performed abortions on women who sought to terminate their pregnancies after exposure to German measles (rubella), which can cause serious harm to a developing fetus. However, as seen by the board, these abortions did not fall within the therapeutic exception, as they were based upon fetal indications, rather than upon a threat to a pregnant woman's life.*

Most reform-minded doctors, however, were not solely concerned with protecting themselves from risk, but were also motivated by a desire to protect their patients from the emotional and physical risks associated with illegal abortion. Many also believed that they, rather than the state, were in a better position to assess patient needs within a more accommodating legal framework.[11]

Other concerned professionals, including members of the clergy and reform-minded lawyers, soon joined these physicians in the call for the liberalization of the nation's abortion laws. Significantly, in 1962, the prestigious American Law Institute (ALI), which develops proposed model legislation for adoption by the states, recommended the codification of a more liberal abortion law along the lines taken by the reform-minded doctors so as to permit abortions in cases of rape or incest, serious physical or mental fetal anomalies, and where "continuance of the pregnancy posed a serious threat to the physical or mental health of the mother."[12] As states took up the question of reform, the ALI approach proved highly influential, with many adopting its recommended exceptions to criminalization.[13]

During this initial phase of liberalization, women's voices were not central in the call for legal change. However, as the feminist movement took hold over the course of the 1960s, the right to control one's body, which included access to legal abortion, became a central plank in the quest for equality. Rather than simply seeking to increase the permissible circumstances under which a doctor could legally perform an abortion, which problematically still left it to the medical profession to police the boundaries of

---

* For a detailed history of how the rubella epidemic contributed to the growing debate over the legal status of abortion, see Reagan (2010).

the law, feminists called for the outright repeal of the existing criminal laws. To the point, their goal was to vest women with ultimate authority over their reproductive bodies.[14]

In a departure from the reformist strategy of the first wave of professional reformers, rather than relying on state legislatures, many feminist activists instead turned to the courts in the hope of winning a more sweeping repudiation of the existing criminal laws. To this end, young lawyers and legal scholars began to develop legal theories and to look for test cases that they could bring to challenge the criminal restrictions on abortion.[15] In 1973, this strategy payed off when the *Roe* court ruled that women have a constitutionally protected right to abortion, thus invalidating the existing state laws.

The case presented the court with two starkly divergent views of abortion. In challenging the law, the plaintiff Jane Roe argued that (among other constitutional protections) the concept of personal privacy, which is anchored in the liberty provision of the Fourteenth Amendment's due process clause, encompasses the right of a woman to make the abortion decision for herself without state interference.[†] In contrast, the state of Texas argued that the fetus has a constitutionally protected right to life either because it is a rights-bearing person indistinguishable from any other human being, or alternatively, because life begins at conception, thus giving it a claim to protection from the outset of pregnancy.

Relying on a line of cases dating back to 1923, in which it had recognized a constitutional right of privacy with regard to important personal rights (including, for example, the choice of a marital partner, the use of contraceptives, and the raising of one's children), the court concluded that the "Fourteenth Amendment's concept of personal liberty and restrictions upon state action . . . is broad enough to encompass a woman's decision whether or not to terminate a pregnancy."[16] In locating the abortion decision within this constitutional zone of personal privacy, the court focused on "[t]he detriment that the State would impose upon the pregnant woman by denying this choice."[17]

---

† Roe's claim was grounded in what is known in legal parlance as "substantive," as distinct from "procedural," due process. Whereas procedural due process is concerned with whether the government followed proper procedures when depriving a person of life, liberty, or property, substantive due process is concerned with whether the government has an adequate justification for the deprivation, regardless of the sufficiency of the procedural safeguards.

Particularly relevant in the present context, in addition to identifying the risk of "medically diagnosable" harms, the court zeroed in on the potential psychological and emotional risks of being compelled to carry an unwanted pregnancy to term:

> Maternity, or additional offspring, may force upon the woman a *distressful* life and future. *Psychological harm* may be imminent. *Mental* and physical health may be taxed by childcare. There is also the *distress,* for all concerned, associated with the unwanted child, and there is the problem of bringing a child into a family already unable *psychologically* and otherwise, to care for it. In other cases, as in this one, the additional difficulties *and stigma* of unwed motherhood may be involved (italics added).[18]

Although failing to account for the dynamic connection between the criminalization of abortion and women's historic subordination, this statement nonetheless stands as a powerful indictment of the harms imposed by denying women control over their bodies.

Although unequivocally ruling that women have a constitutionally protected right to decide for themselves whether or not to terminate a pregnancy, the court nonetheless muted the full feminist force of vesting women with decisional authority over their bodies by inviting physicians into this protected zone of privacy. As it proclaimed in summing up the decision, the result "vindicates the right of the physician to administer medical treatment according to his professional judgment,"[19] thus relegating pregnant women to the margins of the text.

As Linda Greenhouse writes, based on this deference that the *Roe* court paid to the medical profession, a reader of the decision "would come away with no reason to suspect that outside the four corners of this opinion, society was in a ferment over a new discourse of women's rights" and that it "would be quite reasonable for our reader to assume, in fact, that none of this discourse had even been presented to the Court in *Roe*."[20] However, as she goes on to document, the court was indeed presented with vigorous "women's rights arguments that reflected the broader social and political context in which the right to abortion was being debated" by both Jane Roe and by groups who had filed amicus curiae (friend of the court) briefs on her behalf.[21] For example, as Greenhouse quotes, the American Association of University Women asserted in its brief that "[a] woman who the law would force to carry an unwanted pregnancy to term is, quite plainly, restricted and imposed upon to a greater degree than by any other action which the state could take, save execution of a sentence of death or possibly long-term imprisonment."[22]

However, as Greenhouse contends, when compared to the arguments raised by medical groups asserting that the existing criminal laws interfered with "the ability of physicians to practice medicine in accordance with their highest professional standards," the feminist arguments appear to have had minimal impact on the court.[23] As she explains, this most likely reflects the fact that the court was simply not "ready to listen to the feminist voices . . . that were being raised in defense of reproductive freedom," as this would have required it to confront more than it was ready to do at that particular historic juncture.[24] Accordingly, rather than embracing the feminist perspective on the importance of reproductive control, the court instead retreated to the safer framing of abortion as a medical decision within the ambit and expertise of physicians.

Despite it having characterized the abortion right as "fundamental," which in constitutional parlance means it is entitled to a high degree of protection from governmental interference, the court nonetheless made clear that the right was not "absolute," but rather "must be considered against important state interests in regulation."[25] To do so, it shifted its attention away from the harms of compelled maternity to evaluate the countervailing state interests asserted by Texas—namely, the protection of the unborn and safeguarding the health of women seeking an abortion.

The court firmly rejected the argument advanced by Texas that the fetus is a juridical person whose right to life is protected by the Fourteenth Amendment, as well as its fallback position that life begins at conception and is thus deserving of protection from the outset of pregnancy. Nonetheless, it determined that states do have a compelling interest in protecting the "potentiality of life." The court likewise agreed with Texas that states also have a compelling interest in safeguarding the health of pregnant women. Recognizing, however, that pregnancy is a dynamic, rather than a static, process, the court made clear that these interests are not of sufficient magnitude throughout pregnancy to justify the imposition of limitations on the abortion right. Instead, it ruled that each interest grows in significance over the course of a pregnancy and becomes sufficiently "compelling" at distinct stages so as to permit regulation of the abortion right starting at that juncture.

Seeking to balance these interests with a woman's fundamental constitutionally protected right to abortion, the court developed its now famous trimester framework (as discussed in the following, this framework has since been replaced by the "undue burden" standard). Although accommodative of these interests, this framework was nonetheless designed to prevent overreaching by the state. Accordingly, as formulated, during the first trimester of pregnancy, state interest is not considered to be of sufficient magnitude to justify limitations on the abortion right. In the second trimester, when the procedure is potentially riskier, the state's interest in safeguarding the health of the pregnant woman becomes compelling, thus permitting regulations that advance this aim. Lastly, as a pregnancy enters the third trimester and the fetus becomes viable, defined by the court as being capable of "meaningful life outside the mother's womb," the state's interest in the potentiality of life becomes compelling, and it may prohibit abortion unless it is necessary to protect the life or the health of a pregnant woman.[26]

ROE v. WADE: A CRITICAL ANALYSIS OF THE COURT'S READ OF THE HISTORICAL RECORD

The *Roe* court was well aware of the controversial nature of the task that lay before it. Reflecting this awareness, at the outset of the decision, it expressly stated "[w]e forthwith acknowledge our awareness of the sensitive and emotional nature of the abortion controversy, and of the deep and seemingly absolute convictions, even among physicians, that the subject inspires," and it stressed that its responsibility was to resolve the issue by constitutional measurement, free of emotion and of predilection."[27] To assist them in this regard, the justices announced their intention to inquire into what the "medical and medical-legal history . . . reveals about man's attitudes towards the abortion procedure over the centuries."[28]‡

Most likely seeking to head off anticipated criticism that its decision was, as one detractor referred to it, "a bolt out of the blue,"[29] the court stressed the fact that "[i]t perhaps is generally not appreciated that the restrictive criminal abortion laws in a majority of States today are of relatively recent vintage. Those laws . . . are not of ancient or even of common-law origin. Instead they derive from statutory changes effected, for the most part, in the latter half of the 19th century."[30] Underscoring their "relatively recent

---

‡ Although the court starts its historical review with a consideration of "ancient attitudes" toward abortion, our focus is on what it had to say about the legal history of abortion in the United States.

vintage," the court further observed that "[i]t is thus apparent that at common law, at the time of the adoption of our Constitution, and throughout a major portion of the 19th century, abortion was viewed with less disfavor than under most American statutes currently in effect. Phrasing it another way, a woman enjoyed a substantially broader right to terminate a pregnancy than she does in most States today."[31]

In tracing the evolution of the law, the court focused on the major role that the medical profession played in the enactment of the nation's restrictive laws.[§] In particular, to uncover the "attitude of the profession," it directed its attention to the two published reports of the AMA's Committee on Criminal Abortion, which, as we saw in the last chapter, was established at the behest of Horatio Storer as the launching pad for the physicians' antiabortion crusade.

Quoting the 1859 report, the court proclaimed that the medical profession's antiabortion campaign was motivated by the desire to end the "'unwarrantable destruction of human life'" and that doctors attributed the "general demoralization" associated with abortion to the "'wide-spread popular ignorance of the true character of the crime . . . [and] the grave defects of our laws . . . as regards the independent and actual existence of the child before birth, as a living being.'"[32] As further confirmation of the physicians' fetal-centered focus, the court pointed to the admonition in the 1871 report that when dealing with the matter of human life, doctors could "entertain no compromise."[33]

As thus presented by the court, even the most discerning reader of the *Roe* decision would come away with the view that the sole motivating consideration behind the physicians' antiabortion campaign was their desire to protect the unborn. Critically, the reader would have no glimmer of the gendered and racialized tropes that they so passionately invoked in support of their goal of making abortion a strict statutory crime.[**]

---

§ According to the court, the medical profession shared "the anti-abortion mood prevalent in this country in the late 19th century" *(Roe* 1973, 141). However, as discussed in Chapter One, the medical profession did not simply share passively in existing attitudes; rather, it played a major role in shaping the public attitudes toward abortion.

** This same discerning reader might, however, protest that we are the ones who are in fact guilty of a pinched textual reading by pointing out that the *Roe* court also quotes a resolution from the 1871 report that directs "the attention of the clergy of all denominations to the *perverted views of morality* entertained by a large class of females . . . on this important question" *(Roe,* at 142, quoting the 1871 report at 258, emphasis added)—language

At the outset of this discussion, one might appropriately ask whether it is unfair to suggest that the court should have tracked down and analyzed primary source materials of the kind we discuss in the first chapter to accurately capture the multidimensional nature of the physicians' campaign. This is certainly a valid point, and in fact, the *Roe* court is to be commended for its impressive interdisciplinary approach that engages with a wide array of historical material. However, what is puzzling is that a historical source that the court actually relied upon in its decision—specifically, the 1871 report by the AMA Committee on Criminal Abortion—is itself laden with the kinds of gendered and racialized arguments that the profession advanced in support of its goal of criminalization.

In other words, the court had before it a document that provided a direct window into the physicians' view of abortion as a deeply destabilizing act that threatened both the domestic and the national order. Although we discussed these themes in the first chapter, we take a brief look at the 1871 report itself to see what the *Roe* court could have readily gleaned from a document that it actually relied upon in the process of looking into what the "medical and medical-legal history . . . reveals about man's attitudes towards the abortion procedure over the centuries."[34]

The 1871 report positively bristles with indignation over the aborting woman's willful subversion of her divinely defined place in the created world. Recounting God's commandment to Adam and Eve to "increase and multiply," it asserts that woman's "high destiny" is accordingly to "be instrumental in propagating the human family" within the sacred purity of marriage. An abortion-minded woman is thus warned that she who "becomes a participant in the destruction of her own infant" steps down from this high place and is no longer "the appropriate representative of a refined age, a model of purity, [and] the center of honor and affection" as child-murder "was not the intention of the Deity with regard to woman."[35] Perhaps even more calamitous than this fall from her "high position," the report warns that she who "yields to the pleasures but shrinks from the pains of responsibilities of motherhood" in disregard of "the course marked out for her by Providence" should expect to descend "into old age like a withered tree,

---

that suggests the court may indeed have been attuned to the multidimensional nature of the physicians' campaign. However, this quote marks the end of the court's discussion of their effort, except for its final observation that subsequent to the 1871 report, doctors periodically engaged in a "condemnation of the criminal abortionist" (ibid.).

stripped of its foliage, with the stain of blood upon her soul; she dies without the hand of affection to smooth her pillow."[36]

Driving home the AMA committee's contempt for married women who turn to abortion, particularly if they were among "the intelligent, the refined, and the religious," the report glowingly recounts the story of the Roman matron Cornelia, who, even "unaided by the light of Christianity," replies to a friend's request to see her jewels that her children "are my jewels . . . they are the pledges of a virtuous and honorable affection."[37] Noting that such would be the response of "an honest matron of the day" in a well-trod theme, the report continues on to disparage women who instead turned to abortion for selfishly "regarding the care and expense of children as a burden, as well as in preferring pleasure and fashion to domestic duties and responsibilities."[38]

The Committee on Criminal Abortion's conviction that aborting women subverted God's gendered order of the domestic realm was closely entwined with its nativist fears. In addition to specifically expressing concern that abortion was particularly prevalent among "the intelligent, the refined, and the religious," its use of the previously noted descriptive phrases such as "representative of a refined age," "a model of purity," and "the center of honor and affection" clearly communicates the ideals of womanhood that were closely associated with middle-class norms of respectable domesticity.

One does not, however, need to parse these descriptive hints to uncover the AMA committee's deep preoccupation with the depopulation of the nation. More directly to the point, the report relies upon Dr. Nathan Allen's influential census-based study of population shifts in New England and New York to sound the alarm that there was "something of a grave nature, something mischievous, something radically wrong" in the nation.[39] It then highlights his demographic analysis showing that when compared both to their foremothers and the contemporary foreign-born, the birthrate of the "strictly American," meaning those descended from the once "prolific" Puritans, had dropped precipitously—findings that the committee regarded as "well calculated not only to surprise but to excite alarm."[40]

Encapsulating the intersecting nature of the medical profession's concern with aborting matrons' power to simultaneously destabilize the domestic and the national order, the report shares Allen's perplexity as to why the most intelligent, refined, and religious married women placed "so low an estimate . . . upon the value of human life" that they engaged in a "persistent effort . . . to defeat one of the most important objects of the marriage institution."[41] It continues on to endorse his explanation for this state of affairs; namely, that "some radical change in the organization of woman" had blunted her "natural instincts," leading to a situation that was unparalleled "in the history of any other civilized people, race, or nation."[42]

In short, even a cursory reading of the 1871 report of the AMA Committee on Criminal Abortion makes clear that the protection of fetal life, which is barely mentioned, was hardly the sole aim of the physicians' anti-abortion campaign. Casting aborting matrons as subversive for refusing to display a large brood of children as the jeweled exemplars of their unwavering commitment to "a virtuous and honorable affection," the report reveals the activists' overriding interest in restoring moral order by impressing upon married women—most notably those of "original stock"—that their "high destiny" was to propagate the species in accordance with divine command so as to perpetuate the domestic and national order.

In this regard, it should be noted, that Linda Greenhouse's theory regarding the court's "selectivity" with respect to what it "heard in *Roe* and what it chose to say"[43] offers a potentially useful insight as to why it may have also opted to ignore the gendered and nativist themes that permeated the 1871 report. Although we will never know for sure, it is certainly plausible that the court was likewise not ready to confront the fact that our criminal laws were not simply enacted to protect the unborn but were also intended to manage certain women's bodies in accordance with a gendered and racialized conception of their paramount obligation to self, family, and nation. Had the court grappled with this historic reality, it might well have had to reason about the challenged Texas law within the "new feminist discourse of women's rights," as it would have been readily apparent that it was not simply about the preservation of fetal life but was also aimed at the management of women's reproductive bodies.

To do justice to this history, the court would have been compelled to go beyond its individualistic understanding of the harms of compelled maternity and confront the reality that our antiabortion laws were designed to shore up a particular social order, which the doctors believed was at risk of collapsing under the dual threat of the woman's rights movement and the nation's growing "nonnative" population. However, the *Roe* court instead chose to reason about these laws as if their sole aim was the protection of fetal life, thus missing a critical opportunity to examine their gender-coercive function. It is our view that the *Roe* court's elision of the gendered work that these laws were enacted to accomplish in favor of a fetal-focused narrative arc has served to blunt the full weight and meaning of the new pro-woman/pro-life antiabortion position. As we develop in the remaining chapters of this book, this approach is not new, but rather, it resurrects and repackages this earlier essentialized and flattened conception of women's place in a fixed gendered order.††

ROE v. WADE: THE COUNTERMOBILIZATION

The public reaction to the *Roe* decision was swift and impassioned. Needless to say, for abortion rights supporters, the day was one of celebration. Although the victory was somewhat tempered by the court's failure to declare abortion an absolute right within the sole control of women, this did not overshadow the importance of its sweeping invalidation of all existing state criminal abortion laws. By locating the abortion right within the protective mantle of the federal Constitution, the decision was a wholesale repudiation of the legal regime that Storer and his colleagues had worked so hard to install only a century earlier.

It, of course, goes without saying that opponents of abortion had a very different reaction to the decision. As Kristin Luker explains, those who believed that abortion was tantamount to murder had assumed theirs was the majority position. They accordingly experienced the *Roe* decision as a "bolt from the blue," which challenged their fundamental belief that "the embryo was human life as valuable as any."[44] Additionally, by making motherhood optional, the decision was also experienced as a deeply unwelcome assault on the traditional family, and women's pivotal role within it. As Luker writes, abortion "strips the veil of sanctity from motherhood. . . . When pregnancy is discretionary . . . then motherhood has been demoted from a sacred calling to a job."[45]

However, despite common views to the contrary, the *Roe* decision did not actually inaugurate the antiabortion movement. Rather, this countermobilization began a decade earlier when states began considering the liberalization of their antiabortion laws. The opposition at this time was spearheaded by the National Conference of Catholic Bishops (NCCB), which serves as the policy-making body of the Church. The NCCB established the National Right to Life Committee (NRLC) in 1966 to serve "as

---

†† As discussed in Chapter Three, it is more difficult to trace the express use of racialized language forward into the present pro-woman frame. However, as we will see, racialized tropes nonetheless remain tightly woven into the contemporary antiabortion message.

the national umbrella for many of the local organizations" that were mobilizing to fight abortion reform efforts in the various states.[46]‡‡ Moreover, as discussed in the following chapter, crisis pregnancy centers (CPCs), whose primary "service-oriented" mission is to steer women away from abortion toward motherhood, began springing up at this time.[47] Birthright, an organization founded in Canada in 1968, began opening centers in the United States and shortly afterward, Alternatives to Abortion International (now Heartbeat International) was established for the purpose of providing critical resources to the growing network of local CPCs.[48]

As Linda Greenhouse and Reva Siegel write, the Catholic Church's role in opposing abortion in this era was "public, prominent and distinctive," and bishops "increasingly emphasized opposition to abortion as a defining aspect of Catholic identity."[49] Despite this close affiliation between the Church and antiabortion activism, leaders increasingly came to frame their position in secular terms, calling upon, for example, the U.N. Declaration of the Rights of the Child as well as the Declaration of Independence, to broaden their appeal to multiple constituencies.[50]

Following the court's decision in *Roe,* the ranks of the antiabortion movement swelled as "'ordinary citizens' and especially women" took up the cause.[51] In addition, the religious composition and tenor of the movement underwent a profound transformation as young evangelical Protestants affiliated with the deeply conservative New Christian Right (NCR) joined the battle to save the unborn, with many moving into key leadership positions. As their influence increased, the somewhat cautious approach that the predominately Catholic leadership had previously taken with respect to framing their opposition to abortion in religious terms dissipated and antiabortion arguments became increasingly suffused with appeals to religious beliefs and scriptural authority.[52] Over time, as we will see, this turn toward religion served to radicalize the movement and propel it in a more violent direction.

Seeking Change through Political Channels

In the immediate wake of *Roe,* opposition to abortion was dominated by the political branch of the movement, which "consists of organizations and individuals who are trying to shape change through traditional political

---

‡‡ In 1973, NRLC leaders voted to sever the organization's formal tie to the Church.

channels such as lobbying, political campaigns, and litigation" and eschews violent tactics.[53][§§] A favored early strategy was to push for the adoption of a Human Life Amendment to the federal Constitution, which, by declaring the fetus a juridical person entitled to constitutional protection, including the right to life, would nullify *Roe* in a single swoop as abortion would henceforth be the legal equivalent of murder.

For some antiabortion activists, this purist approach was and remains the only morally acceptable strategy as it seeks to actualize the view that *all* life is sacred. In contrast, although likewise hoping in the end for a criminal ban on abortion, incrementalists have adopted what they regard as the more politically expedient strategy of gradually chipping away at *Roe* by enacting restrictive measures, such as waiting periods, funding bans, and spousal/parental consent or notification requirements, with the eventual hope that the Supreme Court would one day overturn the decision.[54] To purists, this approach is an unacceptable compromise with evil as it suggests that the lives of some unborn children can be sacrificed for the sake of expediency, thus undermining the movement's central claim regarding the sanctity of all human life.[55]

Although incrementalists were mainly focused on persuading lawmakers at the state level to enact restrictive laws, when it became clear that a Human Life Amendment was doomed to failure, they layered on a politically more realistic strategy at the national level—namely, seeking to persuade Congress that as the guardian of public fisc, it had a duty to ensure that taxpayer funds not be used to pay for abortion services.[56] This measured approach proved successful, and in 1976, Congress approved what is known as the Hyde Amendment (named after its chief sponsor Congressman Henry Hyde—a staunch conservative from Illinois). This amendment eliminates

---

§§ Munson (2008) identified the robust organizational structure of the pro-life movement as being composed of four distinct "streams," including a politics, direct action, individual outreach, and public outreach stream (ibid., 102). Following similar organizational divisions, Doan (2007) categorizes the pro-life movement's structure into three rather than four branches: political, direct action and outreach, viewing public outreach as an activity that all three branches engage in to engender societal cultural change toward a pro-life perspective. Each branch of the movement relies on different tactics to achieve their branch's specific goal while collectively pursuing the legal and cultural eradication of abortion.

federal Medicaid funding for abortion, with limited exceptions for rape, incest, or endangerment to a woman's life.***

Succinctly encapsulating the intended purpose of this measure, in his testimony before Congress, Representative Hyde explained that it was aimed at preventing federal funds from being used for the "execution of these innocent, defenseless human lives." Positioning himself as the savior of the imperiled fetus, he proclaimed that we should not be saying "poor woman, go destroy your young and we will pay for it," as the "promise of America is that life is not just for the privileged, the planned, or the perfect."[57]

Although certainly not the complete moral victory that the enactment of a Human Life Amendment would have represented, the Hyde Amendment was nonetheless an important accomplishment for the antiabortion movement, particularly because, as discussed in the following section, the Supreme Court subsequently upheld its constitutionality. With this important victory behind them, the political branch of the movement, under the leadership of the NRLC, began earnestly pursuing strategic, incremental changes largely tailored to a more accessible and receptive group of politicians—state legislators.

In subsequent decades, having all but abandoned the absolutist strategy, a constellation of national, state, and local organizations, including the NCCB and Americans United for Life, have toiled alongside the NRLC (including its 50 state affiliates and more than 3,000 local chapters) to reverse course on *Roe* vis-à-vis one restriction at a time.[58] Proponents of this approach were willing to settle in for the long haul in the hopes that a case challenging one of these measures would eventually land before a changed Supreme Court, which would decide to overturn *Roe*.†††

*** The Hyde Amendment was introduced as a "rider" to an appropriation bill that Congress has renewed annually for more than 40 years. Congress has subsequently enacted a variety of "Hyde-like" policies that likewise prohibit the use of federal funding to pay for abortions in a variety of other contexts, while a majority of states have enacted "mini" Hyde laws that prohibit the expenditure of state Medicaid funds for abortion. These public funding restrictions have had a demonstrably negative impact on the ability of low-income women and women of color to access abortion.

††† As this book goes to press in the wake of Justice Anthony Kennedy's resignation from the Supreme Court, this eventuality, which once seemed a remote possibility, suddenly looms as a threat on the horizon with two President Trump appointees now on the court.

This legislative strategy paid off, and within a few years of the *Roe* decision, states across the country had enacted a wide range of laws aimed at making access to abortion more difficult, including spousal and parental consent mandates; informed consent and waiting requirements; bans on the use of any public resources (including funds, facilities, and employees) to pay for abortions; and performance requirements, such as that all second-trimester abortions be performed in a hospital. These laws were promptly challenged in court by abortion rights advocates, notably including Planned Parenthood and the ACLU Reproductive Freedom Project, on the ground that they interfered with women's constitutionally protected right to abortion in contravention of *Roe*. In the final section of this chapter, we will look at how the Supreme Court responded to some of these challenges.

Seeking Change through Direct Action

Fueled by a religious fervor and a growing frustration over the slow pace of change through traditional legislative and judicial channels, within about a decade after *Roe,* rather than patiently waiting for lawmakers and the courts to do the right thing, a more radicalized constituency began actively taking matters into their own hands. For these young evangelical activists, opposition to abortion was forged within the crucible of a fierce resistance to the secularization of society. As Duane Murry Oldfield writes, their resistance was closely linked to "the affirmation of distinct social roles for men and women, opposition to contemporary feminism, and opposition to sex outside of marriage," which they channeled into "a battle to . . . uphold a model of the family capable of resisting secular pressures and transmitting evangelical values to the next generation."[59]

With abortion as the symbolic marker of a world careening madly out of control, these activists increasingly made use of vivid and rage-filled apocryphal and militaristic rhetoric to warn the public that the "legalization of abortion was bringing God's wrath on America."[60] This was not simply a shift in rhetorical tone, but rather it signaled the growth of a more militant form of grassroots direct-action strategies aimed at "saving babies" by forcing the closure of abortion clinics. In short, rather than focusing on "shape[ing] change through traditional political channels," the direct-action branch of the movement aims for more immediate and dramatic results, typically employing unconventional and confrontational tactics to achieve its goal of closing down the abortion "industry."[61]

Operation Rescue, which was officially launched in 1988, is generally credited with inaugurating this new form of confrontational antiabortion activism that proved to be particularly appealing to an emerging generation of conservative Christian activists who were impatient with the pace of change.[62] As James Risen and Judy Thomas describe it, under the leadership of Randall Terry, Operation Rescue "turned what had been a small, ragtag group of easily ignored protestors into a genuine movement, an aggressive national campaign that put the anti-abortion cause back onto America's Page One."[63] Although formally eschewing the increasingly violent tactics of the most radical fringes of the movement, which included the firebombing of clinics, acid attacks, kidnappings, and the murder of abortion doctors and clinic staff, Operation Rescue "functioned as a network for putting militant activists in touch with one another as well as solidifying their commitment to incorporating violence as a justifiable act to end abortion."[64]‡‡‡ Moreover, the group's organizing slogan—"if you think abortion is murder, act like it"—can arguably be seen as fostering an environment in which the murder of doctors and clinic staff came to be viewed as a justifiable and necessary intervention aimed at preventing countless murders from occurring.[65]

A Shared Fetal-Centric Message

There has been considerable tension both within and between the political and the direct-action branches of the antiabortion movement over how to best achieve the desired goal of ending abortion. However, of critical importance for present purposes is that both have historically framed their opposition in fetal-centric terms. As philosopher Francis Beckwith explains, "[s]ince its genesis in the mid-1960s, the movement against abortion rights . . . has made its case in the public square as well as the courts by emphasizing the humanity of the fetus. Its leaders . . . have maintained that if the fetus is a member of the human community, then all the moral obligations and rights that apply to other members of the human community apply to the fetus."[66] Pregnant women were not included within this

---

‡‡‡ For further detail, see Steiner (2006), Mason (2002), Risen and Thomas (1998), and Blanchard (1994).

oppositional frame, expect perhaps by way of an occasional cameo appearance as the murderess of her unborn child.

The near total elision of women from the fetal-centric antiabortion frame did not mean that gender concerns were unimportant to the movement, but rather that they were not enfolded into how it made its case against abortion in the public square. As Susan Faludi argues, many of the male leaders were in fact animated by a deep-seated antagonism toward feminism, and from their vantage point, "sexual independence, not murder, may have been the feminists' greatest crime."[67] For these activists, the sexual freedom ushered in by the availability of birth control and abortion was seen as a violent assault on the gendered ordering of the universe. Highlighting this underlying deeply antifeminist impulse, Faludi quotes both Father Michael Carey, who, in his keynote speech at a National Day of Rescue rally, chastised "feminist-infected" women for interfering with the ability of men to "decide about abortion" as well as John Willke, the president of the NRLC, who charged that "[p]ro-choice women 'do violence to marriage [because they] remove the right of a husband to protect the life of the child he has fathered in his wife's womb.'"[68]

Not only was women's reproductive autonomy regarded as a threat to male authority within marriage, according to Vincent Rue, it threatened to "emasculate men" by diminishing their sexuality.[69] Drawing an explicit link between abortion and emasculation, George Gilder, an outspoken conservative commentator and author, declared that "because a man quite simply cannot father a baby unless his wife is fully and deliberately agreeable," his sexual potency, which was once a "weapon of procreation . . . that women . . . have viewed with some awe . . . is now almost completely lost. The male penis is no longer a decisive organ." He thus explains that in addition to representing a "repudiation of sexual liberation in general," antiabortion sentiments can "be seen as a symbol of resistance to the erosion of male sexuality."[70]

FROM *ROE* TO *CASEY:* THE SUPREME COURT'S EVOLVING ABORTION JURISPRUDENCE

From 1976, when the first post-*Roe* abortion case reached the Supreme Court until its 1992 decision in *Planned Parenthood of Southeastern Pennsylvania v. Casey,* the court, at least in theory, adhered to *Roe*'s trimester framework when assessing the constitutionality of restrictive abortion laws.

With two important exceptions discussed as follows, its adherence to this framework typically resulted in the invalidation of these measures on the ground that they interfered with the constitutionally protected right to abortion.

By way of illustration, a decade after *Roe* was decided, in the case of *Akron v. Akron Center for Reproductive Health*,[71] the court invalidated multiple provisions of a restrictive municipal ordinance. Of key importance, it invalided the closely linked informed consent and waiting period rules. Taken together, these provisions required that physicians provide women with state-scripted information, including that "the unborn child is a human life from the moment of conception" at least 24 hours before performing an abortion, thus presumably giving her time to reconsider her decision.

Although the court made clear that as with other medical procedures, states can mandate informed consent requirements, it concluded that Akron's effort exceeded permissible limits. As it explained, "by insisting upon the recitation of a lengthy and inflexible list of information, Akron has unreasonably placed 'obstacles in the path of the doctor upon whom [the woman is] entitled to rely for advice in connection with her decision.'"[72] In addition to straitjacketing doctors and interfering in the doctor-patient relationship, the court also recognized that "much of the information required is designed not to inform the women's consent but rather to persuade her to withhold it altogether"[73]—a clearly unconstitutional objective under *Roe*. It also invalidated the waiting period requirement on the ground that forcing a woman to delay her abortion procedure for 24 hours after receiving this information did not serve to enhance either the safety of the abortion procedure or the quality of her decision making, and thus did not advance any permissible state interest in accordance with *Roe*'s trimester framework.

The *Akron* court also invalidated the requirement that all second-trimester abortions be performed in a hospital. Although acknowledging that this requirement made abortions more expensive and generally less available, the city of Akron nonetheless asserted that it was a valid health measure intended to ensure that abortions were performed in appropriate settings that minimized potential risks to a woman's health. Noting that the safety of second-trimester abortions had improved dramatically since the ordinance had gone into effect, the court held that (at least as applied to early second-trimester abortions) it imposed a "heavy and unnecessary burden . . . on women's access to a relatively inexpensive, otherwise accessible, and safe abortion procedure," without providing a discernible health benefit.[74]

Although purporting to be reasoning within *Roe*'s trimester framework, the court departed from its general pattern of striking down restrictive laws when it came to measures impacting two groups of women—namely low-income women and teens. With regard to low-income women, the ban on the use of Medicaid funds to pay for most abortions was challenged on the ground that this limitation interfered with the constitutionally protected right of choice. Critically, women asserted that by funding the costs associated with pregnancy and childbirth, but not abortion, the Medicaid program injected coercive financial incentives into the decision-making process.

In a series of cases, the court consistently rejected the challenges to both the federal and state public funding bans. Although agreeing with the plaintiffs that these funding schemas incentivized childbirth over abortion, it did not agree that this was problematic in light of the state's interest in the potentiality of life. In reaching this conclusion, the court distinguished the denial of funds from other types of restrictions. As it explained in the case of *Maher v. Roe,* which involved a challenge to a Connecticut rule limiting the use of Medicaid funds to pay for "medically necessary abortions," there is a "difference between direct state interference with a protected activity and state encouragement of an alternative activity."[75] Elaborating, it maintained that unlike a requirement, such as that a woman obtain the consent of her husband before having an abortion, which is a state-imposed obstacle, the denial of funds "place(s) no obstacles . . . in the pregnant woman's path to an abortion. The State may have made childbirth a more attractive alternative, thereby influencing the woman's decision, but it has imposed no restriction on access to abortions that was not already there."[76]

By identifying the barrier as the woman's own poverty, as distinct from a state-imposed obstacle, the court was able to claim that its decision in these cases did not signal a "retreat" from *Roe* and its progeny. Locating the funding cases within its existing jurisprudential framework, the court thus asserted that protecting a woman's right of choice does not "translate into a constitutional obligation . . . to subsidize abortions."[77]

This result drew scathing dissents from the more liberal justices on the court who viewed the issue quite differently. Rather than regarding the problem as the women's own poverty, these justices recognized that the funding disparities between abortion and childbirth injected a coercive element into the decision-making process, thus steering women toward motherhood. As stated:

> A distressing insensitivity to the plight of impoverished pregnant women is inherent in the Court's analysis. . . . [M]any indigent women will feel they have no choice but to carry their pregnancies to term because the State will pay for the associated medical services, even though they would have chosen to have abortions if the State had also provided funds for that procedure . . . This disparity in funding by the State clearly operates to coerce indigent pregnant women to bear children they would not otherwise choose to have.[78]

In short, rather than identifying the access barrier as a woman's poverty, these justices attributed it to the uneven funding schema that privileged the decision to carry a pregnancy to term over termination. Research has subsequently documented that public funding bans have had an adverse impact on the ability of low-income women to obtain abortions, with a particularly disproportionate impact on poor women of color.[79]

Turning now to the abortion rights of minors, following *Roe,* states began enacting laws that required young women to obtain the consent of or give notice to one or both parents before having an abortion. These laws were promptly challenged, and in the landmark case of *Bellotti v. Baird,* the court confronted the question of whether minors were fully included within *Roe's* promise of reproductive autonomy. Starting with the recognition that a "child, merely on account of his minority, is not beyond the protection of the constitution,"[80] the court sought to reconcile a historic understanding of minors as dependents in need of protection with a more contemporary understanding of them as autonomous rights-bearing individuals.

Pulling in the direction of individual autonomy, the court recognized that the abortion decision is very different in nature from most other decisions young women might make during their teen years due to its temporal nature and enduring impact. As it explained:

> The pregnant minor's options are much different from those facing minors in other situations, such as the decision whether to marry. A minor not permitted to marry before the age of majority is required simply to postpone her decision. . . . A pregnant adolescent, however, cannot preserve for long the possibility of aborting, which effectively expires in a matter of weeks from the onset of pregnancy. . . . [T]here are few situations in which denying a minor the right to make an important decision will have consequences so grave and indelible.[81]

Pulling, however, in the opposite direction, the court also voiced the concern that a young woman might well fail to appreciate that abortion is not necessarily the "best choice," for her, and that she might instead be better off marrying the father, making an adoption plan, or raising the baby with the help of her family.

Although making clear that like adults, teens have a constitutionally protected right to abortion, the court nonetheless concluded that to prevent them from making the wrong choice, their rights can be limited in favor of providing a guiding role for parents in the decision-making process. The court also invoked the "natural" authority of parents over their minor children as a further justification for their involvement. However, the court also was very clear that states cannot vest parents with potential veto power over their minor daughter's abortion decision.

Balancing these considerations, the *Bellotti* court reached what is typically viewed as a compromise between these competing conceptions of young women as reproductive decision makers. Specifically, it held that if a state wishes to enact a parental involvement law, it must provide "an alternative procedure whereby authorization for the abortion can be obtained."[82] Critically, teens cannot be required to first consult with or seek the permission of a parent as some parents might prevent their daughter from ever reaching the courthouse in the first place (in virtually all states, the alternative procedure is in the nature of a court hearing) or from subsequently obtaining an abortion, thus effectively vetoing her decision.

Despite the surface reasonableness of this approach, as in the funding cases, the result tilts firmly toward motherhood. What the court essentially ignores is the fact that in most states, teens can self-consent to sensitive medically related care, such as the diagnosis and treatment of sexually transmitted infections. Most directly relevant is that teens, no matter how young, can make their own decisions to carry a pregnancy to term—an ability that carries with it the right to make all pregnancy-related medical decisions as well as medical decisions for the resulting child—a reality that raises serious doubts about the sincerity of the court's expressed concern that teens are not mature enough to make their own reproductive decision.[83]

In 1992, the Supreme Court handed down its decision in the case of *Planned Parenthood of Southeastern Pennsylvania v. Casey,* in which it both affirmed *and* substantially undercut its prior decision in *Roe v. Wade.* In evaluating the constitutionality of the challenged Pennsylvania law before it, which, among other provisions, included an informed consent and a waiting period requirement akin to those it had invalidated in *Akron,* the court announced that the time had come for it to reevaluate its decision in *Roe*.

The court indicated that if the abortion question was before it for the first time, it might have decided the matter differently. However, any reservations that some of the justices may have had about reaffirming what they referred to as the "central holding" of *Roe* were outweighed by their respect for the concept of individual liberty coupled with the principle of stare decisis (literally meaning "to stand by that which is decided"), which limits the ability of a court to overrule prior decisions.[84] It accordingly upheld what it characterized as the "central principle" of *Roe*—namely, the right of a woman to decide to terminate a pregnancy before viability.

In doing so, the court invoked notions of women's dignity and equality, thus suggesting that the "new feminist discourse of women's rights" had perhaps begun to seep into the consciousness of a least some of the justices. For example, it stressed that regardless of the long-standing historic emphasis on the central importance of motherhood in a woman's life, her "destiny . . . must be shaped to a large extent on her own conception of her spiritual imperatives and her place in society," and further observed that the "ability of women to participate equally in the economic and social life of the Nation has been facilitated by their ability to control their reproductive lives."[85]

This aspect of the decision was clearly an important victory for supporters of the right to abortion and was likewise a major defeat for abortion opponents who had hoped that the court would finally overturn *Roe*. However, this was not the end of the court's analysis. Having focused on the abortion issue from the perspective of the pregnant woman, it then shifted perspectives to consider the state's interest in the potentiality of life. In this shift, the *Casey* decision sharply undercuts the integrity of *Roe*.

In accordance with *Roe*'s trimester framework, states were not permitted to enact restrictive laws to promote their interest in the potentiality of life until the third trimester, at which point, they could prohibit abortion unless necessary to protect the life or health of a pregnant woman. However, according to the *Casey* court, the trimester framework was not part of "the essential holding" of *Roe,* but instead served as a rigid constraint on the ability of states to promote their legitimate interest in the potentiality of life. As explained, "the trimester framework, however, does not fulfill *Roe*'s own promise that the State has an interest in protecting fetal life or potential life. *Roe* began the contradiction by using the trimester framework to forbid any regulation of abortion designed to advance that interest before viability."[86] Dramatically reconfiguring the role of the state, the court accordingly abandoned *Roe*'s trimester framework in favor of an "undue burden standard," which it deemed the "appropriate means of reconciling the State's interest with the woman's constitutionally protected liberty."[87]

Under this newly enunciated standard, laws that are designed to promote the state's interest in the unborn from the outset of pregnancy are now considered to be constitutionally acceptable so long as they do not impose an undue burden, or "substantial obstacle" in the path of a woman seeking to terminate a pregnancy. Highlighting the new place of the unborn in abortion jurisprudence, the *Casey* court concludes its reconsideration of *Roe* as follows:

> What is at stake is the woman's right to make the ultimate decision. . . . Regulations which do no more than create a structural mechanism by which the State, or the parent or guardian of a minor, may express profound respect for the life of the unborn are permitted, if they are not a substantial obstacle to the woman's exercise of the right to choose. Unless it has that effect on her right to choose, a state measure designed to persuade her to choose childbirth over abortion will be upheld if reasonably related to that goal.[88]

Although the *Casey* court made clear that abortion is still a constitutionally protected right, its wholesale repudiation of *Roe*'s trimester framework in favor of the far less protective undue burden standard gave states the green light to enact laws aimed at chipping away at the abortion right.

Pointing the way to the future, the *Casey* court proceeded to uphold the informed consent and waiting period provisions of the Pennsylvania law as valid expressions of the state's "preference for childbirth over abortion," even though they served to increase the "cost and risk of delay of abortions" and the risk of exposure "to the harassment and hostility of antiabortion protestors" as women had to negotiate two trips to the clinic. The court blithely concluded that these burdens were not "undue," because although making things more difficult, they did not amount to actual barriers.[89] In so deciding, the court overturned its prior decision in *Akron v. Akron Center for Reproductive Health,* in which it had held that measures intended "not to inform the woman's consent but rather to persuade her to withhold it altogether" were an unconstitutional infringement on the abortion right.

The changed standard in *Casey* for evaluating the constitutionality of restrictive laws is generally understood as being pro-natalist in orientation given that the court gave states the green light to pass laws expressing their "profound respect for the life of the unborn." However, this shift also can be read as presaging the emergence of the woman-protective approach, which emerges more fully in the 2007 case of *Gonzales v. Carhart*. Specifically, in elaborating on why doctors can be compelled to provide the woman with state-scripted information, the court explained that "in attempting to ensure that a woman apprehends the full consequences of her decision," the state was simply furthering the "legitimate purpose of reducing the risk that [she] may elect an abortion, only to discover later, with devastating consequences, that her decision was not fully informed."[90]

CONCLUSION

In the 1973 landmark case of *Roe v. Wade,* the Supreme Court held that women have a fundamental, although not an absolute, constitutional right to an abortion. Although the *Roe* court addressed the critical role that 19th-century physicians associated with the AMA played in the enactment of these laws, it limited its discussion to their interest in protecting unborn life. As a result of this narrow focus, the decision fails to reckon with the gendered and racialized tropes that were tightly woven into the very fabric of the nation's criminal abortion laws. In turn, we contend that this pinched reading of the history of our criminal abortion laws has contributed to a masking of the deeply paternalistic turn of the law.

Opponents of abortion reacted to the *Roe* decision with a swift and fierce intensity. The political branch of the movement focused on overturning or chipping away at *Roe* through legislation and litigation. Although efforts to overturn *Roe* were unsuccessful, in the years following the decision, a panoply of restrictive laws were enacted. Growing weary with this slow and gradual pace of change, the direct-action branch turned to unconventional tactics to shut down the abortion industry. This frustration was also heighted by the Supreme Court's 1992 decision in *Planned Parenthood of Southeastern Pennsylvania v. Casey,* which reaffirmed the constitutionality of the abortion right.

In making the case against abortion, these two publicly oriented branches of the movement were singularly focused on the protection of fetal life, and they paid little or no attention to the needs or interest of pregnant women. However, as we will see in the next chapter, abortion-minded women occupy a central place in the privatized and feminized outreach branch of the movement, which is dominated by crisis pregnancy centers (CPCs). Rather than seeking to effectuate sweeping change, a primary goal of CPCs is to steer women away from abortion to save them from a life of trauma—a task that is typically attended to by counselors who frequently draw upon their own experiential knowledge of postabortion suffering.

THREE

The Crisis Pregnancy Centers and the Roots of the Contemporary Abortion Regret Narrative

Following the *Roe* court's invalidation of strict criminal abortion laws on constitutional grounds, the political and then the direct-action branches of the antiabortion movement, with their singular focus on the sanctity of fetal life, shifted into high gear to turn back the clock. At the same time, as we will see in this chapter, a very different antiabortion narrative was taking root in the feminized outreach branch of the movement, which is dominated by crisis pregnancy centers (CPCs).* Rather than centering their objections to abortion on the fetus, counselors working in this setting instead turned their gaze to the emotional precarity of abortion-minded women.

This chapter focuses on the place and growing influence of CPCs within the antiabortion movement. As we will see, CPCs have blossomed into women-centered powerhouses where abortion regret narratives are continuously generated and entrenched through the provision of services to abortion-minded women. Following an overview of the origins of the CPC movement in the pre-*Roe* era, we take a close look at the deeply feminized and religious orientation of these privatized spaces and explore how these

_____

* The outreach branch of the pro-life movement recently rebranded crisis pregnancy centers as "crisis resource centers" (Munson 2018).

qualities permeate the efforts of counselors to steer abortion-minded women toward motherhood to safeguard them from regret. These efforts are typically rooted in the experiential knowledge of the counselors, which they parlay into universal truths about the traumatizing effect of abortion. The chapter concludes with an examination of two additional services that are now being offered by CPCs—postabortion support and perinatal hospice care, which both serve to expand the reach of the abortion regret narrative.

We want to note several important dimensions of this chapter. First, it draws heavily upon in-depth interviews we conducted between 2007 and 2012 with 23 CPC counselors (both paid and volunteer), which help to illuminate the feminized care work that is the hallmark of the CPCs.[†] Our deconstruction of these interviews should not be read as a critique of the sincerity of the interviewees' stories, nor as a repudiation of the ways in which they make meaning out of their own experiences. Rather, our critique is directed toward the ways in which their voices have been lifted up and privileged as a representation that claims to speak for all women in order to actualize a political and legal agenda.

Second, in this chapter we pay particularly close attention to comparisons between the 19th-century antiabortion physicians and those who populate today's CPCs to highlight the fact that similar concerns animate both groups' opposition to abortion despite more than a century that separates them. Many of the closely intertwined gendered and religious undertones that enlivened the 19th-century physicians' campaign are threaded throughout the contemporary abortion regret narrative, providing a modern reboot to a rather well-trodden narrative.

In this regard, however, discerning readers might well have noticed that although we indicated our plan to identify many of the "closely entwined gendered and religious motifs" that conjoin the past with the present, we said nothing about our intent to do so with respect to the racial themes that the 19th-century doctors deployed to advance their cause. This omission is not an oversight. Rather, although a similar construction of women as inherently and eternally maternal is manifest across the two generations of antiabortion activists, today's regret narrative is not similarly steeped in the overtly racialized discourses that populated the physicians' antiabortion arguments.

---

† See the methods appendix for additional details.

Instead, abortion regret is framed as a "color-blind" narrative that serves as a universalizing stand-in for all women's abortion experiences. Nesting the regret narrative in the language of "women's rights" serves to erase a multitude of significant racialized dynamics that differently shape women's reproductive experiences based upon a myriad of intersecting factors, including race, class, culture, and gender identity. This unevenness of experience is represented in basic reproductive health measures. For instance, compared to white women, African American women are nearly four times as likely to die from a pregnancy-related cause,[1] and they have significantly higher abortion and unintended birthrates.[2]

The race-neutral deployment of the abortion regret narrative glosses over the ways in which antiabortion policies as a whole are entwined in systems of intersectional and institutionalized racism. As a result, the antiabortion movement, which is dominated by white activists, fails to account for the ways in which the "color-blind" regret narrative may serve to mask racialized dynamics that continue to haunt contemporary antiabortion practices and policies. In short, we may need to look elsewhere to pierce the veil of racial neutrality.

In fact, one need look no farther than the "Black Genocide" billboard campaign to do so. This effort, which Life Always and the Radiance Foundation campaign has spearheaded, involves the strategic location of billboards in predominantly African American neighborhoods. The campaign boasts slogans such as "the most dangerous place for a African American child is in the womb." Fighting back against this initiative, the group SisterSong Women of Color Reproductive Justice Collective makes clear that it is a "misogynistic attack to shame-and-blame black women who choose abortion, alleging that we endanger the future of our children . . . [and] to claim that black women have a racial obligation to have more babies . . . despite our individual circumstances."[3]

The effort to shame black women underscores the campaign's deeply racialized message that black women *should* regret their abortions because their bodies are invested with social meaning that presumptively trumps their own agency. As Jennifer M. Denbow writes, this "representation not only occludes the interests of African American women who symbolically stand against the fetus, it also renders them threats to the polity and precarious citizens."[4] Simultaneously, however, they are also cast as victims of an abortion industry that seeks to strong-arm them into terminating their pregnancies. As a result of this coercion, African American women are thus seen as in need of rescue, which effectively serves to "increase the surveillance of women of color and undermine their decision making."[5‡] Fusing the 19th-century understanding of aborting women as malevolent presences in need of management with the contemporary view of them as victims in need of protection, the billboard campaign helps us to see that the seemingly color-blind abortion regret narrative may in fact be infused with racialized meaning.

Dr. Willie Parker's deep aversion as "an African American abortion provider" toward the "Black genocide" campaign further suggests that this may well be the case. As Parker argues, the groups behind this effort do not actually care about black babies and black women but are using "women of color as pawns in a much bigger game" to eventually "limit access to abortion for all women, including and especially white women." As he continues on to explain, the "thing all too many white antiabortion activists really want, which they can't say out loud, is for white women to have more babies, in order to push back against the browning of America."[6] Reinforcing the eerie similarity to the 19th-century antiabortion campaign, Parker thus argues that despite seemingly being aimed at encouraging women of color to embrace motherhood, the end goal is in fact to turn white women away from abortion to recalibrate the racial balance of the nation.

TURNING WOMEN TOWARD MOTHERHOOD

In the 1960s, Louise Summerhill, a Catholic mother of seven children living in Ontario, Canada, was troubled by what she identified as an absence of concern and the acute familial scrutiny of unmarried women experiencing unplanned pregnancies.[7] Opening a modest, one-room office in 1968, Summerhill's vision was to create a space in which pregnant women could interact with other women and receive "personal, one-on-one contact in helping relationships" to guide them through their "pregnancy dilemmas."[8] With little money to fund her vision, Summerhill relied on the "good hearts and hard work of volunteers" to staff the organization.

In the ensuing decades, Summerhill's vision grew into the first international crisis pregnancy service (Birthright International), including the

---

‡ See Denbow (2016) for an analysis of the ways in which laws seeking to ban race-selective abortions encode similar themes.

opening of offices in the United States, to offer "love, hope and support to each woman [and] to help her make a realistic plan for her future and the future of her unborn child."[9] In contrast to other CPCs that would soon come to dominate the landscape in the United States, Birthright operated within a secular framework. Although most of the leaders in this country were Catholics, Birthright "advised volunteers not to invoke religious arguments against abortion with the women who visited their centers"—a pledge that continues to shape their work today.[10]

Expanding beyond Summerhill's initiative, as individual states began to liberalize their abortion laws in the 1960s, concerned pro-life Catholics began seeking alternatives to abortion clinics by opening CPCs, which, like Birthright, tended to be secular in orientation.[11] In contrast, as evangelical Christians began opening CPCs, these centers adopted an overtly religious orientation where "being Christ" or "sharing Christ" with clients was integral to their counseling work.[12] Growing from a meager cadre of 75 centers in 1971, currently an amorphous constellation of approximately 2,700 CPCs operate in the United States.[13]§

Today, most CPCs in this country are affiliated with one of three Christ-centered federated organizations—Heartbeat International, Care Net, or the National Institute of Family and Life (NIFL). Dominating the landscape, these umbrella organizations provide critical resources for the independently owned and operated affiliates who adhere to their biblical principles and policies.[14] In short, as described on the Care Net website, the umbrella organizations offer "compassion, hope, and help to anyone considering abortion by presenting them with realistic alternatives and Christ-centered support through [a] life-affirming network of pregnancy centers, organizations, and individuals."[15]

In contrast to the political and direct-action branches, which men have historically dominated, CPCs from their inception have mainly

---

§ Although the outreach branch of the antiabortion movement primarily consists of CPCs, a larger pregnancy help movement (PHM) exists, which also includes hotlines, maternity homes, adoption agencies, and independent crisis pregnancy centers. The outreach branch and the PHM share a similar goal of assisting pregnant women; however, they are not necessarily affiliated with each other. Although some antiabortion CPCs may consider themselves as part of the pregnancy help movement, the reverse is atypical. Consequently, due to the large number of organizations that provide services to pregnant women and the absence of a shared definition of what constitutes a CPC, estimates of the number of CPCs operating in this country vary from approximately 2,000 to 4,500.

relied upon female volunteers whose goal is to "reach and rescue as many lives as possible" by turning abortion-minded women toward motherhood to save them from a lifetime of regret.[16] Notably, CPC volunteers contribute the most hours to the antiabortion movement, which has shaped the gendered care work taking place in the centers.[17] Heartbeat International, for instance, has more than 25,000 volunteers working in its network of CPCs,[18] and the Family Research Council concluded that in 2010, roughly 71,000 volunteers contributed an estimated 5,705,000 hours to CPCs.[19]

Although contributing the most volunteer hours to the antiabortion movement as a whole, the intimate and individualized woman-centered ethic of CPCs means that these centers have historically operated in the shadows of the political and direct-action branches of the movement, which, as discussed, have focused on making their case against abortion in the public square.[20] However, as the pro-woman/pro-life antiabortion argument has taken hold as a political strategy for limiting access to abortion, the visibility and stature of CPCs has increased.

Although a detailed discussion is outside the scope of this book, it is important to recognize that many CPCs have been soundly and consistently criticized for deliberately engaging in "high-pressure tactics to guilt, trick, or otherwise coerce women to carry their pregnancies to term."[21] It is also a common practice to provide women with misleading or false information.[22] For example, Amy G. Bryant and Jonas Swartz[23] criticize CPCs as unethical because they often "strive to appear as sites offering clinical services and unbiased advice" when in reality "most CPCs are not licensed, and their staff are not licensed medical professionals."[24] Even more troubling, "regardless of whether a particular location is licensed, CPCs engage in counseling that is misleading or false," and they fail to "meet the standard of patient-centered, quality medical care."[25]

Most CPCs offer free pregnancy testing, which is often the "hook" for bringing women into the centers.[26] Hoping to guide them toward motherhood, many CPCs have added free ultrasound services to facilitate mother-child bonding. During our interview with Ryan, the director of a CPC,** he touted the benefits of advertising his center's free ultrasound exams for women, explaining that ultrasounds are a "secret weapon" for CPCs: "we

---

** It should be noted that most directors of CPCs start out as volunteer counselors, and many continue to counsel women even after moving into a directorship position.

have the 4-D ultrasound machine and we can show them the scan of their own baby. Once they see their own baby, that makes a big difference to them. We've had women that were very hardened to having an abortion. By the time they get through [the exam], usually they've chosen life over abortion."[27] Ryan's sentiments were shared across our interviews with CPC workers who viewed ultrasound exams as an invaluable tool that creates "an immediate bond" between a "mother and her child" because "it confirms the fact that it's a baby and not just a blob."[28]

Seeing the potential for ultrasound technology to persuade abortion-minded women to choose life, starting in 2004, Focus on the Family began providing grant funding through its Project Ultrasound program to help CPCs acquire the equipment. By 2017, 40 percent of CPCs were outfitted with ultrasound equipment, and Focus on the Family credits this technology with changing the minds of 70 to 90 percent of abortion-minded women who seek out crisis pregnancy centers.[29]

Despite this robust claim of success, according to eKROS, a data management company that tracks data for 1,450 "Christ-centered pregnancy resource centers," the impact is far more modest, with data showing that between 2004 and 2017, less than 4 percent of clients changed their minds about abortion as a result of seeing their ultrasound.[30] This result squares with other research findings. For example, in their review of medical records for 15,575 women seeking abortion services at a clinic that conducted ultrasounds prior to the procedure, researchers found that a small number of women who were uncertain about their decision to abort prior to the viewing opted to continue their pregnancy; however, the vast majority (approximately 98 percent) of those who viewed the ultrasound did not change their decision to abort.[31] Tracking these findings, a recent major study demonstrated that women's reactions to viewing an ultrasound prior to an abortion—even when it is mandated by the state—cannot be distilled to a singular emotional response, but rather, reactions are "steeped in a political, social, and personal context."[32] Moreover, in contrast to the experience of women with wanted pregnancies, there was little evidence that viewing an ultrasound inspired a maternal bond in women seeking an abortion.[33]

After a positive pregnancy test followed possibly by an ultrasound exam, the mostly volunteer lay counselors facilitate conversations with women to provide them with alternatives to abortion and emotional support as they navigate the decision-making process. In addition, the majority of CPCs also offer pregnant women a range of free material resources, such as clothing, diapers, and formula, to help alleviate the immediate financial needs that could potentially be influencing their decision to abort.[34][††] However, as interviewee Katherine, director of a CPC, noted, the continued receipt of these free resources is contingent upon a woman's participation in "educational classes." As she explains: "we don't just give everything away for free. We don't just give you free diapers every time you come in. If you come to our classes and you have earned [Mommy Bucks], then you get to buy diapers or wipes or whatever. So, I really see [CPCs] fitting in to some of the social needs of our society."[35]

At Katherine's center, the classes focus on "sexual integrity," which is shorthand for helping clients to understand that sexual intimacy is only to be experienced within the boundaries of a heterosexual marriage. In addition to focusing on appropriate sexual behavior, some CPCs offer secular-oriented classes that are aimed at helping clients to shore up their life skills with the ultimate goal of strengthening their parenting abilities. Importantly, regardless of their primary focus, instructional activities are often tied to religious teachings aimed at strengthening each participant's personal relationship with God.[36]

More directly benchmarking the relationship between religious teachings and services, CPC director Marsha explained:

> If they want to continue to receive our services, it is a requirement that they do a one-page Bible study. We will give it to them twice, and if they haven't completed that on their own, then we would ask that they would stay and fill out that Bible study, just to have a level of accountability because regardless of where you go, you have to have a level of accountability and we feel like a one-page Bible study is a minimum requirement.[37]

Requiring pregnant women to participate in courses guided by religious principles, such as "sexual integrity classes" or a Bible study, underscores the religiosity of both Katherine and Marsha's CPCs—an orientation that is a bedrock identity of most CPCs in this country.[38]

---

†† Some CPCs have intentionally chosen to stay away from providing material support because they believe it detracts from their purpose. For example, in our interview with CPC director Felicity, she explained, "A lot of centers do material support. We really try intentionally to stay away from that. Material support is one tiny piece of a resource that is necessary, but it's not why we exist. And, there are a lot of places in [the community] that we can send clients to get stuff" (interview with Alesha E. Doan, 2012).

Beyond providing some short-term relief for the more immediate pressing financial needs of their clients, CPCs do not have the bandwidth to address the structural poverty facing a significant portion of those seeking their services. Trying to bridge this gap, most CPCs supplement any short-term material support they provide to low-income clients with referrals to social service providers that are potentially better equipped to assist them with the long-term costs (i.e., subsidized housing, food stamps, and Medicaid) associated with parenting.[39]

CRISIS PREGNANCY CENTERS AS FEMINIZED AND RELIGIOUS SPACES

As discussed, the political and direct-action branches of the antiabortion movement have traditionally focused their efforts on safeguarding the rights of the fetus within the highly visible public square. In contrast, the work of the mostly female volunteers of the outreach branch typically takes place within the cloistered spaces of the nation's CPCs—spaces that are both feminized and infused with a quiet but intense religiosity.[40] Thus, as Kimberly Kelly explains, contemporary pro-life activism is dominated by women who have "shifted attention away from the fetus and toward women in unplanned pregnancies."[41]

In this section, we seek to unpack some of the complexities and nuances of the care work that CPC counselors provide to abortion-minded women. Although we discuss gender and religiosity in separate subsections to highlight the themes that are distinctive to each, note that these themes are intertwined, thus leading to some inevitable overlap.

Feminized Care Work: Unpacking the Contemporary Nuances and Historical Continuity of the Construction of Gender within Crisis Pregnancy Centers

CPCs have emerged as the contemporary "intimate confidant" that Dr. Storer imagined himself and other physicians to be in the 1800s. However, in stark contrast to the physicians' masculinized orientation, CPCs have always been deeply feminized spaces. Notably, they are rooted in care work—defined as physical and emotional labor for others, marked by nurturance, empathy, and selflessness.[42] Because these characteristics are so closely identified with traditionally feminized qualities associated with domestic labor, care work is also often thought to be interchangeable with the concept of "women's work." By aligning the mission of CPCs with the interests of women and their unborn children, the care work performed within these centers adheres to a more traditional, gendered, private sphere of activism, which is also imbued with a marked religiosity.

The gendered identity, in the present context, of CPCs affords women the opportunity to move into the public sphere without compromising their sense of identity as domestically oriented and nurturing, particularly because volunteering is conventionally seen as part of the apolitical private sphere.[43] Viewing volunteer work as apolitical is important for many women working in the antiabortion movement, especially among those who volunteer in direct-service programs at crisis pregnancy centers.[44] These volunteers describe their work as educational, empowering, empathetic, and even the "real action"—but never as political.[45] Instead, women like CPC director Claire explain their work in terms of "empowering women with information" and providing resources to clients to help them make an informed decision in a safe space.[46]

The sustained commitment of CPC volunteers and staffers to guard and reify traditional gender roles, particularly those of mother and homemaker, gives buoyancy to their "empowering" work, and aligns them with earlier generations of antiabortion activists who harbored similar trepidations about what they viewed as society's devaluation of homemakers and its elevation of "modern" women. Thus, as we saw in Chapter One, the 19th-century antiabortion physicians positively bristled with animosity toward the "new woman" who purportedly rejected motherhood in the selfish pursuit of other activities better left to men, such as voting. More recently, Luker's interviews with pro-life activists in the post-*Roe* era revealed the concern that by making the continuation of a pregnancy optional, the legalization of abortion had downgraded motherhood from a "sacred calling" to a mere "job," which women could embrace or reject at will, much as they might any other opportunity that happened to come their way.[47]

Embodying traditional gender roles and qualities that exemplify care work, CPC counselors contribute to the overall aims of the antiabortion movement by educating and persuading clients to embrace motherhood without compromising their female-centered identities by affiliating with the more male-identified world of antiabortion politics.[48] Corresponding with prizing traditional gender roles, with its long-standing stress on selfless giving, most of the intensive and time-consuming labor provided at CPCs is performed by volunteers. They gain emotional compensation through assisting clients—almost exclusively pregnant women—in a more intimate, relational setting, as compared to other more public forms of anti-abortion activism, such as protests and sidewalk counseling.[49] Volunteerism thus operates to supply many resource-starved centers with a stream of free labor that fuels their work.[50‡‡]

Embodying many of these characteristics, as a new CPC volunteer, Jennifer did not consider herself political; instead she preferred the rewards of domesticity—nurturing her marriage and raising her children whom she described as healthy, successful young adults. Jennifer's decision to volunteer at a CPC came about as a reaction to a conversation with her sister-in-law who scoffed at the idea of embracing a domestic career and then went on to nonchalantly mention that she aborted an unwanted pregnancy. During our interview, Jennifer recounted the indelible mark this conversation had on her: "it was my sister-in-law's abortion. She just kept on going like it was normal. It just brought it home. It was personal . . . that would have been my niece or nephew. That would have been family."[51]

Although her children were young adults at the time of the conversation with her sister-in-law, Jennifer still treasured being a "stay-at-home mom." She felt stung and marginalized by her sister-in-law's normalization of her own abortion and concomitant rejection of motherhood. Volunteering at a CPC thus served as a way for Jennifer to reclaim her domestic identity *outside* of the home and impart to other women the value of motherhood and child rearing. Operating as a counterweight to the sense of devaluation she felt after the exchange with her sister-in-law, the feminized culture of CPCs appealed to Jennifer, and offered her a seamless transition to a new but familiar and cherished role. Despite the long volunteer hours Jennifer clocked each week, like many other CPC care workers, she quickly pointed out the reward—namely, "seeing those little babies come through the door with those mommies and those happy smiles."[52]

At first blush, younger CPC volunteers, such as Donald, presented a more accepting view of contemporary gender norms. But as his interview unfolded, like Jennifer, he pushed back on what he described as the prevailing social views that devalue domesticity. Having "really benefitted" from a stay-at-home mom who "was always there," Donald wants to see

---

‡‡ In Hussey's (2014) survey of CPC volunteers and paid staff, 80 percent of workers reported being married, and among volunteers, the majority (64 percent) are electively unemployed, while an additional (nearly 18 percent) are employed part-time.

societal norms shift to re-embrace and laud domesticity because "women staying at home should not be discouraged at all," and "it should actually be looked at as a great thing for a woman to do."[53]

Our interviews also highlight the deep commitment that CPC counselors have to the feminized care work in which they are engaged. Critical in this regard is the value they attach to their unique, time-intensive approach to building relationships with clients, which Sandra praises as the "quiet, hidden-away pro-life work that speaks by example and not through argument or fighting."[54] Comparing the work performed in CPCs to that done in the other branches of the pro-life movement, CPC director Lindsey explained, "we can have more personal one-on-one involvement with the people. I think that's probably the big difference. Not just seeing [women] one time or two times but having the long-term relationship with them where we get to know them, include them, and help them in their life."[55] As Lindsey stresses, the real power of CPCs lies in the willingness of counselors to have repeated, personal interactions that facilitate long-term relationships with women. Her reflections echo the findings of Kelly's (2012) research in which she concludes that women working within this branch of the antiabortion movement: "feel that feminized, relational approaches carried out woman-to-woman represent the best strategies for preventing abortion and converting clients." At times this may require counselors to subordinate traditional evangelical solutions to an unplanned pregnancy—namely marriage or the relinquishment of the child for adoption—to advance a client's best interest.[56]

In describing the environment of the local CPC where she volunteers, Felicity also emphasized its relational aspects:

> There is so much compassion in centers like this. You can come in and it's a non-judgmental attitude. Everybody wants to be heard when they're facing something [difficult]. They want to know that there's somebody that cares about them—that has their best interest at heart. I think that's the value of these centers because that's exactly what the foundation is. There is a lot of compassion and a lot of caring that goes out of these centers.[57]

Guided by a woman-centered approach, Felicity makes it clear that her primary loyalty—and that of CPCs as a whole—lies with leading clients to decisions that align with their "best interest." In practice, this means that Felicity willingly supports a client's choice of single motherhood rather than pressuring her to pursue more suitable evangelical solutions to an unplanned pregnancy. However, Felicity does not view her support for a religiously unconventional solution as a slight against her faith. To the contrary, she channels her evangelicalism into establishing trusting relationships with clients and in turn, helps them to cultivate a relationship with God, which she believes is the cornerstone for saving abortion-vulnerable women from regret.

The embrace of traditional gender roles of those working in CPCs is moored to their belief in a divine ordering, which cements into place a fixed understanding of gender that shapes the contours of the feminized care work in which they engage. Akin to the 19th-century antiabortion physicians, CPC counselors embrace a biological construction of gender that supports the traditional evangelical underpinnings of most centers, but with a nod to modernity. CPCs provide a space where women exercise agency and occupy leadership roles in gender-segregated spaces, while upholding and ascribing to traditional gender values.[58] Assuming these leadership positions has enabled "women to identify with men's goals [while] actively recenter[ing] their efforts to reflect women's interest."[59]

Reflecting on the changing opportunities available to today's women, college-age volunteer Brittney pointed out that unlike the women coming of age in the 1950s who were boxed into a domestic life, the women of today have "the same opportunities as men," which she sees as "a good thing."[60] Outlining her future plans, Brittney explained, "Personally I want to have a career first, and then settle down and be able to live comfortably and be a stay-at-home mom."[61] In short, Brittney wants the best of both worlds, a desire that reflects contemporary notions of female agency, which unmoors women—at least temporarily—from a fixed maternal destiny, while ultimately yielding to traditional gender ideologies. Her more fluid, modern embrace of both customary and contemporary roles for women is also reflected in the feminized leadership and culture of CPCs. On the one hand, all interviewees elevated the importance of women's unpaid work as mothers and homemakers; on the other hand, the majority were also supportive of women entering into the labor force so long as they put motherhood first and foremost. Of critical importance is that they do not sacrifice this central identity for that of the career woman, which they believed is the case with today's misguided "liberated" women.

In sharp contrast to the 19th-century physicians who sought to stop abortion by exclusively mobilizing and asserting male authority over women and their reproductive bodies, for contemporary activists, women have a definitive role in this work. Counselors' understanding of gender as divinely fixed somewhat paradoxically provides women with an innate authority within the CPC space. Rather than a limitation, embracing this construction of gender often empowers female care workers to "explicitly claim legitimacy for their positions based on their gender" and to draw on strategies that eclipse patriarchal control and authority.[62] CPC director Evelyn reflects this nuance by carefully articulating the importance of having women support other women. She explained that, "women find themselves having to make these huge decisions all the time, with very little support. We're not saying men aren't great, you know. But there is something to having a female network to understand the complexity of things that you engage in, and we need it in pregnancy."[63] Evelyn's stress on the importance of a "female network" resonates with Kelly's observation that "for the CPC movement, conservative religion created the motivation, space, and legitimacy for activism on behalf of other women."[64]

Within this space, adhering to strict gender roles elevates the status of women, rather than simply serving to oppress them.[65] Ascribing to gender essentialism gave Evelyn, as the full-time director of a CPC, a valid evangelical framework for eschewing male authority and privileging female authority in the realm of pregnancy. According to Evelyn, men—"even the best of them"—have a limited capacity to truly connect with the embodied experience of pregnancy. She accordingly advocated for female-centered support networks because women uniquely possess the expertise to meet other women "in their time of need" and even beyond the initial stages of a "crisis pregnancy."

Unlike in the other branches of the movement, adherence to a gender essentialist model within the confined realm of CPCs ironically creates a space in which men can temporarily acquiesce authority to women. Although limited in scope and reach, within this setting, gender operates as a credentialed, ethereal source of expertise that invites and requires female activism.§§ Underscoring the evolution of activism from a strictly masculine project of repair in the 19th century, in which women were not imagined as worthwhile accomplices, to a contemporary feminized repair project, seasoned activist Mike credited women as making the best volunteers. Firmly rooted in essentialist gendered beliefs, Mike explains that women have a "naturally caring attitude about them that guys don't seem

---

§§ However, dissent does exist. Some male evangelical leaders have criticized the woman-centered approach of the outreach branch for being ineffective and straying from the pressing goal of preventing abortion and evangelizing to clients (Kelly 2012, 203–30).

to have, and they will understand things differently than a guy will ever understand them," thus they are superior "frontline sidewalk counselors and CPC counselors."[66]

Although women may enjoy a prominent status within the cloistered space of the CPCs, this position remains anchored in an immutable understanding of women's special capacities and location in a tightly woven gendered social order. Like the 19th-century antiabortion physicians who singled out the woman's movement for seducing the middle-class matrons away from motherhood, those active today in the CPCs are also preoccupied with the destructive impact of feminism on gender roles. Capturing this view and echoing the cries of the prior generation who proclaimed that "the whole country [was] in an abnormal state" because of recent attempts to "force women into men's places,"[67] Ryan decried the fact that "the women's movement tried to elevate women into thinking that if they became more like men, then they would be equal. Well actually they weren't trying to elevate them. They degraded women down to a man."[68]

The lasting societal changes ushered in by second-wave feminists continue to occupy a place of anxiety and frustration for many interviewees who believe the changes have been "misguided" with a deleterious impact on both men and women—themes that also permeated Luker's interviews with antiabortion activists in the 1980s. Offering a gentler rendition, several interviewees echoed the more caustic views of the women's movement that were voiced more than 30 years earlier by leaders in the direct-action branch of the antiabortion movement.

Although their concerns were expressed in less colorful language than, say, those of George Gilder, who bemoaned the fact that the penis was no longer a "decisive organ,"[69] a fear of emasculation continues to haunt some of the men we interviewed. The consternation that they expressed over a perceived feminist mockery of motherhood and "traditional values" was matched by their angst regarding the deleterious spillover influence they believe the women's movement has had on scores of men who now feel unmoored from their traditional and highly valued roles. Mourning these changes, interviewee Steven believes "men, as a rule, have lost their identity. Men used to have a role. A very definitive role. They were the father, they were the protector. They were the provider."[70] Lamenting the legal changes that have further reduced men's domestic authority, one seasoned male activist dejectedly pointed out that "society's done a disservice to men by telling them 'well it's the woman's right to choose' and usually they don't have any say-so in that, and legally, they don't."[71]

Further elaborating on this critique, many of the interviewees believe that the women's movement's staunch support of abortion rights has altered the natural gender order by falsely liberating men from their duties at the expense of women's well-being. Interviewee Paul thus expressed his bafflement of misguided feminists, who "cling to" abortion as a "woman's reproductive rights issue" because from his perspective "it's the guys who get all the freebies." Underscoring the faulty logic and promise of feminism, Paul points to the women he has counseled to illustrate the deterioration of masculinity in society: "These poor women don't have any idea of the long-term consequences of their actions. And dudes don't care. We have these men who do nothing more than take advantage of women. Predatory males, I call them. And they're out there, and they love abortion. They think it's great."[72] Like Paul, Mike also sees a crisis of masculinity spurred by the women's movement, and he too locates access to abortion at the center of this crisis for permitting men to "have sex conveniently" by liberating them from worrying about the consequences.[73]

The sanctity of the feminized space of the CPCs is continually scripted and complicated by both male and female counselors who construct the innate complexity and fragility of women's agency in opposition to their more simplistic and base construction of the nature of many men. Adopting a binary construction of good versus bad men, interviewees carefully delineated between "real men" who "stand for what's right" and "will get involved to help somebody to do the right thing," and unscrupulous men who "walk away" or "coerce" women into having abortions.[74] Leery of this latter type of men, counselors regard them as posing another roadblock that can easily derail women from motherhood. Drawing on a mix of personal and counseling experiences with clients, staffers frequently described these men as intimidating, manipulative, authoritative figures who pressure women into aborting unplanned pregnancies as a way to shirk their responsibilities as protectors of and providers for women.

CPC staff is well versed in defending against and countering this form of male coercion. Jane insists she simply "will not condone a woman being pressured by a boyfriend or a husband" into having an abortion because the man can "walk away" while the woman is left permanently scarred by regret.[75] Enlisting more acidic language, according to Paul, "predatory men" can simply pressure women to "get rid of the child, to kill the child" as a ruse to avoid paying child support.[76] Interviewees believe that abortion provides a "freebie" for men that harms women, and that the solution lies in reinstating men to their primary role of protector and provider. However, they recognize that, in practice, traversing this restorative path is complicated.

Jumping between a rejection of feminism and an embrace of its ideals, interviewees often borrow and repurpose feminists' calls for female autonomy and empowerment to dissuade women from having abortions in favor of motherhood. Attempting to empower clients, Mike encourages abortion-minded women to level the playing field by taking control of their lives and doling out a dose of revenge:

> I tell women if you're trying to get even with the guy, have the baby. That'll get even with him. For 18 stinking years, every month he is going to have to write you a check. That's the way to get even with him. You think having the abortion is the way to get even with him? No. He's off, he doesn't care about this, he's on to the next woman. You've done nothing to get even with him—have the baby, that'll get even with him.[77]

In softer and less punitive terms, counselors like Katherine carefully explained that they are not trying to be "disagreeable" to men but that they "will not support a woman being pressured." She sees CPCs as creating a safe environment where volunteers and staff can help women remove hurdles at "critical junctures."[78]

The interviewed counselors' portrayal of clients as confused, scared, and pressured into aborting aligns with the larger reverent construction of women within the feminized and religious space of a CPC. Counselors idealized and lauded the virtues of women as mothers, caretakers, and wives, by continuously encouraging clients to visualize the instantaneous joy of motherhood they will experiences as soon as "they see that baby's face."[79] Building on stereotypes of feminists as anti-man, and reappropriating this stereotype into the pro-life framework as a way to "empower" women via revenge, counselors try to expose the self-serving motivations of errant men for steering women toward abortion while emboldening clients to navigate their crisis pregnancies independently of male authority. Blending together an inherently biological construction of women's maternal instinct with the feminist stress on female autonomy and agency, the loyalty of counselors firmly lies with abortion-minded women whom they urge to "think about what's best for you and what's best for your baby," during their counseling sessions.[80]

However, this panegyric construction only envelopes abortion-minded women who are seeking services at CPCs and stands in contrast to the reproachful construction of women who unapologetically choose to abort unwanted pregnancies. The depiction of these women by volunteer counselors is firmly rooted in their deeply held religious objection to casting aside the natural ordering of society. Fusing together sex, sexuality, and agency, Brittney identifies sex and childbirth outside of marriage as a major underlying problem and believes that legalized abortion erodes the institution of marriage. She supports recriminalizing abortion so that women will have to deal with the consequences of engaging in unsanctified sexual activity: "It would kind of make girls think before having sex and think, 'if I do have sex then I could get pregnant, and once I get pregnant, I can't have an abortion. I can't get rid of it. I have to take responsibility for it.' So, I think it'll make girls less slutty, less likely to sleep around. I think it'll make our society a little more wholesome."[81]

In short, Brittney sees legalized abortion as an escape route for promiscuous women who engage in irresponsible sexual activity by allowing them to avoid "taking responsibility" for their actions and to short-circuit marriage. Closely aligning with Brittney's characterization of reckless women, another counselor depicted abortion as a flippant reaction to being inconvenienced because "for the majority of them, the child wouldn't fit into their lifestyle."[82] Their characterization closely fits with that of the 19th-century physicians who chastised married women "for killing their own offspring, and making their bodies dens of murder [to avoid] the inconvenience of having children."[83]

Several interviewees also implicated contraception as an additional accelerant that flames women's promiscuity, increases their demand for abortion, and ultimately undermines their affinity for marriage with impunity. Steven uses an analogy between alcoholism and contraception to describe the detrimental impact the latter has had on women who need to "get better." As he explained:

> It's kind of like giving a drink to an alcoholic. Why would you do that? You know it's going to cause a lot of trouble. So, giving birth control to someone who is not married, what are you saying? Have all the sex you want without any responsibility. Does that mean you want to be an object for someone else? You don't want to get married? You don't want to get better? You don't want to have somebody else join in your life? You don't want to join with somebody in making a life for yourself? That's just like saying, "I want to continue to be used by society and used by men." I have trouble understanding this.[84]

Much as Hodge and Storer castigated 19th-century women for accessing abortion to "destroy the fruits of illicit pleasure," today's CPC counselors are equally troubled by what they view as unbridled promiscuity that they must fight in morally rockier terrain. Akin to many, Steven believes that "the fruit of marriage is not sex, it's children," and the access that unmarried women have to contraception has simply made it easier for them to engage in sex—behavior that is spiritually unmoored from motherhood and marriage.[85]

Expounding on these themes, Donald likewise describes contraception in addictive terms, believing that its availability feeds salacious sexuality, moving it outside of the marital sphere where God intended sexual activity to reside. As he explained, "I'm against contraception because it removes an element of sex that's necessary for the purpose of sex. . . . There should be a law against the manufacture or importing of it. The goal of that law would be to re-implement sex for the three reasons [reproduction, love, recreation in marriage], which would strengthen families, which is basically the basis for what a society runs off of."[86] Augmenting their opposition to abortion, contraception was thus likewise viewed by a number of the interviewees as a modern, profane tool that "removes the reproductive portion of it" thereby "distort[ing] what sex is."[87] By facilitating recreational sex outside of marriage, the availability of contraceptives is dynamically linked with the far graver sin of abortion, which then becomes necessary as a "back-up plan" in the event of a contraceptive failure.

So viewed, birth control further enables women to breach God's sacred order by encouraging them to flaunt their sexuality and lead a self-centered lifestyle, which is incompatible with the religiously derived understanding of the natural social order that fuels the commitment of CPC counselors. This illicit construction of sexually irresponsible women sharply contradicts the interviewees' infantilized construction of the scared, confused, and unknowledgeable abortion-minded women and seems antithetical to the woman-centered ethic of the CPCs. However, these dueling constructions reify the religious identity of CPCs, where retribution and redemption figure as critical elements in the abortion regret narrative.

Called to Action: Unpacking the Contemporary Nuances and Historical Continuity of the Religious Identity of Crisis Pregnancy Centers

A strong religious identity frames the "life-affirming" mission statements of most CPCs,[88] and religiosity is likewise a core element of the identity of our interviewees. Nineteen interviewees self-identified as evangelical Christians belonging to a range of denominations, and the other four self-identified as Catholic. The religious profile of our interviewees matches closely with that Hussey reported in her study of 26 centers in which approximately 83 percent of CPC staff identified as evangelical Christian and about 13 percent as Catholic.[89] Across all interviews, counselors prioritized addressing the immediacy of their clients' needs. However, they all also stressed that a commitment to God was a crucial component of guiding women though the process of evolving from being abortion-minded to embracing motherhood. They firmly believed that their clients "need to know the love of Jesus Christ," but felt that many abortion-minded women were not capable of forming an ethereal relationship with God until a tangible connection was made with a CPC counselor. As Marsha explained, "Women need to know that someone cares and loves them"; only then can they "open their hearts to Jesus Christ—and I love to tell people about Jesus."[90]

The counselors shared an enthusiasm for evangelizing clients, and several interviewees described being called by God to support the woman-centered mission being carried out at CPCs. For many years Sandra's "attention was really drawn socially to babies who were really vulnerable to being murdered," but she did not become active until she "hear[d] that voice, that call" that compelled her to action.[91] Likewise, Katherine felt she was called to do this work even though she felt unprepared. As she explained, "God doesn't call those who are equipped or prepared, he prepares us when called. So, I just settled in with that and thought, well, I'm teachable. I can be taught."[92]

Within this religious context, several historical themes resurface linking modern activists to their predecessors. Walking in lockstep with the 19th-century antiabortion physicians who rallied around the call to end the "slaughter of countless children," CPC staffers uniformly and unequivocally view abortion as murder. Pivoting from a woman-centered to a fetal-centered position, during our interview, Mike fleshed out his perspective on the immorality of abortion, as he put it, "abortion is the most unjust indefensible; it's absolutely wrong. Would you go out and randomly kill innocent members of society at any age? I see no difference between someone going along and killing a two-year-old versus killing a two-month-old in the womb. It's the same baby. It's the same person."[93]

Echoing the beliefs expressed by antiabortion physicians more than a century ago that the fetus was a living being from the moment of conception, Mike sees an equivalency between fetal and human life. Mirroring this stand, Steven refuses to be a passive bystander to abortion because "an unborn child is unjustly being killed and cries out for justice." Realizing that "we have to oppose abortion," Steven migrated from the sidelines of the debate into an active opponent whose passion for the cause was channeled into his life-affirming work as a CPC counselor.[94]

Like their predecessors, without exception, interviewees described life in sacred terms. Tracking the antiabortion physicians, they also believe that the Sixth Commandment's injunction "thou shalt not kill" is a basic tenet of Christianity, which explicitly prohibits abortion. In this spirit, both generations of antiabortionists have invoked the imagery of battle to convey the expansive and fervent nature of their mission. In parallel fashion, the 1871 Report of the AMA Committee on Criminal Abortion proclaimed that in contrast to the uprising of the colonies, "we have not in the present case a British army to meet. We have no foreign enemy to contend with . . . we have a domestic enemy, and that enemy is in our midst . . . [A]nd it now becomes us to do our part faithfully towards God . . . to crush the monster."[95] Likewise, Patricia exclaimed that "it is about war. This whole pro-life movement is spiritual warfare. We know what the Bible says about life."[96] Crediting God as the "author of life," Jane shared Patricia's alarm that "human beings have tried to take that control away from Him and seek abortion."[97] She draws the battle lines of abortion more narrowly around a woman's body, defining "the womb as the most dangerous place for a baby."

Further connecting the two generations of antiabortion activists, both extend the travesty of abortion beyond the destruction of unborn life to encompass a woman's deliberate disruption of God's biological ordering of creation. As Dr. Hodge succinctly wrote in the 19th century, abortion was "in violation of every natural sentiment, and in opposition to the laws of God and man."[98] The firm belief that abortion subverts God's intended plan for women in the created world likewise continues to distress CPC counselors, and fuels their opposition to the practice. As Evelyn explained, "it's not about a medical procedure per se. It's about that woman's welfare and what she's created to be, and we're trying to go against the grain of nature."[99] Once women have broken the maternal oath, Claire believes that the larger "culture is wounded" by the "psychological, emotional, and spiritual" repercussions that trail women after an abortion.[100] In short, as with other interviewees, Claire cannot reconcile abortion with a woman's sacred position as the center of life due to her role of "bring[ing] humanity into the world."[101]

Conceptually tracking with the physicians' antiabortion belief that God has indelibly stamped women's bodies with the impress of maternity, those working in CPCs today likewise view women's well-being as dependent upon their fulfilling their natural and divinely enjoined destiny as mothers. Leaning into and fully embracing God's natural ordering, all interviewees expressed their shared belief that women are created to be mothers. Accordingly, they position abortion as an unnatural act that "is so destructive obviously to children but also to women," because it places them at cross-purposes with their ordained destiny.[102] Across interviews, activists emphasized that a maternal instinct is biologically and spiritually hardwired in women and, as CPC counselor Haley observed, is evidenced throughout the natural world: "Women are created to nurture their young and they follow that pattern even through the animal world."[103]

Organically following from the shared view of abortion as destructive of women's naturally ordained maternalism, like Storer and his colleagues who warned that regret or guilt over an abortion might trigger insanity, CPC counselors understand abortion as an aberration that logically and inevitably leads to severe emotional consequences. Fusing these together, Donald explained that the roots of regret dwell in these crossroads: "Women have some kind of internal thing about being a mother and having babies and stuff like that—relationships, family, [and] the little white picket fence. Abortion just ruins that. Abortion hurts women. Abortion is not the lesser of two evils, it is the only evil. The only one that is not evil is having a baby, having a baby is not evil. So, one is evil, the other is not."[104] According to Donald, abortion permanently tarnishes the idyllic vision of family life he imagines that all women desire. In this respect, Donald lends a modern rendering to the historical words of the antiabortion physicians who glowingly extolled the virtues of the Roman matron who likened her children to jewels.[105]

Adorned with images of maternal purity, Donald's portrait of women was heralded by other counselors who likewise valorized the virtues of a selfless maternity. As Lindsey put it, "moms are heroes, they are so selfsacrificing," and their willingness to "put the needs of children above their own needs" is cast as the naturally preordained outcome of women's ingrained maternity.[106] Gazing more closely at this flat, essentialized portrait of women enables one to grasp the counselors' understanding of the origins and significance of abortion regret. It is not simply an emotion, but rather it is the inescapable consequence of dismantling God's maternal blueprint for women. As Patricia explained, "God says that without vision my people perish. God doesn't make mistakes. This is about saving the lives of women and their babies."[107] So viewed, abortion is the tangible mechanism through which God's gendered ordering of the created world is subverted, which inevitably leads to suffering.

Framed as inimical to women's true nature, the CPC counselors we interviewed were quick to point out that "nobody wants to have an abortion and if they're seeking that, it's because they're in a crisis of some kind."[108] Attempting to avert a second, and more profound crisis for an abortion-seeking woman, counselors "seek to come along beside her to move the roadblocks out of the way for her not to have to go through that experience."[109] Mired in crisis, a woman's decisional incompetence is implicated as a symbolic roadblock that pushes her off God's ordained path unless she is saved through the intervention of a caring counselor who can guide her in the right direction. Strongly reminiscent of the 19th-century antiabortionist physicians, CPC counselors likewise view abortion as an act that women cannot truly consent to because it is antithetical to their true nature.

However, in a significant contrast to the antiabortion physicians who vilified aborting matrons and did not offer them any hope of release from their suffering, those working in CPCs see women who abort as victims in urgent need of support and caring so they can heal. Importantly, they leave open the possibility of redemption for postabortive women who have suffered a life of regret and ruin because, as Donald puts it, they "suppressed [abortion] for years and cannot get over forgiving themselves."[110] For these women, the path of redemption lies in accepting God into their lives and receiving postabortive counseling to help them to heal from their psychological wounds of regret—an option that the antiabortion physicians did not hold open for women who had subverted God's plan by rejecting motherhood.

DEPLOYING EXPERIENTIAL KNOWLEDGE TO STEER WOMEN TOWARD MOTHERHOOD

The fierce and protective stance that CPC counselors take toward their pregnant clients is often fostered by their experientially derived knowledge regarding the emotional harms of abortion. By way of a brief explanation, experiential knowledge is "socially and culturally grounded" knowledge that is unique to an individual's lived experiences. More specifically, it is derived from two types of experiences—embodied or empathetic.[111] The former is derived from a person's own bodily experiences such as, in the present context, having been pregnant or having had an abortion, whereas the latter is gained from the experiences of people close to an individual, such as patients, family members, or friends.[112]

Putting Experiential Knowledge to Work

This is certainly not the first time that experiential knowledge has been used to advance the antiabortion agenda.*** Although the 19th-century physicians derived their primary authority from their status as highly educated "medical men," they augmented their expertise by drawing upon experiential knowledge gleaned from the confidential communications of their patients regarding their abortion experiences. Drawing upon these confidences, Horatio Storer thus proclaimed as certitude that abortion disrupted "the elements of domestic happiness" and eroded "the matron's self-respect."[113] Tracking this reliance on experientially derived knowledge, today's CPC counselors likewise draw upon their experiential knowledge of the harms of abortion to counsel abortion-minded women.

So grounded, experiential knowledge provides a limited perspective, which is not reliably generalizable. It tends to be subjectively interpreted, meaning that people are likely to funnel experiences (their own or those of others) through their beliefs and worldviews to make sense of them.[114] People also tend to "cluster" issues together, projecting their limited experiential knowledge about one situation to inform their understanding of other situations.[115]

These salient characteristics of experientially derived knowledge are frequently at play in the CPC context. Despite the inherent limitations of extrapolating individual experience to arrive at a universal truth, this is a common practice among CPC counselors.[116] For many volunteers and staffers, experiential knowledge of abortion regret has spurred their participation in CPCs and intensified their commitment to leading all women away from what they consider to be the inevitably traumatizing consequence of this pregnancy outcome.[117] Similarly, they also tend to cluster issues together

---

*** It should be noted that experiential knowledge has been used to energize activism across the political spectrum. For example, in the 1960s, feminists used their firsthand experiences with the "horrors, humiliation, and tragedy of illegal abortion" during conscious-raising speak-outs as a subversive mobilizing tactic to publicly challenge the medical community's gatekeeping role in determining who had a compelling enough reason to be granted an approval for an abortion (Doan 2007, 59).

through the attribution of virtually all subsequent psychological, emotional, and physical symptoms to the trauma of abortion regardless of when and how experienced.

These patterns were plainly evident in our interviews. According to CPC director Rachel, "many of our volunteers are postabortive. That's why many of them are here, because they know, they've been there."[118] Following years of hardships and suffering, Lindsey and April found refuge from their post-abortive emotional and spiritual pain at their local CPCs. Leaning into what April described as the "merciful hand of Christ" and the support of counselors, the two of them found redemption and purpose as they progressed through their abortion regret recovery process. Subsequently, they felt called upon to spare other women from the same adverse fate that they attributed to their abortion experiences.

April, who volunteers her time at a CPC, pinpointed her struggles with depression, maintaining relationships, and parenting to her abortion. She explains that as a teenager, her father coerced her into having an abortion and that this lack of agency at the hands of a male authority amplified the trauma of her abortion: "My dad made me have an abortion when I was 16. I didn't have a choice. And, that was the worst day of my life. I tried to commit suicide afterwards. I turned into a mess afterwards. So that experience . . . it haunted me."[119] Lindsey, who ascended from a CPC client to a volunteer to the director of a crisis pregnancy center, also explained the long-term psychological impact abortion regret had on her life after aborting an unplanned pregnancy at age 15: "A procedure that was supposedly going to be a simple procedure, had over 30 years of lasting impact on my life . . . I've had screwed-up relationships because of a fear of people finding out who I was . . . And so masquerading who I really was, and not ever letting people get to know who I was, [was] part of that guilt and the shame that I carried from having had an abortion that really robbed me."[120]

Decades later, April and Lindsey retrospectively understand their abortions as traumatic experiences that have led to years of mental health challenges. Their stories share similar elements—an unplanned pregnancy as teenagers followed by years of emotional instability—that validate for them the authenticity of their trauma. But despite the common threads tying their experiences together, these are individual embodied occurrences that are bound to a specific time and subjective interpretation. Both women view their abortion regret through a prism that is structured by their shared religious and moral beliefs and their ideas about "how life should be lived."[121]

Lindsey and April have embraced their experiences with deep conviction, equating them with a more generalized knowledge and universal truths that are applicable to all women who have abortions. Fearing that all aborting women are manacled to this fate, they use their experiential knowledge as the basis for reaching out to CPC clients in an effort to dissuade them from abortion, even though for most women, as discussed in Chapter Five, abortion is not a significant predictor of poor mental health. And like other CPC counselors, Lindsey and April dismiss the counternarratives from women who have not experienced long-lasting regret as false testimonies riddled with denial. Like most of their peers, they believe that because "abortion is quick, it's immediate," that women can move through life in denial about their regret because "they don't realize the lifetime consequences."[122] Using herself as a case in point, Lindsey's denial of her regret led to decades of silence. She explained how she "couldn't speak" about her abortion until "God's restoration process" gave her "a voice to speak" and enabled her to accept that "it's not hypocritical to have one and then talk, because I have experienced the negative effects."

However, many of the counselors we interviewed expressed their confidence that with enough time, a reckoning awaits these women. Patricia, who spent years recovering from her abortion regret, believes all women will inevitably begin to wrestle with "the pain" of abortion as their personal lives unravel in "broken marriages or liv[ing] in a promiscuous lifestyle, switching partners [and unable] to have lasting relationships."[123] As she explained, she has witnessed women hitting "rock bottom" before shedding their denial and "dealing with the guilt" of their abortion.[124] When this watershed moment happens, CPC counselors are there to provide solace through postabortive redemption and healing. Counseling from her own experience with regret and salvation, Patricia assures other women, "ultimately if you're a believer in Jesus Christ you [will] have the victory. You'll see them again. Jesus is holding them."[125]

Although most of the CPC counselors we interviewed draw on firsthand, embodied experiences with abortion regret when working with abortion-minded and postabortive women, a minority of them—comprised of the few men we interviewed and a handful of women—rely upon empathetic experiential knowledge to guide their conversations with clients. Paul explained that he felt called to stop "the murder of innocents" and help the "poor women" who unwittingly turned to abortion to "take care of their problem." However, lacking embodied experiential knowledge and feeling inadequately prepared to counsel abortion-minded women, he sought out empathetic knowledge from his friends to help prepare him for his role: "I don't have any kids. In fact, when I first got in [the organization] I thought 'now how am I going to talk to people about this?' So, friends of mine, I'd ask them for their stories and I'd share their stories . . . and then over the years people would tell me their stories, so I use almost everybody else's stories."[126] Paul thus acquired an early understanding of abortion regret by relaying compelling anecdotes from friends and retelling secondhand stories to clients. Akin to Paul, the other counselors who did not have embodied experiences with abortion trauma followed a similar pattern. In turn, they harnessed this empathetic experiential knowledge for the benefit of their clients, which vitalized their engagement and strengthened their commitment to the missionizing work performed at their centers.

From Experience to Expertise

As highlighted by our interviews, CPC counselors tend to draw on their embodied and empathetic experiential knowledge to position themselves as the "true" authorities on abortion regret. Grounded in this expertise, they believe they are in the best position to guide women through the decision-making and recovery process. In a corresponding vein, they also frequently underscored the corrupting influence that profits have on the professional integrity of abortion providers. As Deborah put it: "unfortunately if people stand to make money from something, sometimes we can't trust them to tell the whole truth."[127] Building out from here, in a historical—and ironic—twist, contemporary abortion opponents wield experiential knowledge on the larger political stage to subversively challenge and discredit the expertise of those they describe as the biased "pro-abortion" medical profession steered by the AMA.[128] Further underscoring what they see as the medical field's bias, opponents point out that abortion providers have a fiduciary stake in providing abortion services that can motivate them to falsify information or mislead women into aborting for financial gain.

At Deborah's organization, the lived experiences that clients had with abortion regret was embraced as an important source of authoritative evidence to counter the biased information the medical community, particularly abortion providers, circulated. Characterizing medical studies as uncertain, unreliable, and unmoored from women's lived experiences,[129] counselors commonly harnessed their experiential knowledge, pointing to their clients as "living proof" that abortion causes long-term negative health consequences. They hone this experiential "living proof" to undercut counterclaims that abortion is a hallmark of reproductive rights, and instead advance a narrative of regret that identifies abortion as antithetical to women's rights and well-being.

Although everyone we interviewed believed themselves to be experts on abortion regret and in an ideal position to counsel clients, it should be noted that the few men in our sample were far bolder and more assertive about their credentialed expertise than were the women, including those who drew upon their own embodied experiential knowledge of abortion regret as their source of expertise. Although our sample is far too small to draw any firm conclusions from this observation, we simply note it here, as the following discussion reflects this reality.

Turning again to Paul, over time, he progressed from having an elementary grasp of abortion regret to possessing a more intimate empathetic knowledge of it after spending countless hours working with postabortive volunteers and helping clients with their decision-making process. Like Storer and his colleagues, Paul cultivated his expertise as an "intimate confidant" and "witness" to the ravaging impact of abortion. Speaking with authority, Paul explained, "[abortion] does hurt women in a lot of different respects. It's kind of overwhelming to think about the huge number of women that have been victimized or are now just devastated by the abortion itself. . . . The psychological problems are severe. I don't care what [pro-choice activists] say, they are severe."[130] Relying on his empathetic experiential knowledge, Paul clusters issues together while dismissing what he sees as the false counterclaims of pro-choice activists and evidence-based studies. He insists that the aftermath of abortion can blossom into psychological maladies for women.

Similarly drawing on years of empathetic experiential expertise, long-time staffer Mike asserted, "I think almost always—and you're asking a person who has more authority to answer that question than perhaps anyone else you're ever going to talk to—I think that almost always, the woman does not want to have the abortion."[131] Mike has crafted his lay expertise from years of working in the movement and observing abortion-minded women "at the gates of the clinic," as well as interacting with some women within the walls of the CPCs. He continued to explain that women abort when they think "there is no other alternative," because "there is no woman who wants to go in to kill her baby."[132]

Based on his "firsthand experiences" counseling postabortive women, Carl used his lay expertise to confidently diagnose guilt as the source of women's ailments as they age: "I've seen women later in life really struggle with things and they don't really know why they're struggling with depression, anxiety, and difficulties in their marriage. And maybe perhaps some of that is because they haven't really addressed all those things and forgiven themselves of the guilt that comes with [abortion]."[133] Again deploying a retrospective lens, Carl positions himself as able to read backward in time to a woman's earlier abortion experience as the potential cause of her mental and physical unraveling later in life, much as the 19th-century physicians did in warning that a woman can expect to sink "into old age like a withered tree, stripped of its foliage; with the stain of blood upon her soul."[134]

According to Carl and Mike, abortion regret is not time-stamped—years, even decades later, the deep-seated guilt of regret catches up with postabortive women to catastrophic ends. The unraveling over time due to unidentified regret over an abortion is a powerful theme that connects contemporary and historical regret narratives. Dr. Storer also identified guilt from abortion, "a touch of pity for the little being about to be sacrificed—a trace of regret for the child," as a debilitating factor that leads to the mental and physical unhinging of women later in life.[135] Many of the contemporary clients that CPC care workers referenced were middle-aged women who had abortions years, often decades, before they found solace at a CPC.

In short, these counselors have witnessed and supported women struggling with a range of mental health and life issues that they date back to their prior abortions in accordance with their experientially derived expertise on the subject of abortion regret. From this limited and highly subjective retrospective perspective, they have come to understand abortion regret as a condition that plagues all women. These narratives of regret are collected from women who are purposefully seeking out services at a CPC, thereby excluding most women's abortion experiences. Interactions with CPC clients continually corroborate the clinical validity of abortion regret for the counselors, despite drawing from this select pool. Nonetheless, their limited experiential knowledge of women's abortion experiences is now being deployed in the public arena to validate the universal existence of abortion regret.

Foregrounded in experiential expertise, interviewees folded additional story elements into the narrative, creating a more encompassing account of regret that expands well beyond the psychological consequences of abortion.[136] Echoing their 19th-century predecessors who claimed that abortion caused women to suffer from "chronic weaknesses, disease and disarrangement of her organs,"[137] interviewees also made unsubstantiated claims about the physical harms of abortion. Embracing this more inclusive and historical familiar narrative arc, Paul pivoted from listing out the seemingly endless psychological ailments associated with abortion regret to detailing the numerous physical ailments that lie in wait for women who abort, proclaiming that it is "just amazing, the physical ailments they have to deal with; it's just unbelievable."[138]

Reasoning that abortion unnaturally leaves pregnancy hormones in a woman's body that accelerate her likelihood of developing breast cancer, Paul went on to cite unnamed studies that support his position while dismissing the credibility of the American Medical Association:

> The studies show that if you have an abortion on your first pregnancy, in the first trimester, your chances of breast cancer are extremely more likely. And the more I think about it, I think these poor women don't have any idea of the long-term consequences of their actions. . . . I'm going to guess somewhere between 25 and 30 studies have been done. Out of those 25 or 30, all but about 3 maybe 4 of them have proven a connection between abortion and breast cancer. But, 3 of them haven't. The ones that haven't, those are the ones—you know the American Medical Association and everybody else who is in favor of abortion—uses as their reason to say no, no, no that isn't true. The other 20 to 25 say there is a link.[139]

Paul's claim, along with many of the other claims of injury advanced by the antiabortion movement, is highly contested. Although Paul asserts a link between abortion and breast cancer, the American Cancer Society (ACS), hardly a radical feminist organization, disputes this link. According to the ACS, some earlier studies suggested a possible link between breast cancer and abortion; however, the more recent and methodically "rigorous scientific evidence does not support the notion that abortion of any kind raises the risk of breast cancer or any other type of cancer"[140] (discussed further in Chapter Five).

Anchored in their pro-life beliefs, Paul and other interviewees were quick to reject information or alternative perspectives that disputed, diluted, or even nuanced the regret narrative. Their palpable distrust of the medical community was evident in our interviews and was matched by a general distrust of "mainstream" media. Many CPC counselors view the media as complacent institutions that help advance a "pro-abortion" agenda while willfully neglecting to tell society about the hazards of abortion regret. After excoriating the "biased mainstream media's" culpability in misleading the public, one interviewee asserted that "the media refuse to tell people the truth about abortion, or about the complications, or all the associations with abortion."[141]

Although counselors view mainstream media as liberal dead ends for broadcasting the "truth" about abortion regret, the advent of the internet and new social media platforms has been revitalizing for them and the larger outreach branch of the movement. Online user communities are glued together by shared beliefs and worldviews that mirror those embraced by brick-and-mortar CPC communities, thus providing additional emotional credibility to the firsthand and secondhand abortion regret narratives being disseminated therein.[142] Within these spaces, experiential knowledge is held up as tangible evidence that legitimizes postabortion syndrome as an illness, while simultaneously undermining the credibility of contradictory professional expertise.

Online communities have greatly accelerated the outreach branch's capacity to share inaccurate information about the risks of abortion.[143] Within this extensive network, the presumed authenticity of women's experiential knowledge of abortion regret helps strengthen the credibility of online "research," which blends some evidence-based facts with misleading facts.[144] Extending the dissemination of biased knowledge well beyond the reach of the dizzying "list of horribles" touted by 19th-century antiabortion physicians, online platforms have deployed this research into the public arena as seemingly sound evidence to validate and legitimize abortion regret as a medical condition.

Magnifying this robust online presence, the leading CPC umbrella networks have assembled a directory of thousands of crisis pregnancy centers readily available online for anyone seeking pregnancy-related support. Beyond the CPCs, an extensive community of support groups and helplines exist that aid postabortive women. Other organizations, such as Operation Outcry, are dedicated to collecting online abortion regret testimonies, which can also be used to advance the woman-protective agenda on a larger political stage.

This online presence has contributed to the growth and visibility of the outreach branch of the antiabortion movement. More recently, the outreach branch, which is comprised mainly—but not exclusively—of CPCs, has extended the services it provides to include postabortion support and perinatal hospice care, which have helped to extend the abortion regret narrative arc in ways that would have been unimaginable to the 19th-century antiabortion physicians.

EXPANDING NARRATIVES OF REGRET: POSTABORTION CARE AND PERINATAL HOSPICE

In this final section of the chapter, we look at the expansion of the outreach branch of the antiabortion movement into the provision of abortion recovery care and perinatal hospice programs. Although quite different in nature and purpose, these services are thematically united by their stress on the traumatizing impact of abortion regret, thus adding new elements to this ever-expanding narrative arc.

Postabortion Care

In 1986, Theresa Burke (who would go on to co-author *Forbidden Grief: The Unspoken Pain of Abortion* with David C. Reardon) founded the Center for Post Abortion Healing, which was one of the earliest organizations to turn its attention to women on this side of the abortion experience. After publishing *Rachel's Vineyard: A Psychological and Spiritual Journey of Post Abortion Healing* in 1994, Burke began offering weekend retreats for "women who were grieving the loss of their aborted children."[145] Taking the organization's name from biblical scripture, Rachel's Vineyard offers women who have terminated a pregnancy a "spiritual and emotional healing process" to assist in their recovery from the "anguish and intense yearning for someone who cannot be retrieved."[146] Teaming up with Priests for Life, Rachel's Vineyard holds more than 1,000 retreats a year in 48 states and 57 countries, which are hosted by "church based ministries, counseling outreach programs, Project Rachel Offices or Respect Life groups, and crisis pregnancy centers."[147]

Far more common, however, postabortion care is delivered through an extensive ministry of "abortion recovery care centers," which are dedicated to counseling women through the maze of "unresolved psychological, physical and spiritual aspects" of abortion trauma.[148] These centers are typically housed within CPCs, and in keeping with their religious orientation, use a "biblical" counseling model primarily delivered through "support groups, Bible studies, or one-on-one counseling."[149] Abortion recovery centers have also been supplemented with a rapidly growing online network of support groups, resource referrals, blogs, and online videos sponsored by national organizations such as Care Net, which enable women to share their postabortive stories.[150]

Although services were initially only offered to postabortive women, abortion recovery ministries have broadened their realm of services to encompass "those who play a role in an abortion or are impacted by one."[151] Although less commonly featured, men who believe they have been robbed of fatherhood are starting to appear as figures in the abortion regret narrative. Growing out of a conference organized by the National Office of Post-Abortion Reconciliation and Healing, websites such as Reclaiming Fatherhood: A Multifaceted Examination of Men Dealing with Abortion, and Men and Abortion now dot the online community of the outreach branch.[152] Helping to give voice to the regret of such men, Shane Idleman, founder and lead pastor of Westside Christian Fellowship in Lancaster, California, has written blogs and made videos documenting the regret he wrangles with 23 years after "conceding" to his then girlfriend's decision to abort. He describes it as a "decision that still haunts [him] today," and leaves him "heartbroken" when he daydreams about "walking and talking with my child." Praying "deeply to the Lord to remove his guilt and shame," Shane draws strength from "God's unfailing love and compassion," and uses his position as a pastor to encourage other men to come forward with their stories of pain and regret.[153]

Pro-Life Perinatal Hospice Programs

As part of their effort to reach out and dissuade more women from aborting, many CPCs have transformed their centers into more professional "life-affirming" medical facilities, which ironically are molded along the reproductive health clinic model.[†††] These centers are now able to offer limited medical services to clients, such as sexually transmitted infection screening and treatment as well as prenatal and postnatal care under the supervision of a licensed physician or nurse manager.[154]

Emerging from this more professional and medicalized model, a handful of CPCs have begun offering perinatal hospice programs. These programs emerged out of existing secular licensed hospice programs (and most are still so affiliated) to provide support and services to women and their families who decide to continue a pregnancy when a perinatal death—meaning one that occurs during pregnancy, labor, or shortly after birth—is

---

[†††] This effort has been spearheaded by the National Institute of Family and Life Advocates (NIFLA), which provides interested CPCs with consultants who "guide pregnancy centers through medical clinic compliance and conversion with all the necessary legal and medical guidelines" (National Institute of Family and Life Advocates 2018).

imminent. More recently, due to the pioneering efforts of Dr. Byron Calhoun, who recognized that these programs are a natural fit with pro-life ideology and practices, CPCs have begun providing perinatal hospice services, along with a handful of other organizations within the outreach branch of the antiabortion movement.[155] Among our interviewees, 10 worked or volunteered in such programs in addition to their counseling work with abortion-minded women. The following discussion is based on these interviews.

Drawing on the feminized and religious identity of CPCs, counselors extend the intensive one-on-one engagement they are known for to women with wanted pregnancies diagnosed with imminent perinatal death. In short, they call upon the same Christ-centered, nurturing model of care work and experiential knowledge that frames their work with abortion-minded women.

The intimacy of the care work provided through perinatal hospice, coupled with the emotionally intensive environment, constructs a space that can create a transformational experience for both clients and care workers. Even though these fetal abnormalities routinely result in a stillbirth or sudden death after delivery, women are encouraged to recognize their children outside of these diagnoses, making their experiences and fetuses recognizable within a more traditional narrative of childbirth and loss. Stressing that both are equal in the eyes of God, counselors help women see the equivalency between their baby with extreme anomalies and a baby with no health issues.[156]

Witnessing the strength and resilience of her perinatal hospice client, Claire described her own transformative experience as follows: "It occurred to me, and I shared this at the funeral, how much they loved this little baby, with all his anomalies. Who could deny? He had no top on his head and they loved him dearly; and to me, that was this great picture of how God loves us."[157] Claire's story captures what she saw as the purity of a family's grief and love when it was not stained by regret. Growing out of her experience, Claire quickly identified perinatal hospice as another place where CPC care workers can reinforce the importance of reaffirming life in the context of all pregnancies, regardless of circumstances.

Counselors held up the experiential knowledge emanating from perinatal hospice as another source of "truth" that underscores the illegitimacy of abortion as an outcome for any pregnancy.[158] Other CPC counselors used the visibility and empowerment of individual women's experiences as a way to expand the abortion conflict into the "gray areas" of the debate. As Ryan explained, the advent of perinatal hospice centers represents a pioneering front for the pro-life movement and is the answer to the "hard cases" posed by fatal fetal anomalies that pro-choice activists rely upon to "prop up" their arguments in favor of ensuring that women have access to late-term abortion services.[159] Sandra similarly viewed the role of perinatal hospice as so vital that "hopefully one day we'll start opening these in every city because there is a need for this support."[160] By positioning perinatal hospice centers as the preferred alternative to late-term abortions, activists believe they have developed a solution to a major point of contention in the abortion access debate, while simultaneously creating a more expansive narrative of regret.

Regret Regardless of Circumstances

The CPC counselors we interviewed envision pro-life perinatal hospice as a compelling arena in which the reach of the abortion regret narrative can encompass tragic fatal fetal pregnancies. Although none of them had ever interacted with anyone who had chosen to terminate a fatal fetal pregnancy, they nonetheless steadfastly claimed that like all the women they served, these women would likewise suffer from abortion regret. Lacking a comparison group, and based on her relationship with two perinatal clients, Haley expressed her wish that "all parents would carry babies to term" because the "parents will come out of this with no regrets."[161]

With equal certitude, Katherine echoed Haley's concerns about the risk of regret, irrespective of a woman's pregnancy circumstances. The directive counseling Katherine provides to perinatal clients is underscored by warnings of abortion regret that are laced with familiar chords of coercion: "One of the things we stress in our typical counseling is that, to the woman, it is your choice. . . . We're not trying to be ugly to parents or boyfriends or grandmothers, but you are the one who will live with whatever decision you make."[162] Katherine attempts to counter what she sees as a driving force in pushing women toward any abortion—the diminished agency of clients caused by external pressure. Attempting to mitigate the influence of "parents or boyfriends or grandmothers," Katherine stresses to the perinatal clients she advises that they alone will have to shoulder the weight of their decision.

Women's experiences in these centers accord with the dominant abortion regret narrative that is founded on women's divinely ordered destiny as mothers. Emphasizing women's natural role, Carl explained why women are irrevocably physically and emotionally harmed when they terminate a pregnancy, regardless of circumstances: "I think that women naturally, and I think families naturally, don't want to abort. . . . I will argue that the woman and family who spends the time with that child are healthier in the long run. . . . They didn't participate in the termination of that child and all that goes with that and the emotions that are tied within that family and that woman forever."[163] Aborting a terminal pregnancy, as Carl explained, creates additional trauma for a grieving mother. He sees the loss of a child as a recoverable tragedy for a woman, while an abortion, even in this context, will lead to irreparable emotional damage for her—a view shared across the interviews.

Counselors point to perinatal hospice as the solution that closes another loophole in any counterargument for abortion rights—namely, the necessity of giving women the option of terminating pregnancies in situations involving severe fetal anomalies. For individual women, perinatal hospice can be a transgressive and liberating choice when diagnosed with a fatal fetal pregnancy. However, as philosopher and gender theorist Judith Butler emphasizes, "[w]hat is most important is to cease legislating for all lives what is livable only for some, and similarly, to refrain from proscribing for all lives what is unlivable for some."[164] Aggregating their limited experiential knowledge, counselors generalized across all women's fatal fetal pregnancies, implicitly positioning perinatal hospice centers as the universal answer for every woman, just as they positioned the embrace of motherhood as the universal answer to an unplanned pregnancy.

CONCLUSION

In clear contrast to the fetal-centric messaging of the political and direct-action branches, within the cloistered and feminized spaces of crisis pregnancy centers, aborting women are front and center. Within this woman-centered realm, mostly volunteer counselors marshal their experiential knowledge as generalizable evidence regarding the inevitability of abortion regret to dissuade those they counsel from terminating their pregnancies. The regret narrative that is deployed within the CPCs is laced with a sacralized conception of women's essential maternalism, which serves to re-entrench traditional gender roles. Critically, although today's CPC counselors are far more sympathetic toward aborting women, their woman-centric approach rearticulates many of the tropes stressed by the 19th-century physicians in their battle to wrap the law tightly around women's bodies for their own purported benefit.

Now, as then, a deep skepticism of feminism underlies this antiabortion activism, as it is seen as turning women away from the sacred calling of motherhood with devastating consequences. This concern about the impact of feminism on women is closely aligned with a corresponding anxiety about feminism's corrosive effect on men by divesting them of their protective role and position of authority within the family. Yet somewhat paradoxically, a gender essentialist model also creates a space in which men can temporarily acquiesce authority to women based upon a fixed and highly bounded conception of women's expertise.

Highlighting the extent to which the regret narrative has taken hold within the outreach branch of the movement, there has been a gradual proliferation of postabortion regret groups and the emergence of perinatal hospices, which serve to further extend the reach of the abortion regret narrative as a cautionary and therapeutic tool in the antiabortion struggle. As discussed in the next chapter, the strategic secularization and mobilization of this narrative has galvanized the antiabortion movement, ultimately leading the abortion regret narrative into mainstream political and legal discourse.

FOUR

Beyond the Crisis Pregnancy Centers: Regret Moves from the Margins to the Center of the Antiabortion Movement

Within the cloistered spaces of the nation's crisis pregnancy centers, a woman-centered antiabortion message has taken hold in contrast to the fetal-centric messaging of the other branches of the movement. Within this feminized space, counselors seek to build intimate connections with their clients to guide them away from abortion by stressing the beauty and joy of motherhood. Starting in the 1990s, David C. Reardon sought to persuade the broader antiabortion movement to likewise locate women in the center of its message.

To situate his call for this radical shift in orientation, this chapter begins with a discussion of how a series of setbacks to the anti-abortion movement led to the emergence of the increasingly confrontational and violent direct-action branch, which in turn resulted in a growing public perception that activists would readily throw women under the proverbial bus to protect the unborn. From here, we consider how this public relations problem prompted the call for a strategic reframing of the traditional antiabortion message to persuade the public that the movement did indeed care about the welfare of women. Focusing primarily on the work of David C. Reardon, we examine the religious roots of the abortion regret narrative and its subsequent repackaging as a secular concept aimed at persuading the "ambivalent middle" that the antiabortion movement was, in fact, the authentic defender of women's rights. In the final section, we trace how this narrative began to leach out into the public square as an articulated strategy for limiting the abortion rights of women.

SETBACKS TO THE ANTIABORTION MOVEMENT

Over the course of the 1980s and into the early '90s, the antiabortion movement experienced a series of cumulative setbacks. To begin with, Ronald Reagan's presidency proved to be a major disappointment to his pro-life supporters who had hoped he would make good on his commitment to overturn *Roe v. Wade* by way of a constitutional ban on abortion—a challenge that he equated with the "Civil War struggle to end slavery."[1] Capturing the depth and fervor of Reagan's commitment to this goal, supporters were buoyed by the remarks he shared with participants in the annual March for Life rally in 1988: "We're told not to impose our morality on those who wish to allow or participate in the taking of the life of infants before birth. . . . We're told about a woman's right to control her body. But doesn't the unborn child have a higher right, that is to life, liberty, and the pursuit of happiness? . . . America was founded on a moral proposition that human life—all human life—is sacred."[2]

However, Reagan's inability to deliver on his repeated promises to bring about an end to the tragedy of legalized abortion deflated the hopes of those who regarded him as a crusader for their cause, contributing to a rising sense of frustration at the slow pace of change.[3] Subsequently, the election of pro-choice president Bill Clinton in 1992 effectively dashed the antiabortion movement's hope that change would come from the executive office.[4]

Other traditional political channels for sweeping change also appeared increasingly closed off. Congress showed little will for approving a Human Life Amendment, which would have nullified *Roe* by recognizing the fetus as a person. It was also increasingly apparent that there was little support for a more moderate amendment that would have eviscerated *Roe* by declaring that the federal Constitution does not secure the right to abortion, thus leaving its status up to Congress and the individual states.[5] Although this latter option was generally regarded as less desirable (particularly to absolutists), it had at least held out the promise that the rights of the unborn would be protected in some jurisdictions.[6]

Moreover, although the Supreme Court invalidated most of the restrictive laws that the various states enacted in the post-*Roe* era, its 1989 decision in *Webster v. Reproductive Health Services* led many to believe that it was poised to overturn *Roe*. Although stopping short of calling to overturn the decision, three of the nine justices critiqued *Roe*'s trimester framework. Declaring it "inconsistent with the notion of a Constitution cast in general terms," they questioned why "the State's interest in protecting life should come into existence only at the point of viability."[7] A fourth justice openly called upon his colleagues to take the more courageous step of bringing the decision down in its entirety, rather than cautiously dismantling it "doorjam by doorjam."[8]

However, the movement's ardent optimism, fueled by the *Webster* decision that Roe's reversal was imminent, evaporated in 1992. Despite having announced its intention to "review once more the principles that define the rights of the woman and the legitimate authority of the State respecting the termination of pregnancies by abortion procedures,"[9] as we have seen, the *Casey* court voted to reaffirm *Roe*'s holding that the right to abortion is protected by the Constitution. Although the court abandoned *Roe*'s trimester framework in favor of the far less stringent undue burden standard, it nonetheless stopped far short of declaring that the unborn are juridical persons with a protected right to life.

Because of these cumulative setbacks, many activists lost faith in the use of "traditional political channels such as lobbying, political campaigns, and litigation" to effectuate meaningful change,[10] and turned instead to a range of direct-action tactics aimed at shutting down the nation's abortion clinics, which ranged from intense and overt harassment, including massive clinic blockades and picketing homes of abortion providers, to more outright violent approaches, such as the murder of abortion doctors and clinic staff.[11] The spectacular and often devastating nature of these assaults on clinics and their staff served to make the direct-action branch "the most publicly visible and culturally influential segment of the pro-life movement."[12]*

The direct-action branch tended to attract evangelical Protestants affiliated with the New Christian Right. To them, abortion was a symbolic battleground upon which the fight to save the moral soul of the family and

---

* Regarding the gradual decline of intimidating and violent tactics aimed at shutting down the abortion industry, see Doan (2007, 86–89) and Saurette and Gordon (2015, 78–79).

nation was being waged. Hence, deploying violent and confrontational tactics aimed at "changing the political and social culture of American society" appealed to them.[13] Although the dramatic nature of these actions may have succeeded in putting the "anti-abortion cause back onto America's Page One,"[14] they also contributed to another kind of setback for the movement. Notably, the turn to violence did not sit well with much of the American public. Speaking directly to this concern, John C. Willke, the president of the National Right to Life Committee (NRLC), concluded (based on market research) that most of the general public was of the view "that pro-life people were not compassionate to women and that we were only 'fetus lovers' who abandoned the mother after the birth. They felt that we were violent, that we burned down clinics and shot abortionists. We were viewed as religious zealots who were not too well educated."[15]

In addition to their concern that the antiabortion movement was losing support due to its lack of compassion for women, Willke and a handful of other activists were further troubled by what they regarded as a critical moral paradox in the general public's acceptance of women's right to abortion. Namely, that "while three-fourths or more of the people in the United States now admitted that this was a child who was killed, two-thirds of the same people felt that it was all right to give the woman the right to kill."[16] In an influential article, entitled "Abortion: A Failure to Communicate," Paul Swope explained that "[b]ecause pro-lifers find it morally obvious that one cannot simultaneously hold that 'abortion is killing' and 'abortion should be legal,' they have tended to assume that people only need to be shown more clearly that the fetus is a baby." However, as he went on to explain, because "modern American women of childbearing age do not view the abortion issue within the same moral framework as those of us who are pro-life activists"—rather, because they regard an unplanned pregnancy as "equivalent to a 'death of the self,'"—abortion becomes an act "of self-preservation."[17]

Like Willke, Swope stressed the importance of adopting an antiabortion position that responded to these concerns. Emphasizing the strategic importance of deploying a pro-woman approach, he explained that although "we may not agree with how women currently evaluate this issue, the importance of our mission and the imperative to be effective demand that we listen, that we understand, and that we respond to the actual concerns of women who are most likely to choose abortion."[18] Importantly, in contrast to Swope, who clearly viewed the pro-woman approach as being at odds with the moral stance of the pro-life movement, David C. Reardon would seek to persuade his colleagues that this reframed message was in fact "a fuller and more complete expression" of the movement's morally grounded opposition to abortion.[19]

LOCATING GRIEVING MOTHERS AT THE CENTER OF THE ANTIABORTION MESSAGE

In 1996, David C. Reardon published the book *Making Abortion Rare: A Healing Strategy for a Divided Nation,* in which he set out to persuade antiabortion activists that the time had come for the movement to shift its message from one centered on the sanctity of fetal life to one focused on abortion's traumatic impact on women. We begin here with a discussion of what Reardon hoped to gain by unseating the fetus as the central bearer of the pro-life message in favor of grieving mothers, and then turn to the religious roots of this reframed message.

Converting the Middle Majority

In his attempt to persuade antiabortion activists that the time had come for a change in approach, Reardon began by categorizing the public into three basic groups based on their views toward abortion. According to him, 16 percent of the population falls into the "pro-abortion" category based on their investment in keeping abortion legal for their own nefarious ends. More specifically, this cohort is comprised of "population controllers" who rely on abortion as a "tool for social engineering" for the purpose of creating a utopic society, and "abortion profiteers" who stand to gain financially from keeping the industry going.[20] Because pro-abortionists are in it either for social engineering purposes or their own pocketbook, he explained that they will not be moved by the message that abortion harms women, and can thus be written off.

Located at the other end of the spectrum, Reardon characterized 33 percent of the population as "consistently pro-life." This cohort is comprised of devout Christians who clearly do not need any persuading regarding the evils of abortion. However, Reardon does not entirely let them off the hook. Observing that those who fall into this group consistently "scratch their heads in confusion, wondering how God can allow this holocaust of abortion to go on so long," Reardon has a stern message for them. Expounding on his belief that "there is a tremendous good which God intends to resurrect from this great evil," he admonishes them that God will not end the holocaust of abortion until they recognize that women who have terminated a pregnancy are victims of despair, rather than evil monsters.[21]

Reardon then classifies the remaining 51 percent of the population as the "middle majority." Making up his target audience, he characterizes members of this cohort as being "paralyzed by competing feelings of compassion for *both* the unborn and for women."[22]† Laying the groundwork for his advocacy of the pressing need for a change in messaging, Reardon explains that it "is vitally important the pro-life movement understand the feelings of the middle majority so that we can better discern how to develop a strategy which is in alignment with their mixed feelings."[23]

Elaborating, he explains that those falling into this group are "honestly discomfited by the killing of unborn babies. It nags at their conscience. Yet this nagging is offset by their concerns for the welfare of women," which results in "an uneasy acceptance of the status quo."[24] In other words, those in this group are gripped by the moral paradox of believing that abortion is murder, while also believing that it must remain legal for the benefit of women. Although an incomprehensible position to committed pro-lifers, the lynchpin of Reardon's call for a frame shift is that the middle majority are locked in this "paralysis of compassion," and will not be moved by further efforts to persuade them that the "rights of the unborn child to live must always prevail over the needs and desires of women."[25]

Given this intransigence, Reardon forcefully argues that if the middle majority were to be won over, the time had come for antiabortion activists to advance the message that the "proper frame for the abortion issue is not women's rights versus unborn children's rights, but rather women's *and* children's rights versus the schemes of exploiters *and* the profits of the abortion industry."[26] Similarly, as Frederica Mathewes-Green, a prominent advocate of the pro-woman approach, whose "longstanding career of speaking through the CPC movement amplified the feminist cachet of the pro-woman/pro-life stance"[27] put it, "I want us to view the pregnant woman and child as a naturally-linked pair that we strive to keep together and support. Nature puts the mother and the child together: it doesn't make them enemies; it doesn't set one against the other in a battle to death."[28]

Critically, as Reardon argues, by moving away from the "abortion is murder" trope in favor of highlighting the enduring suffering of women who

---

† Reardon further divides the "middle majority" into four subcategories: the "secretly pro-life," the "conveniently pro-life," the "reticently pro-choice," and the "personally opposed pro-choice."

chose to terminate a pregnancy, the antiabortion movement would be in a position to claim that it, rather than the pro-choice side, was the true champion of the "*authentic* rights" of women.[29] By fighting in the name of women's rights, rather than continuing the uphill struggle to persuade the ambivalent middle that it was wrong to sacrifice innocent lives to the needs of women, Reardon predicted that the movement would gain new adherents once they understood that the "pro-woman/pro-life initiative truly do [sic] expand the rights, choices, and opportunities of women."[30]

In seeking to promote the strategic benefits of a reframed message, Reardon credits John C. Willke, president of NRLC, for helping him to recognize that the middle majority will not be ready to focus their attention on the protection of fetal life until they are fully satisfied that the needs of women have been taken into account. As he recounts, Willke learned this lesson on a college circuit tour where he and his wife had been greeted with mounting hostility when they lectured on the stages of fetal development. However, when they modified their approach to address the needs and concerns of women both before and after the presentation on fetal development—what Reardon refers to as a "pro-woman sandwich"—the hostility suddenly disappeared, and audience members committed to taking a "new and serious look" at the pro-life position.[31]

Based upon his experience, coupled with market research on the matter, Willke thus proclaimed, "[w]hat is needed . . . is to shout from the housetops the details of the pro-life movement's obvious compassion for women. When this is done, the folks in the middle once again will listen to us."[32] Willke's plan to shout this woman-friendly message from the housetops was not as sophisticated as Reardon's plan to "reverse the trap," so that those opposing the pro-woman/pro-life initiative would be cast as the enemy of women's rights.[33] Nonetheless, Willke fervently hoped that by adopting the one-liner "Why not love them both?," the antiabortion movement could effectively turn the tide in its favor by correcting the erroneous perception that pro-life people were not compassionate toward women.[34]

Of further benefit, Reardon stressed that arguments about harms to women could be presented to the public in scientific terms, which would be more effective in reaching the middle majority than conventional appeals steeped in moral claims about the sacredness of all life. Highlighting the strategic appeal of cloaking this woman-centric approach in evidence-based vestments, Reardon refers to his plan for converting this cohort to the pro-life cause as one of "teaching morality by teaching science."[35] As he explains, "although believers know that God's moral law is not given to us to enslave us . . . [but] is given to us as a path towards true happiness," nonbelievers can only be reached through "an alternative way of evangelizing," which appeals to their self-interest, rather than to an innate sense of good.[36]

Reardon accordingly urged movement leaders to adopt a research agenda that was aimed at finding "compelling evidence" to demonstrate that acts such as abortion inevitably "lead, in the end not to happiness and freedom, but to sorrow and enslavement."[37] To this end, Reardon founded the Elliot Institute for Social Science Research which, as described on the institute's website, serves as a "major resource for organizations around the world who are concerned about protecting the rights of women and their unborn children."[38] Aiming to provide scientific support for his claim that "when we are talking about the psychological complications of abortion, we are implicitly talking about the physical and behavioral symptoms of a *moral* problem,"[39] Reardon has teamed up with other proponents of this approach in an effort to publish a body of credentialed, secularized articles "proving" that abortion harms women. Although, as discussed in Chapter Five, many of these articles have been soundly critiqued for containing multiple methodological weaknesses, Reardon's secular publication record has nonetheless garnered his reputation as "one of the leading experts on the effects of abortion on women."[40]

Reardon is far from alone in advocating for adopting a scientific approach to what conservatives have traditionally viewed as a moral issue. As journalist Chris Mooney writes, when it comes to abortion and other controversial issues, such as intelligent design and abstinence-only education, "religious conservatives have shifted gears in their battles over science and policy" by adopting "the veneer of scientific and technical expertise instead of merely asserting their heartfelt beliefs."[41] This perfectly describes Reardon's approach for taking the "pro-woman message" into the public square. However, before taking this bold step, he faced the daunting challenge of persuading his colleagues that this shift would not "undercut the moral high ground of opposing abortion simply because all human life is sacred."[42] In short, as he sought to make his new vision a reality, Reardon faced a double burden of persuasion.

Subjecting the Pro-Woman/Pro-Life Position to a Moral Examination

As Reardon ruefully acknowledges in the introduction to *Making Abortion Rare,* the task of persuading his fellow travelers in the antiabortion movement to position grieving mothers at the center of their antiabortion message proved far harder than he originally imagined it would be. As he explains, "I never intended to write this book. For the last twelve years, my goal has been to educate the general public about how women are seriously injured by abortion. I have discovered, however, that I am instead spending most of my time trying to explain to pro-life activists exactly why post-abortion issues are the key to converting hearts—the key to winning the battle for life."[43] As he further grouses, the difficulty of this persuasive task was compounded by the opposition of "many pro-life leaders [who] believe it is both strategically and morally wrong to concentrate the public's attention on anyone other than abortion's primary victim, the unborn child."[44]

Reardon goes on to single out C. Everett Koop, the fiercely pro-life surgeon general of the United States, as the "most significant" example of this kind of obstructionism based on his refusal to issue a report on the health consequences of abortion as then President Ronald Reagan had requested he do.[45] Explaining his decision in a letter to the president, Koop wrote that "despite a diligent review . . . the scientific studies do not provide conclusive data about the health effects of abortion on women."[46] Koop also made his moral opposition to the adoption of such an approach clear, stating in an interview that as "soon as you contaminate the morality of your stand by getting worried about the health effects of abortion on women, you have weakened the whole thing."[47]

Reardon would also come to contest the position as expressed by philosopher Francis Beckwith. Beckwith posited that if the middle majority both believed that abortion was murder and that women should have the right to make this decision for themselves, it meant that the pro-life movement had failed in its efforts to persuade them that the "fetus is a member of the human community" who is entitled to "all the moral obligations and rights that apply to other members of the human community."[48] He also argued that rather than getting sidetracked by the morally irrelevant and relativistic suffering of women, activists should instead redouble their efforts to show that "one cannot be 'prochoice' on abortion and at the same time maintain that fetuses are fully human."[49] Reardon dismissed this view as strategically futile and oblivious to the power of a morally grounded opposition to abortion that simultaneously focuses on women as well as the unborn.[50]

The dual utility of the pro-woman/pro-life approach should now be apparent. Not only could it be presented to the ambivalent middle as a seemingly morally neutral scientific argument against abortion, it could also be marketed to the antiabortion camp as a fuller expression of its traditional moral imperative. Reardon brilliantly encapsulates this dualism in the concept of "teaching morality by teaching science," which has been folded into the antiabortion movement's strategy to obscure the religious underpinnings of the abortion regret narrative.

In seeking to convince his colleagues that the adoption of a pro-woman/pro-life message would not weaken the "moral high ground of opposing abortion simply because all life is sacred,"[51] Reardon subjected this approach to a "moral examination" to demonstrate that it is "not only consistent with the pro-life moral imperative, it is, in fact, a fuller and more complete expression of it."[52] Reardon begins this examination with what he describes as a very simple observation, namely that "[i]n God's ordering of creation it is only the mother who can nurture her unborn child. All that the rest of us can do, then is to nurture the mother. . . ."[53] Grounded in God's dictate that "the interests of the child and the mother are always joined," he accordingly insists that "from a natural law perspective, we can know in advance that abortion is inherently harmful to women. It is simply impossible to rip a child from the womb of his mother without tearing out a part of the woman herself."[54] Driving home this message, he stresses that "when we are talking about the psychological complications of abortion, we are implicitly talking about the physical and behavioral symptoms of a *moral* problem" (italics added).[55]

Elucidating why the abortion decision resides in the moral domain, Reardon, in keeping with some of the CPC counselors we interviewed, depicts the decision-making process as a pitched battle between Christ and Satan. As he explains, pulling the woman in one direction, Christ urges her not to "do this thing," and implores her to "[p]lace your trust in Me." Pulling her in the opposite direction, Satan insists "[y]ou must get rid of it. . . . You have no choice. . . . Do this one thing and then you will be back in the driver's seat of life."[56] Likewise drawing the battleground motif, during our interview with Michelle, she explained that "this whole pro-life movement is spiritual warfare. We know what the Bible says about life. . . . One of the things I teach on sometimes is that Satan hates women—hates women—because she brings humanity into the world. So, the attack on women . . . is strong and it's powerful because if he can get rid of her, if he can kill babies, you're killing humanity."[57] Michelle went on to further contextualize this battle through scripture. Drawing from the passage in Revelations where "the dragon [is] at the womb of the woman," she internalizes abortion as Satan's tool that he wields to destroy women's powerful position as gifting humanity to the world. In this scenario, abortion transcends the bodily realm and takes up occupancy in the spiritual plane where the battle over humanity is being waged.

But Reardon reassures us that all is not necessarily lost for the "desperate woman" who rejects God's gift of life and instead follows Satan to the abortionist's door. If she subsequently repents and embraces His gift of forgiveness, and allows God to use her as "an instrument for showing the abundant glory of his mercy," she will, he promises, "escape from the tar pit of despair," where she would otherwise be trapped.[58] Embracing Reardon's perspective, all of our interviewees endorsed this idea of a second chance, succinctly relayed in the description of their service model—"our purpose is to save lives. And our goal is to save souls. We talk about holistic health care and taking care of body, mind, and spirit."[59]

If, however, a postabortive woman is paralyzed by the "horror of [her] sin" and does not believe she deserves God's mercy, Reardon warns that she will instead find herself consigned to a living hell where Satan seeks to "pump as much despair into [her life] as he can generate."[60] Standing now as her "fiercest accuser," he will taunt her that she is "beyond redemption. . . . There is no one who can love YOU—a murderer. You are alone." In turn, he will entreat her to escape this misery by seeking "what little comfort you can in the bottom of a booze bottle, in the silence of suicide, or in the embrace of an affair."[61] Shadowing Reardon's grim picture, one counselor explained that for women devoid of a strong religious faith, redemption and peace lay out of reach—"without a relationship with Christ, without spiritual reasons for doing what you do, it's just natural for people to want to take the low road and make it as easy as they can on themselves."[62]

This "devil's bargain" by which Satan first encourages a woman to abort and then fans the flames of despair, is, according to Reardon, aimed at separating women from God. Unmoored from their faith, unrepentant postabortive women spiral toward atheism, which he identifies as the "greatest tragedy of abortion."[63] Tracking Satan's jeering admonition that their only hope for comfort lies in death, adultery, or addiction, Reardon likewise asserts that "annihilation of the self," either through the literal act of suicide or through "death's semblance in abusive relationships or the mind-deadening effects of drug or alcohol abuse," is their only chance for escape from a life of despair.[64]

The concept of the "devil's bargain" crystalizes the animating religiosity of Reardon's pro-woman antiabortion strategy. The tragic figure of a wounded woman postabortion stands as the literal embodiment of Satan's victory over God, and her despair is the direct consequence of having repudiated his sacred design for her life. So viewed, antiabortion activists assume the mantle of avenging angel come to wrest suffering womanhood from Satan's vicious grasp.

By way of further reassurance to those who might still be concerned that the adoption of a pro-woman message would dilute the movement's moral center, Reardon stressed that grieving mothers are the best spokespeople for the sacred humanity of unborn children. As he explains, by listening to the "testimony of women who grieve over their lost children," the ambivalent majority will inexorably be "drawn into implicitly acknowledging the unborn for whom the tears are wept."[65] He thus proclaims that "by focusing on women's rights, we are not ignoring the unborn, but, instead, are preparing the stage for the most compelling advocates of all for the unborn—their mothers."[66]

TAKING THE MESSAGE PUBLIC

In this section, we look at the ways in which the pro-woman message moved out of the cloistered spaces of the nation's CPCs into the public square where it began to coalesce into a cohesive political and legal strategy for restricting access to abortion. In a somewhat earlier transitional phase, this message began to take hold in other somewhat more public, but still predominantly female spaces. As Karissa Haugeberg documents, during the 1980s, carefully scripted "regret tracts" began circulating in antiabortion publications. In these tracts, anonymous authors described "how their lives fell into turmoil after their abortions, with accounts of suicide attempts, sexual promiscuity, eating disorders, and drug and alcohol abuse." This was followed by a "spiritual awakening that caused them to identify as born-again Christians," resulting in a promise that in exchange for Jesus's forgiveness, they would share their redemption stories to dissuade others from aborting.[67] Presaging an approach that Reardon would soon urge the movement to adopt, the writers of these regret tracts typically called upon abortion opponents to regard them with compassion rather than with the traditional animosity reserved for women who chose to terminate a pregnancy rather than embracing motherhood.[68]

The woman-centric approach got an important boost in 1981, when Vincent Rue, then a professor of family relations, testified before the Senate Subcommittee on the Constitution in hearings on an antiabortion amendment to the Constitution. In his opening statement, Subcommittee Chair

Orrin Hatch, a conservative senator from Utah, made his own views on the matter known. As he stated, "I believe that abortion under virtually all circumstances is wrong because it involves the taking of a human life [and that] because it is a human life that we are talking about, I personally have no reservations about elevating this protection into the Constitution."[69]

Although Hatch framed the issue before the subcommittee as one involving the matter of securing constitutional protection for the unborn, Vincent Rue turned his gaze upon the injured women with his testimony that abortion is a "psychological Trojan horse for women," which inexorably leads to "guilt, anxiety, depression . . . deterioration of self-image, regret [and] remorse," among other negative reactions.[70] Zeroing in on guilt, Rue proclaimed that "[i]t is superfluous to ask whether patients experience guilt; it is axiomatic that they will."[71] Consonant with the views articulated by some of the CPC counselors we interviewed, Rue further testified that abortion "emasculates men" and is destructive of the relationship between the sexes, as women are empowered to make this decision without involving their partners.[72]

Building on this testimony, Rue famously went on to develop a theory of "postabortion syndrome" (PAS), which he proclaimed was similar to the post-traumatic stress disorder (PTSD) Vietnam veterans experienced in that both are "characterized by the chronic or delayed development of symptoms resulting from impacted emotional reactions to the perceived physical and emotional trauma of abortion."[73] The concept of PAS meshed well with the CPCs' mission of steering women toward motherhood, and it thus quickly gained a foothold within the centers. In addition, several women who heard Rue speak at the 1982 National Right to Life Convention, and who themselves had had a negative experience with abortion, were inspired to "take the first fragile steps" toward forming the nation's first postabortion support group—Women Exploited by Abortion (WEBA).

As Olivia Gans, a WEBA founder put it, the organization was founded at a time when, outside of the CPC context, "few people in the pro-life movement had ever had any intimate contact with women who'd had an abortion [and] . . . few if any women who'd had abortions were active in the pro-life movement." WEBA was thus intended to offer postabortive women like herself, who were "lost in a limbo of . . . denial and painful secrets," a safe space in which to talk about their pain and to begin the process of "tear[ing] away the screen of lies that were spread by every pro-abortion slogan."[74] Despite its lack of clinical validity, the idea of PAS resonated with WEBA members. Helping to get the word out, as Siegel writes, the group "was able to disseminate large volumes of PAS broadcasts and publications through the Christian Broadcast Network (CBN) and other evangelical institutions."[75]

Giving further voice to WEBA's perspective on abortion trauma, in 1987, David C. Reardon published the book *Aborted Women: Silent No More,* in which he detailed the traumatizing impact of abortion based on his survey of WEBA members whom he described as "representative of the aborting population as a whole."[76] However, it should be noted that the accuracy of this descriptor is belied by the fact that respondents were all members of a group founded to specifically provide support to those who were struggling with the aftermath of abortion. Giving voice to WEBA's staunch antiabortion perspective, founding member, Nancyjo Mann, proclaimed in the book's preface that the "pro-abortion mentality [is an] attempt to desex women" by "separate[ing] them from their reproductive potential," which, in turn, erodes "the unique value of female sexuality [and] the natural pride which women enjoy in being able to conceive and bear children."[77]

Most of the women Reardon surveyed had terminated their pregnancies a decade earlier. Touting the benefits of hindsight, he declared that their many years of "self-examination, learning and change" gave them a "matured, reflective point of view of their abortion experience." He further noted that "after facing the physical and psychological aftereffects . . . [and] seeing their lives unimproved or worsened," the overwhelming majority of respondents now recognized that their decision to abort was a mistake.[78] Dismissive of alternative narratives, Reardon asserted that in contrast to the enlightened women in his study, postabortive women who did not report being mired in despair had not yet achieved "this level of insight, this level of inner peace" nor confronted how they had been "manipulated, exploited, and deceived for the convenience of others"[79]—a process that he claimed required time, patience, and support.

Politicizing Regret

Reardon's plan to transform the pro-woman approach, which had initially been cloistered within intimate female spaces, into a cohesive political strategy for revitalizing the antiabortion movement has born considerable fruit. As Reva Siegel meticulously documents, many antiabortion groups have moved away from their previously exclusive focus on the morally grounded claim that abortion is wrong because it is tantamount to murder to also include a woman-protective message. As she details, some have adopted this as their primary oppositional frame, whereas others now include it alongside a more traditional fetal-focused frame.[80] In this section, we trace the ways in which Reardon's pro-woman/pro-life message began to gain traction in the political arena, which helped to lay the groundwork for its consolidation as a rationale for increasing governmental surveillance of and control over women's reproductive bodies.

Reardon's push to locate grieving mothers at the center of the antiabortion platform was aided by a shift in the larger opportunity environment in which "cultural and ideological contexts" align with political openings that can help shape the "trajectories of social movement tactics and frames." In turn, this convergence can lead to the advancement of a movement's aims.[81] For the antiabortion movement, the opportunity environment began to change course through several key political openings, most visibly, the campaign and election of President George W. Bush in 2000.

During the campaign, then Governor Bush delivered a videotaped address at the National Right to Life Convention in 1999. Mirroring the softer, pro-woman discourse that had been percolating throughout the antiabortion movement, he told attendees, "I do not believe the promises of the Declaration of Independence are just for the strong, the independent, the healthy. They are for everyone—including unborn children. We are a society with enough compassion and wealth and love to care *for both mothers and their children,* to seek the promise and potential in every life" (italics added).[82]

Further drawing out Reardon's gentler, curated face of the antiabortion movement into the public mainstream, Governor Bush during his acceptance speech at the Republican National Convention shone a spotlight on crisis pregnancy centers, folding them into the "next bold step of welfare reform," in which their "heroic work"—alongside that of "homeless shelters and hospices, [and] food pantries"—will, he predicted, aid citizens in "reclaiming their communities block-by-block and heart-by-heart."[83] Articulating his perspective more fully, he told the nation, "Government cannot do this work. It can feed the body, but it cannot reach the soul. Yet government can take the side of these groups, helping the helper, encouraging the inspired."[84]

Firmly anchored to a pro-life position, President George W. Bush, once elected, governed from a philosophy of compassionate conservatism trussed to his fundamental belief in the "absolute nature of God . . . the existence of evil, not as an abstract idea, a philosophy, but as something that's real and tangible."[85] He used his bully pulpit to remind society that "[e]very child is a priority and a blessing" who "should be welcomed in life and protected by law."[86] As evidenced by these remarks, President Bush clearly embraced the antiabortion movement's long-standing fetal-centric framing, but he also helped to pull threads from the emerging woman-centric framing into the public spotlight. Proclaiming January 19, 2003 as National Sanctity of Human Life Day, President Bush called for "compassionate alternatives to abortion, such as *helping women in crisis* through maternity group homes, encouraging adoption [and] promoting abstinence education" to "build a culture that respects life" (italics added).[87] Employing this dualistic framing of the antiabortion message, Bush thus closely tracked Reardon's admonition that the well-being of a pregnant woman is conjoined with that of her fetus and that resolution of a crisis pregnancy requires the embrace of motherhood.

In this regard, it should be noted that President Bush's predecessor, President Ronald Reagan, did on occasion make isolated references that were suggestive of a woman-centered view. For example, Reagan mentioned three specific "crisis counseling" centers in Texas during his remarks at the 1984 Annual Convention of the National Religious Broadcasters,[88] and a few years later, he referenced "the suffering of women who have had abortions" in his remarks to antiabortion supporters participating in the 1988 March for Life rally.[89] However, Reagan's remarks were directed at limited audiences of committed antiabortionists, whereas Bush integrated his into mainstream speeches, and more importantly, he helped to channel federal funds into the CPCs, thus signaling a notably more robust embrace of a frame shift.

Seeing an opportunity to realize this vision of "helping women in crisis," President Bush actively worked to forge strong partnerships between government and faith-based organizations, whereby bureaucracies would come to view "faith-based charities as partners, not as rivals."[90] President Bush's earlier campaign promise to "[help] the helper" materialized into more than rhetorical support for faith-based organizations; rather, it became a funded initiative. As he explained, "[w]hen it comes to providing resources the government should not discriminate against these groups that often inspire life-changing faith in a way that government should never."[91]

Prior to 2001, very few CPCs received federal funding.[92] However, President Bush's enthusiasm for building partnerships between the government and faith-based organizations opened the door to a new funding stream for CPCs through an abstinence-only education initiative. A handful of CPCs moved quickly to take advantage of this funding by folding an abstinence curriculum into their existing evangelical programming. Importantly, applicants for these Community-Based Abstinence Education (CBAE) funds were not required to go through the state government vetting process that was required under the existing abstinence-only education funding programs; rather, they could apply directly to the federal government for CBAE monies.[93][‡]

As taxpayer funds flowed into the CBAE program, CPCs were quick to jump on this abstinence bandwagon. As word of this innovative, repurposed use of taxpayer money quickly diffused through antiabortion networks, Care Net began teaching its affiliates about the benefits of obtaining CBAE funding.[94] Seeing this as a lucrative enterprise that could raise the financial and professional stature of CPCs, both new and established centers successfully applied for CBAE grants, resulting in a twofold to sevenfold increase in their budgets.[95] The influx of taxpayer money into the outreach branch of the antiabortion movement dramatically elevated the importance of the missionizing work and messaging of CPCs within the movement, while also increasing their visibility in communities across the country.

Once President Bush termed out of office, the partisan change in presidential administrations did little to stem the flow of taxpayer money into CPCs or the political uptake of the woman-centered framing emanating from them. State governments, aided by state-level partisan changes, continued to help move the messaging and work of CPCs out of the shadows of the antiabortion movement into the public arena. By way of example, several Republican-controlled state legislatures emulated Pennsylvania's strategy of siphoning off a portion of their Temporary Assistance for Needy Families (TANF) block grant funding to support CPCs, while others expanded the pool of available funds by including line items in their budgets for them.[96][§] Wanting to lift up the visibility and shore up government support for the state's CPCs, under the leadership of then Governor Mike Pence, Indiana diverted a portion of its TANF grant in 2015 to fund the antiabortion organization Real Alternatives, which provides financial assistance to

---

‡ For detail on abstinence-only programs, see Doan and Williams (2008).

§ In 1996 the Personal Responsibility and Work Opportunity Reconciliation Act (PRWORA) repealed the entitlement status of Aid to Families with Dependent Children (AFDC) and replaced the previous program's unlimited federal funds with a fixed block grant allocation to the states.

CPCs operating throughout the state while helping to establish new ones.[97]**

Taxpayer funding and support for CPCs has been buoyed by other creative funding strategies that have further raised their stature and organizational capacity.[98] A prime example of this is the spread of "Choose Life" motor vehicle license plates. In addition to providing a financial boost to CPCs, this national project provides an additional channel through which state governments can express support for their woman-centered antiabortion message.

In 1996, building on the antiabortion movement's cultural shift toward a pro-woman/pro-life message, Randy Harris, the commissioner of Marion County, Florida, came up with the idea of creating a specialty motor vehicle license plate with a simple and targeted message to women—"Choose Life." In addition to spreading this message on the state's roadways, his plan also included funneling the bulk of the proceeds from plate sales to CPCs and "other life affirming agencies" that "help pregnant women choose life for their babies."[99]

To this end, Harris founded the organization Choose Life, Inc. In 2000, after several political starts and stops, the Florida legislature, as is required under state law, enacted a specific statute approving the manufacture of Choose Life license plates. Since then, Florida residents have had the option of paying a surcharge to the state over and above the usual fee to acquire a standard license plate displaying the Choose Life message. The additional revenue stream generated from this surcharge is then used to fund "life-affirming pregnancy resource centers, maternity homes, and nonprofit adoption agencies within Florida" that are not involved with abortion in any way.[100]

Inspired by this victory, Choose Life took its campaign national under the aegis of Choose Life America. Aided by this organizational support, today 32 states offer drivers the option of a Choose Life specialty plate. These plates, which typically sport a crayoned drawing of a beaming young

---

** In 2015, Missouri earmarked 2 percent of the state's TANF funds ($4.5 million) to help fund CPCs, eventually supplementing that amount with an additional $2 million in state funds in 2017 (Covert 2016). In 2015, Indiana used $3.5 million from its TANF grant to fund the antiabortion organization Real Alternatives (Stanley 2016). Among states using welfare funds for CPCs, Texas is the biggest spender, having doled out more than $23 million in TANF money to CPCs between 2013 through 2016.

boy and girl with a similarly crayoned "Choose Life" message, have raised more than $26 million. Following Florida's lead, many of these states explicitly prohibit the distribution of funds to any organization that provides abortion-related services of any kind.[101] The antiabortion messaging of this national campaign is hybrid in nature, as it combines elements of the traditional fetal-focused message, namely "Choose Life," while also funding the supporting agencies that have a pro-maternalist mission focusing on the "life-affirming" role of women.

It is important to recognize that motor vehicle licenses are state issued and owned, and the issuance of specialty plates in all states requires formal approval in accordance with the applicable state law procedures. As a result, courts have had to wrestle with the question of whether specialty license plates signal the views of drivers or the state. Resolution of this question has significant constitutional implications. Specifically, if license plates speak for drivers, states that issue "Choose Life" plates would, upon request, most likely have to offer drivers the option of "Respect Choice" plates. Under the First Amendment's guarantee of free speech, states cannot discriminate against viewpoints that they disagree with or find offensive, as this would impinge upon the free speech rights of car owners with a pro-choice view. If, however, license plates are deemed to speak for the government, states would be exempted from this First Amendment constraint on viewpoint discrimination, because "when the government speaks it is entitled to promote a program, to espouse a policy, or to take a position. In doing so, it represents its citizens and it carries out its duties on their behalf."[102]

In 2015, the Supreme Court resolved this thorny question in the case of *Walker v. Texas Division, Sons of Confederate Veterans,* which involved a challenge by the Texas division of the Sons of Confederate Veterans to the denial of their request for the issuance of a specialty plate bearing their logo of a square confederate flag by the Texas Board of Motor Vehicles. In part, the denial was based on public comments that the design was an offensive expression of hate. In affirming the denial, the court concluded that license plates speak for the state rather than for the driver, and that the messaging therefore comes within the "government speech" exception to the First Amendment.††

---

†† For further discussion of the *Walker* decision, including a critique of its free speech analysis in which the author argues that it opens the door to governmental censorship of messages it does not like, see Calvert (2017).

In reaching this conclusion, the court drew a critical distinction between bumper stickers on the one hand and license plates on the other, reasoning that in "contrast to the purely private speech expressed through bumper stickers," an individual who displays a message on a state-approved license plate "likely intends to convey to the public that the State has endorsed the message."[103] Underscoring the distinction, it stressed that the messaging and design of specialty plates are incorporated into "government-mandated, government-controlled, and government-issued IDs,"[104] in contrast to bumper stickers whose messaging falls under the sole authority and control of the driver of a vehicle. Consonant with the *Walker* decision, Choose Life plates can be said to speak for the state, thus amplifying the political reach of the pro-woman/pro-life antiabortion message in the very public space of the nation's roadways.

In direct keeping with the underlying religiosity of the pro-woman/pro-life message, testimonials on the Choose Life America website are saturated with devotional gratitude. As exemplified by the following two testimonials, many regard the Choose Life specialty plates as doing the Lord's work by turning women way from abortion:

Teresa (not her real name) arrived at a pregnancy center in Tampa, FL and told her story to a counselor. She was coming to have an abortion and saw several Choose Life license plates on the 10 mile drive. When she arrived at the abortion clinic, she told Judy, the counselor out front "You are a sign and seal that what I was about to do was wrong." She drove off knowing her future was going to be rough, but pretty well assured that God was going to use her in His plan.

I went in to have my oil changed. . . . the attendant . . . mentioned that he had noticed my license plate and had a close friend who was six months pregnant and her boyfriend was threatening her life if she didn't get an abortion. . . . I told him that she had other options . . . I asked him if he would like the number of the Crisis Pregnancy Center in Baton Rouge and he said yes. . . . I sensed that God was using that license plate to communicate and allow that young man to enter into the conversation. . . .

In addition to testimonials from individuals who witnessed the life-changing power of these plates, others simply expressed their hope of eventually seeing their state make a full throttle endorsement of God's pro-life messaging: *". . . it is our prayerful desire to see those tags the official state tag for the state of Mississippi. God can do it!"* Adding to these sentiments, some organizations expressed their gratitude to God for the distribution of funds from the sale of the plates—*"the first distribution of funds came at the Lord's timing. . . . We have been steadily seeking to expand our services to reach more of the abortion vulnerable women in our area, so the check from Choose Life Fund . . . has enabled us to implement our progressing vision . . ."*[105] Although it certainly would be a stretch to say that these testimonials speak for the state rather than the individuals giving voice to these expressions of gratitude, it is nonetheless critical to bear in mind they consider God to be expressing his will through the Choose Life plates (and the resulting funding stream), which the *Walker* decision makes eminently clear do in fact speak for the state.

In sum, the imprimatur of governmental approval coupled with the influx of taxpayer (and private) money into the outreach branch of the antiabortion movement has dramatically elevated the importance of the missionizing work of CPCs and raised the visibility of their pro-woman messaging within the movement, while increasing their profile in communities across the country. With the growing reputational cache of the outreach branch as a backdrop, elected officials have increasingly begun to incorporate woman-centered rhetoric into their common vernacular. In turn, this has given political flight to Reardon's strategy of moving this feminized message beyond the confines of the antiabortion movement to reshape the nature of the debate and gain new converts.

Marshaling Women's Experience to Document the "Truth" about Abortion Trauma

Armed with growing political and monetary support, antiabortion activists began seeking out "compelling evidence" to buttress the years of experiential evidence that had been garnered from the care work occurring in CPCs to establish that abortion causes women irreparable spiritual, psychological, and physical harm resulting in a lifetime of regret. Operation Outcry has been a critical leader in this effort. A self-described ministry of the Justice Foundation, Operation Outcry is dedicated to "end[ing] the pain of abortion in America and around the world by mobilizing women and men hurt by abortion who share their true stories of the devastating effects of abortion" so that "others will be spared the suffering and tragic consequences."[106] To this end, it has gathered more than 5,000 sworn declarations (meaning that they are signed under the pain of perjury that the information is true) for use in court cases and legislative hearings aimed at restricting or banning abortion.

Directly linking this project to the deep wellspring of religiosity that animates Reardon's pro-woman/pro-life message, an embedded video on the Operation Outcry website opens and closes with the quote from Proverbs 14:25 that a "truthful witness rescues lives."[107] Although this could be read as a fetal-focused framing of the organization's message, the video is entirely focused on the pain of women postabortion, with speakers urging viewers to invite members of their church congregations to fill out declarations as an act of healing and of shedding light on the truth about the traumatizing impact of abortion on women.

Seeking to distill and crystalize experiential knowledge about abortion, while also reinforcing the religiosity that quietly permeates this effort, each declaration is referred to as a "hail stone which will ultimately destroy the refuge, the shelter, the legal structure that supports the injustice of abortion" through its contribution to a veritable "hail storm of voices of those hurt by abortion."[108] This imagery comes from the Prophet Isaiah, whom has long inspired the work of the Justice Foundation and Operation Outcry.[109] The reduction of the abortion experience to a singular fixed truth also tracks Reardon's admonition that "from a natural law perspective, we can know in advance that abortion is inherently harmful to women. It is simply impossible to rip a child from the womb of a mother without tearing out a part of the woman herself"—a recognition that he likewise declares to be the "truth."[110] This project of marshaling experiential knowledge regarding the "truth" of abortion by way of written declarations has borne considerable fruit. In the final portion of this chapter, we look at the role women's experiential knowledge played in the legislative hearings conducted by the South Dakota Task Force to Study Abortion.

In 2005, the South Dakota legislature enacted House Bill 1233, which authorized the creation of a Task Force to Study Abortion (Task Force) after the state senate heard testimony by postabortive women regarding their struggles with depression and "suicidal ideation." In so doing, the state thus effectively answered Reardon's earlier call for "an alternative way of evangelizing" aimed at producing scientific evidence to persuade the middle majority that abortions "lead, in the end not to happiness and freedom, but to sorrow and enslavement."[111]

Moved by the women's testimonies, the legislature charged the Task Force with the responsibility of looking into, among other issues, "the degree to which decisions to undergo abortions are voluntary and informed, the effect and health risk that undergoing abortions has on the women, including the effects on the women's physical and mental health, including the delayed onset of cancer, and her subsequent life and socioeconomic experiences."[112] The Task Force was further empowered to translate its findings into actionable steps by determining "whether the need exists for additional protections of the rights of pregnant women contemplating abortion, and whether there is any interest of the state or the mother or the child which would justify changing the laws relative to abortion."[113]

The Task Force held four days of hearings in which it purportedly strove to achieve "a balanced viewpoint" by inviting experts who both supported and opposed the legality of abortion. Despite this nod to neutrality, the *Report of the South Dakota Task Force to Study Abortion* (Task Force Report or report) concluded that the "evidence was overwhelmingly in support of protecting life and preventing harm to women caused by abortion."[114] In building its support for this conclusion, it elevated the published works of Reardon, along with Rue's discredited studies about postabortion syndrome, over more credible research by leading professional organizations it described as ideologically biased such as the American Medical Association, the American Psychological Association, and the American College of Obstetricians and Gynecologists.[115]

Further underscoring the biased nature of the Task Force's process, the report paid particular attention to the postabortion statements of close to 2,000 women that Operation Outcry submitted.[116]‡‡ Heeding Reardon's 1996 call to the antiabortion movement to place women at the center of their opposition to abortion, it explained the significance of these statements as follows: "The focus we place on the experiences of women harmed by abortion is appropriate because in many ways it is only now that we are realizing in an appropriate way, the magnitude of the injustice of abortion. For most of us, the injustice to the child has long been apparent; but we have never before seen the magnitude of the injustice to the mothers as witnessed from their personal testimonies."[117] Seeking to convey the "magnitude of

---

‡‡ As we discuss at length in Chapter Five, 180 of these same testimonies resurfaced two years later in an appendix to the amicus curiae brief the Justice Foundation filed in the Supreme Court's *Gonzales v. Carhart* case.

the injustice to the mothers," the Task Force Report stressed that "a pattern of shared experiences and trauma and common sense of loss emerge" from the testimonies.[118]

According to the Task Force Report, "[a] majority of these women stated that they were not told the truth that the abortion would terminate the life of a living human being, and if they had been, they would not have submitted to the procedure because of their sense of duty and their relationship with the child."[119] After weighing the "powerful oral and written" testimony of women, which it characterized as "virtually all of the credible objective evidence" that had been submitted, the report took a deft turn, concluding that women do not possess sufficient knowledge of fetal development to understand what they are agreeing to when they consent to an abortion.[120] Grounded in this fundamental ignorance, as understood by the Task Force, a mother's unknowing destruction of her relationship with her unborn child becomes the cornerstone of regret. In a thinly veiled secular rewrite of what Reardon describes as God's natural law where it is "simply impossible to rip a child from the womb of his mother without tearing out a part of the woman herself,"[121] the report claims that it "is simply unrealistic to expect that a pregnant mother is capable of being involved in the termination of the life of her own child without risk of suffering significant psychological trauma and distress."[122]

The wisdom gleaned from women's experiential knowledge of abortion was bolstered by the testimonies of CPC personnel, which the report characterized as "particularly helpful because they are free of any conflict of interest." Thus, for example, Ms. Cynthia Collins, an executive director of a CPC for 18 years, using coded language to underscore women's witless but devout role in society, informed the Task Force that the women counseled at her center are unaware they are terminating a life, and once informed, they "commonly conclude that a mother should protect, not terminate, the life of her own child."[123] Supplying the Task Force with statistics generated at the center, Ms. Collins testified that after receiving counseling, "only 45 of the 1,860 pregnant mothers (2%) ultimately had an abortion."[124] Illustrating the scope and consequences of women's ignorance, she goes on to discuss the postabortive women counseled at her center, stating that 70 to 85 percent of them "made their decision under some form of coercion" and 80 percent were not provided accurate information from abortion clinics.[125] Further authenticating the legitimacy of Ms. Collins's information, the report includes testimony from other CPC personnel who report similar figures.

These numbers, however, stand in stark contrast to other research (omitted from the report) that concludes that less than one percent of women cite the desire of either a parent or a partner to abort as the most important reason for their decision.[126] Moreover, Ms. Collins's allegations regarding abortion providers run counter to the practices that govern their medical profession, including the legal requirement that providers "must verify that patients possess the capacity to make decisions about their care, that their participation in these decisions is voluntary, and that they receive adequate and appropriate information."[127] Rather, as studies have shown, any misinformation or inaccurate information injected in the informed consent protocol is a product of antiabortion state laws, rather than as Ms. Collins asserts in the report, neglect on the part of abortion providers.[128]

Supplied with this "credible" data that were "free of conflict," the Task Force Report concluded that the "many pressures and coercive forces and elements," including "misleading information" from abortion providers, coalesce making "most abortions not truly voluntary."[129] Expounding on its findings, the report goes on to more explicitly incorporate the issues of coercion and consent into the regret narrative:

> It is so far outside the normal conduct of a mother to implicate herself in the killing of her own child. Either the abortion provider must deceive the mother into thinking the unborn child does not yet exist, and thereby induce her consent without being informed, or the abortion provider must encourage her to defy her very nature as a mother to protect her child. . . . Our state must not overlook the harm to the mother and the fact that her fundamental rights are often terminated without informed or voluntary consent, and we must not overlook the injustice of the loss of life that results from abortion.[130]

Far from introducing new data or novel insights about abortion, the Task Force Report has been soundly critiqued for downplaying, dismissing, or simply excluding expert testimony and research that draws contradictory conclusions about women's abortion experiences,[131] while doubling down on an inherently maternal social construction of women to bolster its conclusions.

The Task Force's failure to include credible studies, coupled with its reliance on a highly selective pool of women's experiential testimonies, was so egregious that the antiabortion chairwoman was compelled to vote against the report.[132] Reinforcing these types of concerns, Caitlin Borgmann has roundly critiqued the spectacle of legislative "fact finding" expeditions like South Dakota's where witnesses are discriminately selected to "transform moral pronouncements about abortion into scientific fact," allowing activists to engineer the "ultimate conflation of science and morality on the issue of abortion."[133]

Having cast abortion as an unnatural act, the Task Force Report seeks to preserve the morality of the postabortive woman by impugning her competence and ability to make informed reproductive decisions. Much as the 19th-century antiabortion physician Dr. Hodge sought to defend the morality of "educated, refined" women who sought abortions, by claiming that "they seem not to realize that the being within them is indeed animate . . . a human being,"[134] and Reardon sought to present aborting women as driven by despair and confusion, the Task Force likewise drew from the same gendered playbook to restore the moral virtue of aborting women by proclaiming that they cannot be held accountable for consenting to an act that "asks far too much of the mother." It thus shifts the moral blame to the abortion provider "whose interests and philosophies are in direct conflict with the interests of the mother in her relationship with her child."[135]

Abandoning all secular pretense and reading like a page scripted from Reardon's *Making Abortion Rare,* the end of the report reifies women's divine place in the world by reminding the South Dakota legislature "that the intrinsic beauty of womanhood is inseparable from the beauty of motherhood" and that women therefore are "the touchstone and core of all civilized society."[136] Syncing with the conclusions Dr. Storer drew and then Reardon more than a century later, the report presents a picture of female vulnerability largely fueled by ignorance that society must guard against vis-à-vis legislation to stem women's victimization through the unwitting disruption of their "intrinsic beauty."

Resurrecting the plea of 19th-century physicians to lawmakers to enact "better and more effective safeguards" to protect women from themselves, the Task Force Report "recommend[s], and even urge[s], a legal ban on abortion."[137] However, acknowledging that criminalization of abortion may be too lofty a goal to achieve at the present moment, it implores the state to enact stopgap "legislation in an effort to lessen the loss of life and harm caused by abortion until such a ban can be implemented."[138] Capitalizing on the report's policy recommendations to protect women from abortion regret, South Dakota subsequently introduced new incremental legislation that tracks the growing migration of the pro-woman/pro-life antiabortion message from the CPCs into the public square by way of laws aimed at restricting abortion access.

CONCLUSION

As the 1990s got underway, David C. Reardon and John C. Willke, along with a handful of other antiabortion leaders, actively sought to repair the movement's extremist image by lifting up the woman-centered care work that had been quietly occurring within the nation's feminized crisis pregnancy centers. In seeking to persuade others in the movement that this shift would not dilute the moral integrity of its message, Reardon stressed that women's postabortive grief was the inevitable result of disrupting God's gendered order of creation. Critically, however, this message was divested of sacred meaning for public consumption and repackaged as the secular concept of abortion regret. By repositioning the movement as an advocate for and protector of "woman's rights," and capitalizing on political openings, antiabortion leaders gained the "political high ground" and garnered support from people outside of the movement.

The election of President Bush in 2000 further elevated the compassionate, woman-centered framing of the antiabortion message and opened new government-supported funding streams for the movement. The Choose Life license plates stand as a robust example of the phenomenon of channeling monies into "life-affirming" programs aimed at encouraging women to embrace motherhood. Putting Reardon's strategy of "teaching morality by teaching science," into action, the report of the South Dakota Task Force to Study Abortion presented the testimony of women who grieve over their lost children as evidence-based proof of the traumatizing nature of abortion. This helped to move this regret narrative to the center of the antiabortion movement and onto the national political stage.

The experiential knowledge of "women injured by abortion" made its way to the Supreme Court in the 2007 case of *Gonzales v. Carhart* and became embedded in a two-tiered woman-protective legal framework. The first tier focuses on protecting women from abortion regret, while the second tier highlights their vulnerability to coercion and exploitation by health care providers.

FIVE

Protecting Women for Their Own Good: The Reemergence of Legal Paternalism

Toward the end of the 20th century, David C. Reardon spearheaded a move to locate grieving mothers in the center of the antiabortion platform in an effort to persuade the ambivalent majority that abortion harms women. However, to succeed in this effort, he first had to persuade others in the antiabortion movement that the privileging of women's voices would not dilute the moral integrity of its message. To this end, he stressed that post-abortion grief emanates from the disruption of the mother-child bond in disregard of God's plan for women, thus making it clear that the regret narrative is permeated with sacred meaning.

As discussed in this chapter, the abortion regret narrative has continued to expand outward from its originating point in the cloistered spaces of the crisis pregnancy centers. Having taken root as an ideological reframing of the antiabortion message, it has since become firmly embedded in the law as a rationale for limiting access to abortion. We begin our exploration of this critical development by looking at the Supreme Court's 2007 decision in *Gonzales v. Carhart,* in which it embraced the idea that women require protection from the harms of abortion. Of central importance, we critically examine the court's singular reliance on the amicus curiae (friend of the court) brief that the conservative and religiously inspired Justice Foundation filed in this case. From here, we examine how the regret narrative has been encoded into a wide swath of restrictive measures based upon a two-tiered protective legal framework, which tracks the legislative strategy that Americans United for Life laid out. In the final section of the chapter, we examine the growing body of scholarship that both challenges the clinical validity of abortion regret and offers a far more robust and nuanced understanding of women's postabortion experiences.

THE SUPREME COURT'S EMBRACE OF THE ABORTION REGRET TROPE

In the 2007 case of *Gonzales v. Carhart*,[1] the Supreme Court upheld the federal Partial-Birth Abortion Ban Act of 2003 that criminalized the performance of intact dilation and evacuation (D and E) abortions unless the procedure was deemed necessary to save the life of a pregnant woman. Disregarding expert testimony that this late second-trimester procedure, in which the fetus is removed from the uterus intact, may be the safest option, the court instead agreed with the congressional findings that it bears a "in certain circumstances, disturbing similarity" to the "killing of a newborn infant."[2] Anchored in the view that "respect for human life finds an ultimate expression in the bond of love the mother has for her child," the court concluded, out of deference to these maternal instincts, that a ban was necessary to draw "a bright line that clearly distinguishes abortion and infanticide."[3]

Although expressly acknowledging the lack of "reliable data to measure the phenomena," anchored in this maternalist framing of female identity, the court asserted as a general proposition that it is "unexceptionable to conclude that some women come to regret their choice to abort the infant life they once created and sustained" and that "[s]evere depression and loss of esteem can follow."[4] Pivoting to the intact D and E abortion procedure that was at issue in the case, the court expressed concern that doctors might choose not to disclose the details of the procedure. Accordingly, it concluded that, due to her underlying emotional precarity, a woman who did not learn until after the fact that she had allowed her doctor "to pierce the skull and vacuum the fast-developing brains of her unborn child" was likely to suffer a "grief more anguished and a sorrow more profound" than she might have otherwise experienced.[5]

The court's decision to uphold the federal ban on this abortion procedure to protect women from regret drew a scathing dissent from Justice Ruth

Bader Ginsburg, who forcefully asserted that its protectionist approach relied upon "ancient notions about women's place in the family and under the Constitution [that] have long been discredited." Accordingly, rather than depriving women "of the right to make an autonomous choice," she instead advocated that doctors be required to provide women with all the necessary details so as to promote a fully informed decision.[6]

Not surprisingly, the court did not expressly invoke religious principles to justify its embrace of the abortion regret trope as this would have violated the First Amendment's mandate that church and state remain separate. However, its association of pregnant women with regretful mothers who have taken the life of the *"infant life* they once created and sustained" (italics added)[7] tracks the maternalist thinking of both Reardon and the South Dakota Task Force to Study Abortion, which, as we have seen, is anchored in a religious view of the world. Although expressed in secular terms, the court's invocation of regret reverberates with Reardon's core teaching regarding the maternal bond that God has created between a mother and her child.[8]

Put slightly differently, Terry Maroney writes that by invoking regret in "close narrative conjunction with the invocation of mother-love," the *Gonzales* court has infused the concept with a relativistic cultural meaning. Specifically, she argues that by giving "regret pride of place," the court is "subtly signaling endorsement of an account of the world in which abortion properly is regarded as the killing of a child by its mother" and that women are therefore likely to experience regret as "part of the natural order of things."[9] Maroney further argues that these underlying assumptions are reinforced by the court's reliance upon the declarations contained in the Justice Foundation's amicus curiae brief that are laced with religious sentiments regarding the inevitability of abortion trauma.[10]

Accordingly, although the court's invocation of abortion regret was framed in purely secular terms, it nonetheless implicitly impressed a religiously grounded view of woman's essential maternal destiny upon her body—one that cannot be disrupted without the risk of serious emotional injury. We cannot, of course, know for certain what was in the court's mind when it declared that "respect for life" finds its fullest expression in the bond of love between a mother and child. However, what we do know is that the religiously inspired amicus curie brief of the Justice Foundation was the sole authority that it relied upon in support of its assertion regarding the unexceptional nature of abortion regret.

BRINGING THE VOICES OF WOMEN HARMED BY ABORTION TO THE SUPREME COURT

Playing forward Reardon's lesson plan of "teaching morality by teaching science" to spread the truth that abortion is bad for women, the Justice Foundation filed an amicus curiae brief in the *Gonzales* case on behalf of Sandra Cano (the original plaintiff in the companion case to *Roe v. Wade)* and 180 "women injured by abortion." The suffering of these women was detailed in declarations that Operation Outcry had gathered for the purpose of amassing a body of evidence aimed at refuting the lie that "abortion is safe and good for women."[11] These intimate testimonies were, in turn, provided to the court in an appendix to the brief and through excerpted passages contained within the body of the brief itself.

By way of a short and general explanation, amicus briefs are filed by non-parties in cases to educate the justices and in hopes of swaying them to rule in favor of one party or the other. These briefs often draw heavily upon social science studies to provide expert guidance on what are known as legislative or social facts that, in contrast to case-specific adjudicative facts, make a generalized claim about the world such as that, for example, many women come to regret their abortions resulting in depression and a loss of self-esteem.

Before taking a closer look at the Justice Foundation's brief, we want to reiterate that our intent here is not to question the sincerity of the religious beliefs that prompted either the declarations themselves or the decision to file the brief. Nor do we seek to minimize the suffering recounted in these testimonies. Rather, as noted in the introduction, our concern is with the effort to persuade the court to elevate a single cultural belief structure—which is, as Maroney puts it, that "pregnant women see themselves as mothers, their aborted fetuses as dead children, and the abortion as murder"—into an objective and generalizable statement of reality to "cabin the rights of all pregnant women . . . even those for whom regret is a nonissue."[12]

A Revelation

According to Allan Parker, in 2000, God instructed him to pursue a legal reform strategy aimed at ending the nation's covenant with death. More specifically, as recounted to his followers, he was on his way home from the March for Life rally in Washington, D.C., when the Lord spoke to him in the Dallas-Fort Worth airport to inform him that "only through the testimonies of women hurt by abortion could [they] refute the lie that abortion is good for women."[13] Providing him with a blueprint for action, the Lord subsequently advised Parker to bring these testimonies to the Supreme Court to persuade the justices of this truth, and also gifted him with scriptural inspirations, including a passage from Isaiah, predicting that ". . . [h]ail shall sweep away the refuge of lies and the waters will overflow the hiding place. Your covenant with death will be annulled. . . ."—a passage that Parker notes has long sustained the work of the Justice Foundation and its Operation Outcry ministry.[14]

Seeking to carry out this plan, the Justice Foundation subsequently filed its amicus curiae brief in the *Gonzales* case. Although not identified as such in the brief itself, according to Parker the appended declarations are the direct "fruit of [God's] revelation."[15] Given their originating source coupled with Operation Outcry's characterization of the declarations as the equivalent of biblical hailstones aimed at "sweep[ing] away the refuge of lies" that abortion is good and safe for women,[16] it is not surprising to learn that the testimonies are laced through with sacred themes.

Although spiritually oriented motifs are implicitly embedded in a number of the narratives in which, for example, women speak of their guilt at having murdered their child, or of the unborn child's humanity, our review of them reveals that 22 percent of the declarations contain explicit religious motifs. These include, for example, a fear of divine retribution, emotional distress over the loss of a relationship with God, and guilt at having intentionally interfered with God's procreative plans.*

Illustrating the use of unambiguously religious references, J. L. M., for example, explains that her overly protective relationship with her son emanates from her fear that "God could still punish me by taking this child away." She goes on to explain that this fear has "mired my motivation and hindered my career (ironically since my reasoning in part to have an abortion was so my career wouldn't be hindered). It has cut the soul out of my entire life."[17] Although shorn of its religious references in the body of the brief, D. R.'s full testimony captures her highly freighted relationship with God following her abortion:

> Deep regret—initially I was suicidal—as the years have progressed I
> have developed a heightened level of bitterness and anger and self-
> hate. I feared God, have not been able to attend church because of my

---

* We have chosen to use initials for all the declarants, even where the authors themselves used their full names.

fear of God, forgiveness, shame, guilt, condemnation, inability to bond and fit in with other women, inability to be intimate. The deep emotional scars were a large contributing factor in my divorce—a very, very catastrophic choice! Great sense of loss and grief.[18]

Identifying another potent source of anguish, S. B. M.'s testimony cogently captures Reardon's natural law ideology. As she writes, "[f]or years, I was in denial, but I was bound by shame and guilt. It is the unspeakable deed and harms a woman deep to her core—As a woman, nurturer, child of God . . . it distorts the image of my life."[19]

S. B. M. is far from alone in mentioning shame. It is a theme that runs through many of the testimonies, and in many instances, the articulated feelings of shame are likewise interwoven with religious concerns. For example, C. M. explains that she has suffered from "[d]epression, low self-esteem, guilt, condemnation, and shame, sleepless nights, nightmares and torment, thoughts of self-hate and suicide, lost, confused, destroyed relationships throughout my life, unloved, unlovable, unable to trust God or anyone."[20] Expressing similar feelings of shame, F. K. states that even though she "believe[d] God would forgive me," she too was plagued with "[d]eep shame and remorse."[21]

Hewing, however, to Reardon's admonition that the moral underpinnings of the pro-woman/pro-life message must be packaged in secular terms to reach those who do not appreciate that "God's moral law is given to us as a path . . . toward true happiness,"[22] the excerpts that are included in the body of the brief have either been stripped of religious referents or most likely included because they lacked them in the first place. The brief thus adheres to Reardon's plan to reach nonbelievers through "an alternative way of evangelizing"—namely the garnering of "compelling evidence" demonstrating that abortion leads "not to happiness and freedom, but to sorrow and enslavement."[23]

The "Raging Battle between Darkness and Light": The Army of Justice

On the surface, the Justice Foundation appears to be a secular legal organization that seeks to "protect and restore justice" through litigation focusing on issues such as limited government, free markets, private property, parental rights in education, and the enforcement of laws to protect women's health.[24] However, a closer examination of the foundation's website in conjunction with President Allan Parker's email communications to supporters makes it clear that its mission to "protect and restore justice" is divinely inspired.

The religious orientation of the Justice Foundation is underscored by the embedded video on the website's mission statement page asking viewers, "Whose side are you on?" and inviting them to join the "Army of Justice." Following a recitation of the historic good that God has done, including for example, destroying both communism and Hitler, viewers are informed that "God is sending a Deliverer who is greater than all the deliverers of the past," namely the "King of Kings" and the "Lord of Lords," who is "coming to bring Justice to the Earth with an Army of the Redeemed," and once again they are asked to consider, "Whose side are you on?"[25]

Further underscoring the deeply religious orientation of the Justice Foundation, Allan Parker signs the emails that he sends in his capacity as president of the foundation "Advancing Life, Liberty, and Justice in Him," and he describes himself in a video on the Operation Outcry website as a "born-again Christian who trusts in Jesus Christ as his savior."[26] His email communications and press releases are also saturated with religious references. For example, in 2016, following the court's invalidation in *Whole Woman's Health v. Hellerstedt* of two provisions of a Texas law that held abortion clinics to a higher standard of care than other medical providers, the Justice Foundation issued a press release characterizing the result as a "crime against humanity." Quoting Isaiah, it warned:

> Without massive repentance America is doomed as a nation. We are going to experience much more destruction and more terror and the probable elimination of America as a nation. But God is still saying "America, return to me and I will return to you." But time is very short. . . . [T]he words of Isaiah still ring true today that God himself says "Your covenant with death will be annulled, your agreement with the grave will not stand" and "it will be sheer terror to understand the message."[27]

And in a same-day email communiqué to supporters, Parker also issued a stern cautionary message about the likely consequences of this decision, stating that there "is not much fear of the Lord left in the land, or even more sadly, in ourselves as the Body of Christ. There needs to be! I believe the Day of the Lord is coming, a day of burning like an oven. . . . So fear God, and do not give up on doing good!" He therefore advised them that the "only way to prepare fully for the disaster ahead is to know Jesus as your Savior and Lord! (Boss!)."[28]

In a similar vein, in a 2018 email to pastors, Parker urged them to send letters to their congregants requesting that they record their "opposition to abortion in the sight of God (who sees everything) and at the Supreme Court" by signing the Justice Foundation's "moral outcry" petition. The sample form letter Parker provided described the petition as a "cry for revival and a prayer for ending the covenant with death, the agreement with the grave that is legalized abortion entered into by the highest court in America under God. Isaiah 28:14–22."[29] Underscoring the urgency of this mission, the letter also stressed that, "God hates the shedding of innocent blood. Proverbs 6:16–17. Human blood from our abortion clinics cries out from the ground for justice! Genesis 4:10, Ezekiel 35:6."[30] However, in a comforting gesture to those who may have participated in the shedding of innocent blood, the letter also reassures readers, in keeping with Reardon's promise of redemption through repentance, that "[n]o matter how badly you may feel if you have participated in abortion as a man or woman, Jesus is willing to forgive you if you confess your sin and ask for forgiveness and healing."[31]

The Court's Problematic Reliance on the Justice Foundation's Amicus Brief

The *Gonzales* court's reliance upon the Justice Foundation's amicus brief as the sole source of factual authority in support of its assertion regarding the unexceptional nature of abortion regret is quite troubling. To begin with, it effectively elevates the Justice Foundation to the status of a leading national expert on women's postabortion experiences. In turn, this implicitly signals the court's acceptance of a particular worldview, which, as we have stressed, is saturated with religious meaning. Rather than generalizing this view to all women, the court could have instead relied upon the admonition in the *Casey* decision that at "the heart of liberty is the right to define one's own concept of existence . . . and of the mystery of human life," thus leaving each woman free to decide for herself whether or not an intact D and E abortion was right for her based upon, to again quote *Casey*, her own "conception of her spiritual destiny and place in society."[32]

Characterizing the *Gonzales* decision as "counterfactual," Linda Greenhouse stresses that the court had access to existing scientific literature on the subject, much of which dissenting Justice Ginsberg cited. She also points out that it had ready access to other amicus briefs, which would have provided a much richer and varied understanding of women's postabortion experiences.[33] For instance, the justices could have turned to the brief filed by experts in the field such as the American Medical Women's Association and the American Public Health Association, which poignantly explains that in the context of a wanted pregnancy, which is terminated due to serious health considerations or fetal anomalies, an intact procedure may be a woman's preferred option. Quoting the brief, Greenhouse takes note of the fact that an intact D and E procedure can offer "'psychological benefits'" as it enables "the patient 'to see and hold the fetus, and mourn its death.'"[34] Greenhouse likewise suggests that the justices could have turned to an amicus brief filed by the Institute for Reproductive Health, in which women recounted their second-trimester abortion experiences. Again, quoting from the brief, Greenhouse underlines that in doing so, these women drew upon "intimate, moral, religious, and personal values to make the right decisions for themselves and their families."[35] These examples make it clear that the *Gonzales* court selectively zeroed in on the brief that supported its paternalistic result while ignoring counternarratives that would have supported a different outcome.

The problematic nature of the court's dependence on this single authority is compounded by the fact that the Justice Foundation's brief itself draws upon questionable sources. To begin with, the pages of the brief that the court specifically cites in support of its assertion regarding abortion regret reference the work of David C. Reardon, whom is described as "one of the leading experts on the effects of abortion in women,"[36] despite the fact that, as discussed in the following section, his minority views about the traumatic nature of abortion have been called into question. Moreover, as we have seen, Reardon's expertise is rooted in his underlying religious belief that abortion is a repudiation of God's plan for women.

In addition to referencing the work of Reardon, the specific pages the court cites also include excerpts from the appended declarations of the 180 women injured by abortion. However, this is hardly a representative sample of women who have had abortions, as those who respond to a request for testimonies from an organization that is dedicated to refuting the lie that "abortion is good and safe for women," are more likely than other women to attribute difficulties in their lives to their abortions, which significantly diminishes the generalizability of their experience.[37] Raising further concerns about the court's reliance on these declarations, although the excerpted portions in the body of the brief have been stripped of any religious motifs, as we have seen, the declarations as a whole clearly invest the regret narrative with religious meaning.

In this regard, it should be noted that a growing body of scholarship has begun to question the soundness of the court's liberal reliance on amicus briefs. Although a detailed discussion of this work is beyond the scope of this book, it is nonetheless instructive to consider a few key points that authors have raised, as they reinforce the concerns we have identified regarding the court's reliance on the Justice Foundation's brief as its sole source of factual authority on women's postabortion experiences.

One critical apprehension is that in this "data-rich" world in which vast amounts of information are but a click away, coupled with the fact that the number of amicus filings have skyrocketed, it has become increasingly difficult for the justices "to sort the reliable amici information from the unreliable."[38] As research has shown, this unreliability can result from a number of different factors. For example, it may be attributable to the distortion or misstatement of social science data for partisan aims, or to the use of studies that do not conform to standard research protocols, or possibly to the use of data or studies created for litigation purposes.[39]

Compounding this essential problem, the court may well rely upon a single amicus brief to support a factual determination without any accompanying evidence, which effectively treats the "amici as experts" rather than as "a research tool."[40] Taking this a step further, this reliance can occur in situations where the determination is central to the outcome of the case, and the cited brief "presents a minority view in the relevant field without presenting any countervailing evidence."[41]

As we have just seen, these flaws coexist in the *Gonzales* case, which, it should be noted, is often cited as a prime example of the court's problematic reliance upon amicus briefs. It is crucial in this regard to recognize that this is not simply a technical legal matter that can be neatly contained within the four corners of a single court decision. Significantly, once the Supreme Court has declared a "truth," it is likely to take on a life of its own.

Speaking the Truth

The Supreme Court's singular reliance on the Justice Foundation's amicus brief serves to elevate the organization to the status of expert with regard to women's postabortion experiences. By direct implication then, Reardon and the 180 women injured by abortion can be said to be speaking *the truth* about abortion regret, which serves to reduce a complex and multidimensional reality to a flat and essentialized narrative of harm. This "truth" has the power to both reshape the existing legal approach to abortion with a spillover effect into the dynamics and strategy of the antiabortion movement.

To begin with, once the court makes a factual finding of such significance, it is likely to become "embedded in the law as [an] immutable statement . . . of reality," and treated as "gospel" by lower courts regardless of its problematic nature.[42] Exemplifying this practice, in the case of *Planned Parenthood v. Rounds,* the Eighth Circuit Court of Appeals cited *Gonzales* for the proposition that abortion may lead to "Severe depression and loss of esteem" in support of its decision to uphold a South Dakota law requiring doctors to inform women that an abortion "will terminate the life of a whole, separate, unique being" and increase their risk of suicide and suicidal ideation.[43] Stripped of its original citation to the Justice Foundation's amicus brief, the Eighth Circuit represented this claim as the Supreme Court's freestanding gospel truth regarding women's postabortion experiences—a move that served to elide the foundation of the court's presumed expertise in this matter.

In addition to the obvious goal of seeking to persuade the justices in *Gonzales* to rule a particular way, in filing the amicus brief, the Justice Foundation may well have also been animated by another objective. As political scientists have observed, in addition to seeking to sway a court, organizations may decide to file an amicus brief as a way to "strengthen ties with their constituents and to contribute to organizational unity," thus making its supporters an additional intended audience.[44] Moreover, a citation in a Supreme Court decision may offer legitimacy to a group, and signal that it "has 'access' to or 'influence' with the Court," which, in turn, can be used to "obtain new members and contributions."[45]

Although there is no way to know for certain whether Allan Parker, in filing the amicus brief in *Gonzales,* was motivated by the goal of strengthening the Justice Foundation's ties with existing constituents and building its support base, he has since sought to consolidate its success at the court under the proud banner of "the Supreme Court is listening."[46] Reinforcing this message, a Justice Foundation memo thanks the Lord for "the progress being made" with respect to the court's willingness to listen to the "'wailing women' who can 'teach our nation to mourn' for children lost to abortion," and stresses that it was "the power of testimony," rather than the brief's legal arguments that touched the justices. Seeking to inspire other women to tell their stories, the memo casts the *Gonzales* decision as "an invitation to provide further evidence of the harm of abortion," and it calls upon "all who have experienced the devastating and life-impacting effects of abortion to come forth as witnesses for truth."[47]

This outreach strategy has paid off. To date, Operation Outcry has gathered more than 5,000 declarations that, according to its website, gives it the distinction of having the "largest collection of legally admissible sworn written testimonies from women hurt by abortion."[48] By way of further galvanizing supporters and building its base, women (and men) who have submitted a declaration are invited to be a "part of the amazing women and men of Operation Outcry who are ministering hope and healing all around the world. . . . Many of us testify before legislatures and work in our communities to end the pain of abortion. We are a loving group who support and minister to one another."[49]

The Justice Foundation has continued to submit these declarations at both the Supreme Court and lower court levels and in legislative hearings as evidence of women's postabortion suffering. Perhaps most famously, in 2016, it submitted an amicus brief in the case of *Whole Woman's Health v. Hellerstedt* on behalf of more than 3,000 women injured by abortion.[50] As proclaimed in the brief, "[a] woman's abortion experience is often a deep, dark, and painful secret . . . For years, even decades following their abortion, most women who have experienced an abortion are still not willing to speak about it publicly. This is true even when the women were injured physically or are tormented by thoughts of suicide, substance abuse, eating disorders, guilt, shame, nightmares, sleeplessness, and depression. Amici's unique perspective will assist this Court in making a just decision."[51] The brief further seeks to link these harms to the "callous reality of the abortion industry," in which high-volume facilities (read Planned Parenthood) treat women as "business assets."[52]

In stark contrast to the impact that its brief had in the *Gonzales* case, this time around, the court was not swayed by the Justice Foundation's narrative of harm. Rather, in evaluating the constitutionality of two provisions of a Texas TRAP law (this acronym stands for "targeted regulation of abortion providers") that required doctors who perform abortion to have admitting privileges at a local hospital and that abortion clinics meet the standards of an ambulatory surgical center, the justices were persuaded by an extensive evidence-based factual record showing that these requirements imposed an undue burden on the abortion right without providing a counterbalancing health benefit.† Significantly, abortion regret did not find its way into the court's opinion—an omission that triggered Parker's apocryphal warning that the Lord's fiery day of reckoning was imminent.[53]‡

THE LEGISLATIVE BLUEPRINT

The legal map sketched out in *Casey,* combined with the antiabortion movement's embrace of the regret narrative that the *Report of the South Dakota Task Force to Study Abortion* (Task Force Report) and the *Gonzales* decision legitimized, has prompted a wave of restrictive laws at the state level aimed at protecting women from the trauma of abortion. Before turning to an examination of these legislative efforts, it is instructive to consider the changing partisan trends in state politics across the country as these shifts laid the groundwork for this gender-paternalist turn.

Priming the Playing Field: Partisan Changes in the States

In 1990, a paltry six states had Republican-controlled state legislatures, but by 2000, this number had swelled to 18.[54] In large part, this partisan shift reflected the ascendancy of the conservative right, which had been toiling against "modern liberalism and the New Deal political order" since the 1960s.[55] Troubled by what they saw as the erosion of Christian virtues and traditional values in America, postwar conservative leaders "proved critical in transforming the Republican Party into a voice of conservatism."[56] These far right thought leaders were "prepared to press those issues that the GOP establishment was eager to avoid, namely the cultural issues," even

---

† This case should not be read as overturning *Gonzales,* as the legal questions before the court in each case were quite different. However, the *Whole Woman's Health v. Hellerstedt* court's careful reliance on credentialed evidence-based studies is a hopeful sign that it has moved away from making pronouncements that lack credible factual support— nonetheless, the future direction of the high court's abortion jurisprudence is uncertain at best given President Trump's recent appointees.

‡ Perhaps seeking to regain the ear of the Supreme Court, in 2017, the Justice Foundation launched the Moral Outcry—a petition drive to gather and submit signatures from a wide swath of the American people demanding the Supreme Court put an end to the travesty of legalized abortion.

if that required mounting an "ideological battle with the GOP and their opponents on the Left."[57]

In the ensuing decades, the rise of far right activists within the Republican Party led to periods of contentious infighting and disarray. However, they successfully managed to maneuver around these political minefields and press their conservative social and economic agenda into the 21st century. Their ascension served to cleave a stronger partisan and ideological divide among the political parties as well as the electorate.[58] These divisions were colorfully displayed in the wake of President Obama's election in 2008 when the deeply conservative Tea Party was born.[§] Emerging out of the increasingly conservative electoral base of the Republican Party, Tea Party members were galvanized into action by Obama's victory, which "symbolized the culmination of generations of societal change" that "provoke[d] deep anxiety" among sectors of the electorate.[59]

Espousing the belief that average Americans were being left behind in this new social order, the Tea Party was predominately populated with older, white, middle-class men who were vociferously opposed to immigration, skeptical of "establishment" politicians, and leery of President Obama's economic and social policies. Vocal and enthusiastic, the Tea Party's right-wing activism and its fierce opposition to President Obama helped to forge a dynamic, renewed conservative political identity. In turn, this helped to fuel the Republican Party's ascending dominance in national and state politics.[60] In discussing the influence of the Tea Party on the political landscape, journalist Tom Cohen observed that, "[t]he coming together of frustrated conservatives fearing American ruin . . . has altered the national discussion to raise the profile of people and policies previously relegated to the right-wing fringe."[61] As a result of this surge in conservative activism, following the 2014 midterm elections, Republicans took over the Senate, which gave them control of both chambers of Congress, and in 2016, they won the ultimate prize—the presidency. While media attention to these national electoral victories was dominating the headlines, a quieter, partisan revolution was also occurring in the states. Following the 2014 midterm

---

§ Although the Tea Party "revitalize[d] right-wing activism in the lead-up to the 2010 midterm elections," scholars note that it has its roots in a long-standing conservatism built on promoting a political agenda that is low-tax, antiregulation and anti-big government (Critchlow 2011; Williamson et al. 2011).

elections, 30 state legislatures were controlled by Republicans, and after 2016, this number climbed to 32.[62]

As the Republican Party's foothold strengthened in statehouses across the country, the fervor of the growing right-wing of the party pushed policymakers to support positions that swung right of the general election voter.[63] Although the party had endorsed an antiabortion platform since the mid-1970s, in the wake of its historic victories, scores of state-elected officials endorsed a decidedly harder-line approach to the issue. This hardening of views in part reflects the influence of Tea Party members whose opposition to abortion is pronouncedly more absolutist when compared to other party constituencies. For instance, only 17 percent of Tea Partiers believe that "by law, a woman should always be able to obtain an abortion as a matter of personal choice,"[64] compared to 33 percent of Republicans, 50 percent of Independents, and 71 percent of Democrats.[65] Similarly, whereas 46 percent of Tea Party supporters would like to see abortion limited to cases of rape, incest, or imminent death of the woman, only 14 percent of Democrats, 26 percent of Independents, and 36 percent of Republicans share this view.[66]

Rewarding the conservative constituents who elected them, state lawmakers wrapped themselves in an unprecedented antiabortion legislative agenda, resulting in an upsurge in restrictive laws aimed at chipping away at *Roe* through the imposition of burdensome requirements, such as mandatory ultrasounds, lengthy waiting periods, and fetal pain measures.** Putting this latest flurry of legislative activity into context, between 2011 and 2017, states enacted 401 new antiabortion policies, which accounts for 34 percent of all abortion restrictions in the states since the Supreme Court legalized abortion in 1973.[67] Critically, as developed in the following section, rather than simply taking aim at saving the unborn, many of these

---

** In 2010, 950 provisions related to reproductive health and rights were introduced in the states and 89 were enacted. By 2011, the number of provisions had climbed to 1,100, and a historic high of 135 were enacted in one year (Gold and Nash 2012). Although the number of enacted restrictions declined to 42 in 2012, it climbed back up to 70 enacted restrictions in 2013 (Nash and Gold 2015). The subsequent years have witnessed a significant but fluctuating number of provisions introduced and enacted. In 2014, 335 were introduced and 26 enacted, and in 2015, these numbers increased to 400 and 47, respectively (Nash and Gold 2015). An additional 50 restrictions were enacted in 2016, and 63 more in 2017 (Nash et al. 2018).

laws are laced with the paternalistic goal of protecting women from the ostensible harms that flow from the choice of abortion over motherhood.

Turning Regret into an Actionable Policy Plan

In endorsing the abortion regret narrative, both the South Dakota Task Force to Study Abortion and the Supreme Court relied upon a narrow conception of gender norms, a biased selection of experts, and cherry-picked information that was sanctified as relevant and credible. Designing public policy to be implemented through legislation can operate in the same way, with similarly consequential outcomes. As scholars have noted, assessing "[p]olicy design offers a way to describe and analyze the policy content as well as the processes leading up to the choice of policy design elements" that "shape institutions and the broader culture through both the instrumental (resources) effects of policy . . . and the rhetorical/symbolic (interpretive) effects."[68]

Policies may impose different sets of rules and structures in accordance with how lawmakers construct a group, which often reflects existing stereotypes and prejudices. Through this recursive process, politicians can script socially constructed categories of people into legislation. In turn, these scripted categories often assume a "natural" quality that appears to reflect a fixed truth, irrespective of the validity of the representation. Over time, a socially constructed historical narrative is created through such policies, which establishes an institutionalized interpretation of the world that subsequently shapes future policies designed on behalf of the group.[69]

Although feminists have long critiqued the social constructions of gender and interrogated the social contexts and processes that give rise to particular constructions of it,[70] gender remains a salient category that is singled out, particularly in reproductive policies, for protection or punishment.[71] The reproductive capacity of women's bodies—and its formative role in maintaining and propagating "traditional" families—has historically marked women, particularly women of color and poor women, for state scrutiny and social control.[72] For example, women of color and poor women have been targeted by the state for sterilization through coercive formal and informal policies,[73] while those who "resisted cultural control over their sexual and reproductive lives by having babies," have been punished through a variety of methods, such as being sent to "correctional facilities" for "wanton and wayward" females, having their babies taken away from them and being denied public assistance or expelled from public housing.[74]

Barbara Gurr interrogates the connection between the state as both controlling reproductive choices *and* mandating appropriate social roles for women.[75] As she explains, "[m]otherhood is central to both the nationalized family ideal and the construction of deviant families and therefore women's reproductive bodies become a specific target of regulation" by the state and society writ large.[76] Gurr further contends that policing the "ideological borders around motherhood" delineates women who adhere to the hegemonic norms of motherhood from "others" who reject it. As a result, women falling outside of these borders became subjugated to further state intervention.[77]

To this end, Americans United for Life (AUL), which bills itself as the "premier pro-life legal team . . . on the frontlines of the policy debates" has spearheaded many of the legislative efforts in the post-*Roe* era to recriminalize abortion "through deliberate, legal strategies that accumulate victories, build momentum, and restore a culture of life."[††] At the state level, AUL collaborates with lawmakers to "craft tailored strategies and legislative tools" aimed at assisting them to enact restrictive abortion measures.[78] Coinciding with the 2005 release of the Task Force Report, AUL created *Defending Life,* a "pro-life playbook" that includes model legislative packages designed to usher in "immediate legal protection [for women] while also laying the groundwork for the day when women reject the fraudulent promises of the abortion industry and see abortion—not as a false panacea— but as a real threat to both their welfare and to their unborn children."[79] The model legislation detailed in *Defending Life* is drawn from two of AUL's signature projects, the Women's Protection Project, which it describes as the "premier legal blueprint for protecting women and their children from an increasingly under-regulated and rapacious abortion industry," and the Infants' Protection Project, which is grounded in the acknowledgement "of the humanity and promise of every child including those yet unborn."[80]

Distributed annually to every legislator in state and national government, *Defending Life* offers lawmakers a road map for encoding the abortion regret narrative into state law through a broad protectionist legal framework. Tracking the themes that populate the Task Force Report, it sets out a model two-tiered legislative framework. The first tier of the model laws is aimed at protecting women from abortion regret by preventing the severance of

†† The AUL was founded in 1971, during "a time when life was under assault and pressure was rising to legalize abortion the United States" (AUL 2018).

the mother-child bond—an occurrence that is believed to inexorably lead to a cascade of emotional and physical harms. The second tier aims to protect women from unscrupulous abortionists who are thought to prey upon their ignorance and vulnerability. Although these two tiers are dynamically related in that an unscrupulous abortion industry is believed to heighten the harms of abortion, regret is also presented as a freestanding and inevitable outcome of defying one's maternal nature. In short, it would remain a salient concern even if the abortion industry were tightly regulated to the satisfaction of the antiabortion movement.

Servicing the twin goals of protecting women from regret by preserving the inherent unity of the mother-child bond and safeguarding them from unethical abortion providers who seek to unbraid this unity for profit, AUL's model legislation foregrounds a construction of women as a vulnerable population. They are presented as unaware of the "negative consequences of abortion" and of "the lie propagated by the abortion industry that a woman's interests are often at odds with those of her unborn child."[81]

Turning to the first tier, *Defending Life* cements into place Reardon's earlier efforts to bridge the movement's conflict between centering on women or the unborn by soldering the two together in an indissoluble bond. Echoing his injunction that it is "simply impossible to rip a child from the womb of a mother without tearing out a part of the mother herself,"[82] *Defending Life* "affirms that to effectively protect women, you must legally protect the unborn. Similarly, to protect the unborn, you must protect their mother."[83] Underscoring this approach, AUL president and CEO Catherine Glenn Foster notes that the current edition of *Defending Life* "highlights both AUL's "Women's Protection Project" and our "Infants' Protection Project."[84] In advancing this strategy, Foster also lauds *Defending Life* for honoring the experiential knowledge of women, including her own. As she explains, "Wyoming passed legislation that is particularly meaningful to me due to my personal abortion experience, ensuring that abortionists allow mothers to see their babies on ultrasound—and we know that when they do, most choose life."[85]

Vowing to never "abandon women," to the "well-documented physical and psychological harms of abortion," *Defending Life* rolls out wellworn antiabortion tropes of women crippled by regret, stripped of agency and susceptible to deception and coercion, thus pinning down their infantilized positioning in the abortion regret narrative. In turn, it assembles these tropes into actionable items through a battery of model legislation. Extirpating women's agency, these measures offer lawmakers a constellation of options to protect them from the harms of abortion. Common examples include fetal pain laws to educate women about "the consequences of their abortion decision—specifically that abortion may cause fetal pain"; expanded informed consent requirements "with detailed information regarding her medical and psychological risks"; and extending waiting periods.[86]

Pivoting to the second tier of the protective framework, AUL's utter disdain for the abortion industry is on full display in *Defending Life,* which describes "abortionists" as players in "an under-regulated, profit-driven abortion industry."[87] Complementing women's precarious position in the abortion regret narrative, *Defending Life* offers model legislation aimed at redressing the fact that "mothers are . . . victimized by a corrupt and profit-driven abortion industry."[88] To this end, model laws seek to rein in "dangerous abortion clinics" through a host of regulatory measures that operate as a check on "'back alley' abortion mills."[89] In an effort to advance what she refers to as its "woman-empowering" approach, Foster explains that AUL decided to revise and republish the investigative report, *Unsafe: America's Abortion Industry Endangers Women,* that it first published in 2016, as a companion volume to *Defending Life 2018.*[90]

In part, AUL's decision to update and reissue *Unsafe* was prompted by the disturbing and gruesome case of abortion provider Kermit Gosnell who was charged with, among other acts of criminal wrongdoing, eight counts of murder against adult patients and seven newborns. Despite its highly unusual nature, Gosnell's case served to reinforce the prevailing construction of abortion providers that AUL and other antiabortion advocates have been promoting for more than two decades. Serving as a stand-in for the industry, AUL asserts that Gosnell "is not an aberration, but rather the norm in an industry desperate to avoid meaningful regulation and oversight."[91] To this end, it characterizes abortion providers as "circuit riders" who travel from one clinic to another, so they can "cut and run" after being paid for their services, leaving women's health in the balance to accommodate the "abortion industry's preferred practice."[92]

In the case of the model laws aimed at protecting women from harm, *Defending Life* likewise offers a range of options that are geared toward reining in the predatory abortion industry for the benefit of women. For example, bills such as those restricting medical abortion and mandating that "women be told that drug-induced abortions can be reversed,"[93] as well as those banning abortions in cases of genetic anomalies or sex selection, prohibiting "buying, selling and experimentation on unborn infants,"[94] requiring abortion providers to tell women about perinatal hospice, and protecting women from coercion, are designed to safeguard women from a second level of harm at the hands of a "rapacious industry."[95]

ENCODING REGRET

As we have sought to show throughout this book, antiabortion laws are not simply about the protection of fetal life. Although this may be an aim, the laws are also aimed at managing women's bodies in accordance with ascribed gender roles as shaped by religious beliefs about women's proper place in the created order. This codification of a particular social construction of women into law establishes a policy trajectory that functions to reinforce a historical narrative, which, as in the present case, may be moored to harmful and outdated stereotypes.[96]

Seeking to assess the extent to which a deeply gendered protective framework has been expressed in the legislative arena, we collected data on all of the abortion policies that passed in either a state's house or senate chamber in the 50 states between 2010 to 2015.[‡‡] All states introduced abortion-related legislation during this time period, but 10 states did not pass a bill in at least one chamber.[§§] Accordingly, the data set we analyzed consisted of 299 pieces of legislation from 40 states. Although some of these policies have not been codified into law, we included them in our study to provide a more comprehensive picture of the extent to which woman-protective motifs have been embedded in the policy context. The vast majority of these bills (79 percent) were antiabortion in nature, 4 percent were abortion rights bills, and the remaining 17 percent were neutral, meaning that they did not advance either a pro-choice or an antiabortion position.

Using a content analysis, we examined the scope and implicit meaning of these 299 legislative policies.[***] By way of a brief explanation, this approach to analyzing data permits both a systematic categorization and analysis of general patterns while also allowing for a more nuanced analysis of the social constructions underlying the legislation.[97] The latter analysis

---

[‡‡] Nebraska is the only state in the United States that has a unicameral legislature; consequently, we included any abortion legislation passed in Nebraska's legislature.

[§§] These states include Connecticut, Delaware, Hawaii, Kentucky, Maine, Massachusetts, Montana, New Mexico, Rhode Island, and Wyoming.

[***] See the methods appendix for more detailed information about the content analysis.

Table 5.1 Content of State Abortion Legislation, 2010–2015

Category	Number of Bills Passed	Percent of Total Bills
Regulate Providers	84	28%
General Regulation	77	26%
Protect Women	51	17%
Insurance	32	11%
Minors	17	6%
Taxes	15	5%
Conscience	8	3%
Public Safety	7	2%
Power of Attorney	4	1%
License Plates	4	1%
Total Bills	299	100%

focuses on the meaning of the data within a specific cultural context, which "goes outside the immediately observable physical vehicles of communication and relies on their symbolic qualities . . . thus rendering the (unobserved) context of data analyzable."[98] Hence, a content analysis can illuminate the meaning and consequences of the data even if they are unobvious to casual observers.

Our first step in the process was to code the content of each piece of legislation to reflect the main topic being discussed. We identified 21 content categories that we then clustered into primary themes. These are set out in Table 5.1, together with the corresponding number of bills that were passed in at least one chamber. As the table makes clear, Reardon's pro-woman/pro-life message has permeated the legislative landscape as a framing strategy for policing the "ideological borders around motherhood." Reflecting this legislative direction, our analysis tracks the two-tiered legal strategy laid out in *Defending Life*. Notably, 45 percent of the legislation we analyzed focused either on safeguarding women from the inevitability of abortion regret with its cascade of emotional and physical injuries (17 percent) or on sheltering them from the "rapacious abortion industry" (28 percent).

We now delve more closely into the content of these bills to illuminate how the full arc of the antiabortion regret narrative has blossomed into a two-tiered woman-protective legal framework, which has been legislatively assembled across a substantial swath of antiabortion policies.

Constructing the Abortion-Minded Woman

To advance the first tier of the woman-protective framework, key components of the regret narrative have been incrementally assembled across multiple state policies that track the narrative's construction of the maternal, unknowledgeable woman. Across this legislation, the more muted terms of *fetus* and *woman* have been replaced with more personalized terms such as *unborn child, baby,* and *mother.* Moreover, within these bills, *woman* and *mother* are assumed to be coterminus identities. By erasing this distinction, the merged self is represented as naturalized in policy design, as it is in the regret narrative. Further reifying this conflated identity, mother and child are commonly represented as a fused policy entity, even in the context of an unwanted pregnancy.[†††] Essentially rubber-stamping this now familiar construction of women, much of the legislation encodes a maternalism that is inextricably tied to women's ignorance and vulnerability in the realm of reproduction. Essentialist in their nature, many of the policy prescriptions treat this construction as a biological truism.

Oklahoma's Enrolled Senate Bill 1274,[99] the Heartbeat Informed Consent Act, exemplifies how the naturalness of the maternal bond coupled with women's decisional incompetence has been deployed in the development of protective legislation. Specifically, the legislative findings explicitly adopt AUL's "mother-child" strategy of linking the fate of one to the other. Appealing to women's maternal instincts, the bill notes that the "presence of a heartbeat in a woman's unborn child may be a material consideration to many women contemplating abortion."[100] Latent within this construction is the ascription and acceptance of a biological unity between mother and

---

[†††] Although beyond the scope of this chapter, it should be noted that in many reproductive health policies outside of the abortion context, such as those dealing with substance abuse and pregnancy, mother and child are not conceptualized as a fused entity that deserves protection. For instance, 43 states have punitive laws sanctioning pregnant women for consuming alcohol although there is no evidence indicating that these policies reduce the harm of drinking while pregnant; in fact, these policies may increase the risk of adverse birth outcomes by deterring women from seeking prenatal care (Advancing New Standards in Reproductive Health 2018; Dailard and Nash 2000).

fetus, which as AUL president and CEO Foster proclaims, is easily awakened by "ensuring that abortionists allow mothers to see their babies on ultrasound."[101] Highlighting the encoding of the "maternal, unknowledgeable" woman, the bill is grounded in the assumption that "[t]he presence of a heartbeat in a woman's unborn child is a developmental fact that illustrates to the woman that her baby is alive."[102] Presumably, once she understands that her intended abortion will terminate the life of her living child, she will instead choose to embrace motherhood. In this regard, it should be noted that reaching back more than a century earlier, Horatio Storer noted that ignorance of this fact "would seem incredible" given the diffusion of "physiological knowledge."[103]

Bringing these plaited threads of the regret narrative together, this bill claims that "[e]nsuring full informed consent for an abortion is imperative because of the profound physical and psychological risks of an abortion."[104] The bill then legitimizes women's risk of regret by referencing several Supreme Court cases and alluding to vague "recent research" findings purporting that women who have abortions have an "eighty-one percent increased risk for mental health problems."[105] Driving home its position, the legislative findings highlight key quotes from *Gonzales* that are premised on the unsubstantiated assertion about the severity and longevity of abortion regret caused by disrupting the unity of the mother-child bond. Operating from this social construction, among other measures, the bill instructs health care professionals to inform pregnant women that it "may be possible" to hear the "fetal heartbeat of the unborn child" and offer them the opportunity to hear it. If the heartbeat is not audible, providers are mandated to offer "to attempt to make the heartbeat audible at a subsequent date."[106]

In a similar mold, Indiana's Public Law 113-2015 stresses the linked fate of mother and child while also redressing women's presumed ignorance about pregnancy. It uses the language of conception to educate women about when life begins while also impressing upon them that the fetus is a child through simple lesson plans which, for example, explain that "human physical life begins when a human ovum is fertilized by a human sperm."[107] Seeking to reinforce the maternal bond, the legislation mandates that women view "a picture of the fetus," accompanied with a description of "the dimensions of the fetus." Hoping to further awaken women's fierce maternalism, the bill pivots to fetal pain, enlightening women "[t]hat objective scientific information shows that a fetus can feel pain at or before twenty (20) weeks of postfertilzation age"[108]—a claim that, as noted in the following section, medical experts have refuted. Thus, Indiana's law rises to remedy the problem identified in the Task Force Report, namely, that women are unaware of the "direct injury to the child that leads to its death," and that if they were made aware, they would instead naturally seek to protect their child from harm and to preserve their relationship with that child.[109]

Likewise, under the auspices of strengthening what constitutes informed consent, Kansas House Bill 2035[110] requires schooling women in the fact that "the abortion will terminate the life of a whole, separate, unique, living human being." Leaning into the maternal bond, it also mandates that printed materials be provided to pregnant women that include the "probable anatomical and physiological characteristics of the unborn child at two-week gestational increments from fertilization to full term."[111] Attempting to further ignite women's maternalism, this legislation requires that a woman be told that "she has the right to view the ultrasound image of her unborn child . . . [and] listen to the heartbeat of her unborn child, at no additional expense to her."[112]

Women's maternalism and illegible knowledge is similarly constructed across multiple state policies that use titles lifted from AUL's "woman-empowering" model legislation, such as North Carolina, Georgia, and West Virginia's "Woman's Right to Know Act" or Oklahoma's "Heartbeat Informed Consent Act." The titles and content of these policies reflect assumptions about women's ignorance on the subject, while framing the legislation as a vestment of women's waxing power. Within the design of these policies, mandated ultrasounds discursively construct uninformed women who unwittingly seek an abortion. As represented, they know nothing about fetal development or the images they must view during the ultrasound and require a doctor—closely guided by a state-mandated protocol—to explain exactly what they should be witnessing. Following the ultrasound viewing, many states mandate a 24-hour (or longer) reflection period aimed at encouraging women to recognize that their fate is cojoined with that of their unborn child and to carefully weigh the consequences of unbraiding that natural unity.

In sum, these informed consent requirements are intended to do the work of preserving the unity of the mother-child bond by persuading women to become mothers. They seek to highlight the humanity of their unborn child, while attempting to bridge their ignorance about reproduction with state-issued lessons about fetal development. These measures seek to remedy one of the problems the Task Force Report flagged that emerged from its probe of women's experiential knowledge. Namely, its allegation that most women were "not told the truth that the abortion would terminate the life of a living human being," and that if they had known this, they would not have followed through with an abortion "because of their sense of duty and their relationship with the child."[113]

Constructing the Abortion Providers

Presented as the second potent level of threat to an aborting woman's well-being, abortion providers are central fixtures in the sweep of bills we examined. Policy prescriptions aimed at reining them in track the Task Force Report's construction of abortion providers as unethical "profit-driven" physicians who "must deceive the mother into thinking the unborn child does not yet exist . . . or encourage her to defy her very nature as a mother to protect her child."[114] Likewise, they trail *Defending Life*'s pledge to protect women from the "whims of an under-regulated, predatory abortion industry" by urging states to curb "abortion industry profiteers" through regulatory policies that strengthen their oversight powers, including the strict enforcement of all existing abortion law.[115]

Looping back to the first tier of the protective framework, the construction of women as inherently maternal and incapable of making informed abortion decisions, is deemed to intensify the urgent nature of this regulatory task. Although protecting women from abortion regret is, as noted, a freestanding legislative objective, the alleged callous and unscrupulous behavior of abortion providers is thought to act upon a vulnerable self, thus compounding the harms that are inexorably linked to the intentional rejection of motherhood.

Seeking to redress this vulnerability, policies coming within the second tier of the woman-protective framework hone in on AUL's model legislation aimed at curbing the abusive practices of abortion providers. In turn, these laws echo and reinforce the construction of abortion providers as reprehensible, thus reaffirming the urgent need for these laws. For example, Utah House Bill 171,[116] which focuses on the licensing and regulation of abortion clinics, includes a full-throttle endorsement of this negative construction of abortion providers in its explanation of why these additional clinic regulations are necessary. In setting out the intent of the law, the legislature explains that it

> is aware of the discovery, nationwide, of abortion clinics that operate in unsafe and unsanitary conditions, risking the health and safety

of women. The Legislature is very concerned of the risks posed to women in these circumstances and intends to take action to help ensure that these conditions do not exist in Utah. The purpose of this bill is to protect women in Utah from these risks in a manner that does not conflict with the rights, held by state and federal courts to be protected by the United States Constitution, in relation to abortion.[117]

Although lawmakers do not provide any specific examples from Utah of these problems, channeling AUL's lead, they suggests that abortion providers are comfortable working in unsafe and unsanitary conditions. Therefore, the state must position itself as a shield to defend women from their dubious medical ethics and practices.

A second related, but distinct, policy genre reflects the regret narrative's preoccupation with women's susceptibility to coercion as spelled out in the Task Force Report. The report concluded that one of the "common experiences" that surfaced in its review of the testimony of 1,940 women was that many "were coerced into having the abortion by the father of the child or a parent, and that the abortion clinics also apply pressure to have the abortion."[118] Narrowing in on providers, the report goes on to directly address the fundamentally coercive practice of abortion and crystalizes the state's obligation to intervene by explaining "the procedure is, as has been seen, inherently coercive. The inherent coercion precludes this method from being an appropriate way for the mother to give up her right."[119] In a similar vein, *Defending Life*'s model legislation also includes measures that "prohibit coercing a woman to undergo an abortion and requires abortion facilities to post signs about coercion and to report suspected cases of coercive abuse."[120]

Although regulating potentially coercive men or parents would pose significant obstacles for states, it is far easier for them to regulate abortion providers through the imposition of mandated anti-coercion warning signage. Accordingly, legislation such as Louisiana's House Bill 586[121] "Forced Abortion Prevention Sign Act" mandates that abortion providers alert women: "You can't be forced. It is unlawful for an abortion to be forced on you without your voluntary and informed consent."[122]

Underscoring the distrust of providers that is built into this law, House Bill 586 preempts them from diluting the visibility or placement of the sign by including stringent directives regarding signage placement, as stated, "[a]ny ambulatory surgical center, private office, freestanding outpatient clinic, or other facility or clinic in which abortions are performed, induced, prescribed for, or where the means for an abortion are provided shall conspicuously post a sign . . . which is clearly visible to patients. . . . [It] shall be posted in each patient admission area, waiting room, and patient consultation room used by patients." The bill does not end with sign placement alone but continues to stipulate design requirement—"All signs produced shall incorporate color graphics and shall be printed on durable signage material measuring at least sixteen inches by twenty inches with lettering presented in a size and style of font design to be clearly visible to the patient."[123]

Other state laws require more inclusive anti-coercion language. For example, pursuant to Tennessee's "Freedom from Coercion Act," medical facilities where abortions are performed must post signs in a visible location with the following language:

> Notice: It is against the law for anyone, regardless of the person's relationship to you, to coerce you to have an abortion. By law, we cannot perform an abortion on you unless we have your freely given and voluntary consent. It is against the law to perform an abortion on you against your will. You have the right to contact any local or state law enforcement agency to receive protection from any actual or threatened criminal offense to coerce an abortion.[124]

This notice implicates a range of unnamed, potentially coercive actors—a woman's family, friends, coworkers, or medical providers—who could be pushing her toward abortion. However, the requirement that this sign be posted in a medical facility also affirms the construction of doctors and other health care providers as people who are prone to acting in bad faith in disregard of a woman's reproductive choice.

This discussion is not intended to ignore the possibility that some women may indeed feel pressured into terminating a pregnancy, just as some may feel pressured into carrying an unintended pregnancy to term, or into having unprotected sex. In this regard, many public health professionals argue that "anti-coercion policies that single out abortion sidestep the broader issue of domestic and sexual violence," which they stress is the root of the problem. Sexual coercion, rather than abortion, is the culprit that "often leads to unwanted pregnancies, followed by abusive partners trying to control the outcome of the pregnancy, be it by trying to force the woman to continue with the pregnancy or to abort." However, by lifting abortion coercion up as a freestanding and unique reproductive risk that women must be protected from, abortion opponents fail to account for the underlying dynamics of abuse and control that could as equally identify motherhood as the desired reproductive outcome.[125‡‡‡]

Other bills, such as those prohibiting abortion for sex selection or genetic abnormalities, are also aimed at incrementally flushing out the perceived unethical and profit-driven providers who stand ready and willing to terminate any pregnancy under all circumstance to increase their bottom line. As a part of the second-tier legislative strategy, these bills return to a common tenet—greed—that runs through both the Task Force Report and *Defending Life*. The latter of which, as we have seen, draws on the egregious actions of Kermit Gosnell to promote a view of abortion providers as being only too willing to disregard the law and their ethical obligations toward their patients to increase their profit margins.[126]

Acting as another line of defense to counter the compromised morals of providers, legislation such as North Dakota's House Bill 1350 makes it clear that "a physician may not intentionally perform or attempt to perform an abortion with knowledge that the pregnant woman is seeking the abortion solely on the account of the sex of the unborn child; or because the unborn child has been diagnosed with either a genetic abnormality or a potential for a genetic abnormality."[127] Like other bills of its kind, House Bill 1350 attempts to close any potential loopholes that providers might shamelessly take advantage of by spelling out what qualifies as a genetic abnormality: "'Down syndrome' refers to a chromosome disorder associated with an extra chromosome twenty-one, in whole or in part, or an effective trisomy for chromosome twenty-one. 'Genetic abnormality' means any defect, disease, or disorder that is inherited genetically. The term includes any physical disfigurement, scoliosis, dwarfism, Down syndrome, albinism, amelia, or any other type of physical or mental disability, abnormality, or disease."[128] By providing this extremely detailed description of genetic abnormality, and then adding a catchall clause that includes "any other type of physical or mental disability, abnormality, or disease," this bill implicitly constructs providers in base terms by suggesting that they might either be ignorant of or deliberately flout the requirements of this law.

When examined collectively, the legislation passed in the states between 2010 and 2015 suggests that both women seeking abortions and abortion providers will continue to be subjected to surveillance practices through a

---

‡‡‡ Regarding the link between reproductive coercion and intimate partner violence, see Moore et al. (2010); Planned Parenthood Federation of American (2012).

trajectory of laws that reinforce the antiabortion movement's construction of them. Once a target population is socially constructed into policy, a narrative takes hold that, in this context, creates a precedent for enacting more invasive policies under the pretext of protecting women from harm. With the passage of each new measure, the justification for the enactment of future protective laws becomes less important, exemplifying what Anne L. Schneider and Helen M. Ingram refer to as the feed forward process of degenerative politics.[129]

Women seeking abortions are treated in antiabortion policy as deviant and unknowing, and in need of corrective state action aimed at guiding them toward motherhood.[130] State paternalism also becomes normalized, even expected, in the face of socially constructed women who depend upon the knowledge that can only be imparted to them through the folds of the protective state, regardless of its accuracy. The infantilization of women that is inherent in the regret narrative invites the state to use its legislative authority to supplant women's agency and decisional competence, which reinforces the representation of them as unknowing and vulnerable.

The idea of deviance is not limited to abortion-seeking women. Abortion providers are also marked as a target group in the legislation we examined. Many of the antiabortion state policies are presented as a corrective to their proclivity toward "misrepresentation of fact," including withholding information about the "substantial mental and physical health risks," and the "totally irreversible nature of the decision [to abort]."[131] However, unlike women, the deviance of providers is to be subjected to the punitive, rather than to the protective, arm of the state. Medical professionals are reframed through this legislation as unethical members of an industry that requires ongoing surveillance to stem its corruption and limit the scope of harm it poses to women. In parallel fashion, the representation of abortion providers in the narrative of regret as "rapaciously" taking advantage of abortion-minded women invites the state to use its authority to tightly monitor their practices, which reinforces the representation of them as predatory and driven by the bottom line.

Echoing the unwarranted charges contained in both the Task Force Report and *Defending Life,* many of the antiabortion state policies we have looked at implicitly circle us back to Reardon's original plan to "teach morality by teaching science." They are grounded in naturalized assumptions about women's place in the created world, which inexorably renders abortion a traumatizing event—a view that the Supreme Court embraced in *Gonzales.* However, as we discuss in the following section, the "science" of regret muddles the line between credible and subjective knowledge, and a substantial body of highly credentialed studies has soundly critiqued it.

MISINFORMATION AND ABORTION REGRET

Notwithstanding the result in *Gonzales* and the proliferation of legislation aimed at protecting women from abortion regret, a body of credentialed research challenges the underlying premise of this phenomena and the deluge of associated mental and physical health risks attributed to it. In the decades following David C. Reardon's plea to bring women's experiential knowledge to the forefront of the antiabortion cause, the regret narrative has firmly taken root, inspiring policy initiatives that foreground its contours. As discussed in Chapter Three, interviewees in this study relied on experiential knowledge to wholeheartedly embrace the regret narrative, and they often expanded it beyond the purview of emotional suffering to include a range of physical injuries that they attributed to their abortion. However, the abortion regret narrative has come under fire from a litany of pro-choice advocates, and it has been challenged by evidence-based studies conducted by researchers with expertise in fields such as psychology and women's reproductive health.

Attempting to counter this enduring narrative of regret, the pro-choice movement has worked to reframe it. However, by claiming that women feel relief rather than regret after an abortion, they likewise can be said to have composed a unidimensional script to encapsulate the experience of all women. Within the narrow relief-not-regret framework, the complexities of women's lived abortion experiences have been muted, which Jody Lyneé Madeira suggests, leads to some troubling consequences.[132] As she explains, "[p]ro-choice women can feel troubled if they experience emotions other than relief," thus exacerbating the stigma and secrecy enveloping abortion decision making and ultimately leaving the abortion regret narrative uncontested in public discourse.[133] However, engaging with the range of women's experiences does not diminish the pro-choice position but rather it can facilitate an "understanding of why new laws that transmit misinformation and force a one-size-fits-all approach to the clinical care experience are not the way to promote women's well-being."[134] As policy debates currently stand, pro-choice advocates have not been able to persuade policymakers that abortion restrictions are inimical to women's well-being; in fact, the opposite has occurred.

The dominance of the abortion regret narrative, coupled with the complex and pointed social expectations surrounding abortion discourse, have contributed to the selective use of evidence, the dissemination of misinformation, and the marginalization of more accurate science in legislation addressing abortion regret.[135] Key among the abortion regret claims is the purported causal link between abortion and long-term mental health illness, a "condition" that Vincent Rue pointedly labeled as postabortion syndrome (PAS) in his testimony before Congress in 1981.§§§ Rue eventually went on to team up with David C. Reardon who sought to harness the pro-woman approach of the CPCs into a cohesive political strategy to reinvigorate the antiabortion movement. Eager to supplement women's experiential knowledge, in 1988 Reardon pivoted toward conducting original research to show that abortion harms women, a strategy that he characterized as "teaching morality by teaching science."[136] Founding the Elliot Institute for this purpose, he envisioned it as a "major resource for organizations around the world who are concerned with protecting the rights of women and their unborn children" and safeguarding against the "injustice and trauma" of abortion.[137]

Obscuring his religiously saturated pro-woman/pro-life beliefs under "the veneer of scientific and technical expertise," since founding the Elliot Institute, Reardon has sought to develop a cohesive collection of credentialed, secularized articles "proving" abortion regret.[138] To this end, in collaboration with other outspoken pro-life advocates including Vincent Rue and a few other academically affiliated authors such as Priscilla Coleman, Reardon has published several peer-reviewed articles in academic journals, but not without controversy.[139]

A growing number of scientific studies have discredited postabortion syndrome, and neither the American Psychological Association nor the American Psychiatric Association recognize it as a syndrome.[140] Notably, a 2009 review of 216 studies on abortion and mental health findings published in the *Harvard Review of Psychiatry* concluded that the research

§§§ On more than one occasion, a court has concluded that Rue was not qualified to provide expert testimony on the subject of abortion. For example, the trial judge in *Planned Parenthood v. Casey* stated that Rue's testimony, "which is based primarily, if not solely, upon his limited clinical experience, is not credible. His testimony is devoid of . . . analytical force and scientific rigor. . . . Moreover, his admitted personal opposition to abortion, even in cases of rape and incest, suggests a possible personal bias" (Kolbert 2015).

identifying a connection between abortion and poor mental health was plagued by serious methodological flaws, while the more rigorous and methodologically sound studies showed that experiences of sexual assault or violence or preexisting psychological disorders, rather than the abortion itself, are the strongest predictors of mental health concerns following abortion.[141]

Several of Reardon's coauthored articles have been soundly critiqued for containing similar methodological weaknesses that were present in *Aborted Women: Silent No More,* including relying on biased samples that were "not representative of women in general" let alone "the population of women who obtain abortions"; using unreliable retrospective self-reports; and crafting dubious measures to represent "mental health."[142] The caliber of his colleagues' research has also faded under more rigorous scrutiny. For example, in 2009, Priscilla Coleman, Vincent Rue, Catherine Coyle, and Martha Shuping published an article in which they made sweeping claims about the perilous impact of abortion on women's mental health. As they reported, "[a]bortion was found to be related to an increased risk for a variety of mental health problems (panic attacks, panic disorder, agoraphobia, PTSD, bipolar disorder, major depression with and without hierarchy), and substance abuse disorders."[143] However, when other researchers tried to replicate their findings using the identical survey data, they found egregious errors with the research design and analysis, including the authors' use of "untrue statements" about their measurements and "associated false claims about the implications of their findings."[144]

Seeking to prove abortion regret from a different angle, in 2011, Priscilla Coleman published a meta-analysis in which she drew the bold conclusion that abortion resulted in an 81 percent increase in women's risk of mental health problems. But in a similar pattern to the previously mentioned study, once subjected to review by a robust group of researchers, the integrity of her analysis was eviscerated.[145] Researchers have severely critiqued Coleman's inclusion of methodologically flawed studies in the meta-analysis—notably, 50 percent of these were authored by Coleman herself or coauthored with colleagues, including both Reardon and Rue.[146] Even more damning, Coleman's meta-analysis was woefully pockmarked with significant methodological and analysis errors, ranging from "violating guidelines for conducting a meta-analysis" to asserting dubious inferences from flawed studies that she included in the meta-analysis, which had received a prior rating of "poor" from the Royal College of Psychiatrists.[147] Despite the limitations contained in much of Reardon and his colleagues' research, according to the Elliot Institute's website, his secular publication record has secured his reputation as "one of the leading experts on the after-effects of abortion on women," and has been cited by lawmakers as evidence to justify the enactment of laws to "protect women."[148]

In stark contrast to the conclusions Reardon and his colleagues have reached, a more reliable and extensive body of research stresses that "stigma and other social factors play a significant role in women's emotional outcomes following an abortion," and highlights that feelings—including negative ones such as regret, sorrow, or sadness—are "distinct from mental health issues and should not be conflated."[149] Importantly, although some women are mournful after an abortion, their feelings are often tied not to "the fetal loss, but [to] other losses, including the loss of a romantic relationship," whereas other women "experience guilt or anger at themselves for becoming pregnant unintentionally," and yet other women predominantly feel relief.[150] These studies illuminate that mental health issues and negative emotions are not synonymous, and the complexities of women's emotions cannot be distilled to a singular emotion, particularly the branding of their postabortion experience as one of lifelong regret.

Although the primary emphasis dating back to Reardon and Willke has been on the urgent need to protect women from the emotional pain of abortion, a linked claim is the further need to protect women from the physical hazards of abortion. Central in this regard is the assertion regarding the increased risk of breast cancer. Organizations, including Heartbeat International and Care Net, commonly cite the ABC (abortion-breast-cancer) link as one of the most guarded secrets that pro-choice advocates and the medical community cover up. Care Net boldly asserts on its Abundant Life Blog that research indicates an elective abortion can "increase the risk of breast cancer 30–79%." Turning to the usual suspect—the biased media—the blog goes on to assert that "[w]hile the media is comfortable telling women not to take hormone replacement therapy because of the increased risk of breast cancer, it *refuses* to extend the same logic to abortion."[151] Similar to many of the other highly contested claims asserted by the antiabortion movement, to date, the ABC link has not held up to conventional scientific scrutiny.[152] To be sure, several individuals in the medical community have written about and promoted the purported ABC link, but when vetted by their peers and weighed against other research, substantial weaknesses have been revealed. For example, several of the studies asserting an ABC link have been authored by doctors or researchers at the pro-life Breast Cancer Prevention Institute.[153]

Perhaps most significantly, after a rigorous review, the National Cancer Institute (NCI) released an unequivocal statement that "[i]nduced abortion is not associated with an increase in breast cancer risk."[154] The NCI arrived at its conclusion after convening a panel of the world's leading geneticists, epidemiologists, oncologists, and other experts to investigate the link between abortion and breast cancer.[155] Its findings were further supported by British studies, and there has not been any new evidence on the subject to alter the NCI's statement.[156] Corroborating this position, after reviewing the available evidence in 2003, 2009, and reaffirming its position in 2018, the American College of Obstetricians and Gynecologists (ACOG's) Committee on Gynecologic Practice summarized its findings, stating "[e]arly studies of the relationship between prior induced abortion and breast cancer were methodologically flawed. More rigorous recent studies demonstrate no causal relationship between induced abortion and a subsequent increase in breast cancer."[157] Disregarding this conclusion, five states nonetheless mandate that women be counseled about the alleged link between abortion and breast cancer prior to obtaining the procedure.[158]

Research has also refuted several other policy initiatives flying under the "protect women" banner. AUL has successfully lobbied for bans on telemedicine, which it describes as a "dangerous practice," to restrict women's access to medical abortion remotely in 19 states.[159] Yet running directly counter to AUL's claim, ACOG, the American Hospital Association, and the American Medical Association support telemedicine as a new and evolving way to deliver patient care, particularly in geographically isolated areas.[160] Likewise, misinformation has been promulgated in the policies of four states regarding the risk that abortion poses to women's future fertility. Also of great concern, AUL's *Defending Life* includes a model law that advocates for erroneously counseling a woman that once underway, "it may be possible to reverse the effects of the [medical] abortion should she change her mind."[161] Highlighting this worrisome trend, a recent study by the Guttmacher Institute found that 28 states have abortion restrictions in effect that run afoul of science.[162]

Although not usually thought of in this way, fetal pain legislation is also encapsulated in the first tier of AUL's protective framework. Arguing that "women deserve to know," AUL advocates for folding fetal pain measures into informed consent requirements. As explained in a publication on the subject, notifying women about "the consequences of their abortion decision—specifically, that abortion may cause fetal pain," may influence their decision "on whether or not to obtain an abortion" while also aligning with the state's cojoined interest "in the well-being of women and developing life."[163] To this end, its model legislation asserts that "an unborn child who is twenty (20) weeks' gestation or more is fully capable of experiencing pain," and prescribes clinical treatments for women to "minimize and/or alleviate pain to the fetus."[164]

However, medical researchers have hotly contested the accuracy of these claims about fetal pain and have also expressed serious reservations concerning the safety of administering fetal anesthetic to women who are terminating a pregnancy.[165] In 2013, the ACOG, representing over 57,000 ob-gyns issued a message stating that "a human fetus does not have the capacity to experience pain until after viability," which it based on "rigorous scientific studies."[166] Irrespective of this position, 13 states require women to be counseled about fetal pain.[167]

CONCLUSION

In the 2007 case of *Gonzales v. Carhart,* the Supreme Court concluded that abortion regret with its cascade of emotional harms was unexceptional in nature. In support of this supposition, the court cited the Justice Foundation's amicus brief, which drew on women's experiential knowledge to narrate this reality. The court's reliance on this brief as its sole source of authority on women's postabortion experience is deeply troubling on multiple levels, including centrally that it effectively singles out the Justice Foundation as a leading expert on the topic. Although the court treated regret as a wholly secular concept, as we have seen, the decision nonetheless tracks with Reardon's core teaching about the sanctity of the mother-child relationship."[168]

Extending outward into the legislative realm, following decades of right-wing activism, the states were primed to carry forward the mantle of regret. With the assistance of the legal blueprint provided in AUL's *Defending Life,* the abortion regret narrative has been packaged into a two-tier woman-protective framework that seeks to protect women by preventing the destruction of the mother-child bond and by reining in the efforts of the abortion industry to unbraid this sacred unity. In examining the content of the legislation that traces these twin goals, we found elements of the regret narrative assembled across a wide swath of state laws that reinforce the social construction of infantilized women whose vulnerability is heightened by the unethical practices of the abortion industry. In conclusion, we highlighted the substantial body of highly credentialed evidence-based research that both challenges this flattened and essentialized representation of women's postabortion experiences while also revealing a more nuanced picture that links women's responses to an abortion to a range of preexisting considerations.

Stepping back from this chapter, as we have stressed across the book, the regret narrative reifies a religiously grounded view of women as primarily maternal in nature. This construction reverberates with the admonition of 19th-century antiabortion physicians who asserted that women's holiest duty was to bring forth living children. To this end, two generations of activists have cast abortion as a disruptive event that must be managed for the purported benefit of women—a paternalistic rendering of the pregnant self that has paved the way for the regulatory force of the law.

Despite the commonalities in approach, there are also some important historic discontinuities between the two generations of antiabortion activists. For instance, although the 19th-century antiabortion physicians typically characterized the "aborting woman" as transgressive and in need of the supervisory authority of the state, proponents of today's pro-woman antiabortion message typically portray these women as hapless victims who must be protected. Breaking further with their predecessors, contemporary antiabortionists claim that they are seeking to empower women by vesting them with authentic control over their reproductive bodies. However, as we have shown, the end result is the same—namely the reification of religiously saturated gender conventions that present abortion as an unnatural rupture with nature. Accordingly, across generations, women occupy an infantilized position in the regret narrative that beckons the state to intervene by enacting laws aimed at steering them away from the brink of disaster.

Another critical distinction is the role that race plays in the narratives. Nineteenth-century antiabortion physicians drew heavily upon racialized themes in their campaign to criminalize abortion. Invoking overtly racist language laced with eugenic arguments, they presented abortion as a looming threat that not only disrupted domestic hierarchies, but also threatened the identity of the nation. Accordingly, physicians oriented their campaign toward encouraging white, middle-class women to bear more children as an expression of their gendered national duty. In contrast, today's regret narrative deploys color-blind language that obscures the extent to which the contemporary antiabortion movement has disfigured the reality of the historically intersectional and institutionalized racism that continues to limit black women's reproductive health. This is best exemplified by the Black Genocide campaign, which, in stark contrast to the subprime reproductive landscape available to black women, presents them as the real threat to black babies and to their race writ large. Thus, although the regret narrative is leveraged as a color-blind, universalizing narrative, its pages contain an unspoken and hidden message for black women that implicates them in expediting racial genocide.

Throughout this book, we have also shown that the strategic mobilization of the message that abortion harms women has flourished across multiple institutional venues. It has been deployed as a vehicle for limiting women's rights of decisional autonomy and authority over their reproductive well-being by calling upon the state to police the ideological boundaries around motherhood while institutionally fixing a static construction of both women and abortion providers into law through an expansive array of regulatory measures. As we speak, hundreds of additional policy initiatives are percolating in the states that likewise seek to manage both women's bodies as well as abortion providers through heightened surveillance.

Although abortion rights advocates have turned to the courts to challenge these measures, on balance, the antiabortion movement has successfully actualized its quest to incrementally curtail access to abortion through state policies. As this book goes to press, the Supreme Court's decision in *Whole Woman's Health v. Hellerstedt* stands as a hopeful signal that going forward, it will insist on far more than a single culturally specific amicus brief as the basis for upholding further restrictions on abortion rights. However, as its ideological composition hangs precariously in the balance, the task of countering the abortion regret narrative has become even more urgent.

Methods Appendix

Throughout the book, we use several analyses drawn from different methods, which we detail as follows. All of the methods used in this book are inductive and process-oriented rather than outcome-oriented, meaning we are not trying to assert claims of causality from our qualitative data.[1] Our choice of data and analyses are grounded in our interest in tracing the implicit meaning embedded in the abortion regret narrative from its experiential origins in crisis pregnancy centers to the antiabortion movement's use of it as a cohesive political narrative strategy through to its manifestation in law.

INTERVIEWS

The interviews initially presented in Chapter Three are drawn from a larger sample of 50 in-depth interviews conducted by Alesha E. Doan with 26 pro-life activists, 24 pro-choice activists, and elected officials from 2007 to 2012. In our book, we exclusively focus on the interviews with 23 of the 26 pro-life activists. Three of the interviews are excluded from our analysis because these individuals did not work or volunteer in a crisis pregnancy center, but rather were active in other aspects of the movements. Our sample was chosen using a combination of a purposive and snowball-sampling strategy centralized in a midwestern state that has an active and strong antiabortion movement. Focusing on one state provided an opportunity to contextualize participants' relationships with their clientele, colleagues, and organization in depth.

Most interviews (20) were conducted between April 2010 and November 2012, and three were conducted in 2007. Prior to each interview, individuals filled out a short questionnaire containing 16 demographic questions. Each interview lasted an average of 90 minutes. The initial purposive sample was obtained through an online search to identify grassroots organizations operating at different locations in the state, with a focus on crisis pregnancy centers. Participants were recruited via multiple phone calls and emails to their organizations, and interviews were scheduled with individuals who expressed interest. Initially, 15 individuals affiliated with 10 different organizations were interviewed. After completing these interviews, a snowball sampling strategy was employed, which yielded eight additional interviews.

Apart from one phone interview, the remaining 22 were conducted in person using a semistructured, open-ended format. Participants were asked general questions pertaining to two broad themes related to their personal beliefs and organizational strategies. For example, they were asked about their belief system, their beliefs about women in general and about those seeking abortions, and about their involvement in the antiabortion movement. Organizational questions probed participants about the strategies and tactics their respective organizations use, the horizontal and vertical relationships between their organization and other groups in the movement, and the influence of the movement on policy and culture. Follow-up questions were asked to clarify information or to probe respondents about a topic, feeling, or idea that they introduced while answering open-ended questions.

Seventeen of the in-person interviews were conducted at the CPC where the interviewee worked or volunteered. Five of the participants preferred to be interviewed elsewhere, such as at a coffee shop, hotel lobby, or private office. The demographics of the interviewees are heavily skewed toward female, white, married, and college educated. Seventeen were women, and six were men. Two women identified as African American, and the remaining 21 participants identified as white. Most activists (18) were married, and 20 were college graduates. Nineteen interviewees identified as evangelical Christian, and the other four identified as Catholic. All interviewees identified as heterosexual, and their ages ranged from 20 to 74 years old, with 50 through 59 being the median age category.

In addition to the interviews, the author spent several months engaging in observations at interviewees' organizations, attending events and webinars hosted by pro-life organizations. Detailed field notes were taken, and the hours of observation provided rich contextual information for the analysis.

Pseudonyms are used for all participants, and human subjects' approval was granted for this research. Participants were given a verbal and written description of the project and each participant was required to read and sign a written consent form. Interviewees were provided with a copy of the consent form that apprised them of their rights and contained contact information for the researcher, and the human subjects committee that approved the project.

We used a grounded theoretical approach in the interviews to provide us with flexibility to adapt and pursue unanticipated concepts that surfaced.[2] Ultimately, more themes emerged from the data than we present in the book. Although we did not directly ask interviewees about abortion regret while pursuing these broad, open-ended questions, it quickly surfaced across interviews as an overarching theme.

All the interviews were audio-recorded and transcribed verbatim. Using an inductive approach, the interviews were initially analyzed based on a repeated, line-by-line reading of the transcripts to develop emerging themes.[3] An open-coded, in vivo format (using the words of our interviewees) was used whenever possible to catalog dominant and frequent themes. These themes were then used to continually compare across participants to support themes, refine subthemes, and identify additional themes that surfaced over the course of the interviews, which we present in the book.[4] The interview quotes have been edited to eliminate filler words to enhance readability.

Limitations

Our ability to make causal assertions from our findings is inhibited by the qualitative approach of our study. In this case, we are focusing on the process of how interviewees interpret and make meaning out of their experiential knowledge. In other words, we are interested in understanding their beliefs, and how they make sense of the world rather than seeking to establish strong causality claims.[5]

Although the in-depth interviews are suited for examining process-orientated questions, the small purposive sample poses two specific limitations. The first relates to bias within the purposive sample. During the targeted recruitment phase, many of the individuals contacted never returned phone calls or emails (including three follow-up attempts). Several other individuals declined to be interviewed after the disclosure of our identity as academic researchers. Our interview sample is populated solely with individuals who were willing to be interviewed. We do not have the ability to compare participants to the individuals who declined to be interviewed; consequently, there may be a clear bias in our purposive sample that we are unable to account for.

The second limitation of our sample is the concentration of interviewees in one midwestern state even though the antiabortion movement is active in all 50 states. Sociopolitical cultures vary from state to state, which we do not capture in our geographically targeted group of interviewees. Despite the limitations inherent to the sample and method we have employed, the insights generated from the interviews may be cautiously generalized beyond the limited sample for two reasons. First, although the antiabortion movement has organizational and membership diversity, it also has continuity across states. The movement has a large network of professional and grassroots organizations that share strategies and tactics within and across state lines.[6] Many state and local activists borrow these strategies and deploy them through national networks. Second, the concentration of in-depth interviews in one state allowed us to examine the nuances that shape the participation of individuals in the movement while exploring how they work within and across different organizations in the movement. Finally, the demographic characteristics of interviewees generally tracks with those found in other studies,[7] and therefore the insights stemming from our results may have some applicability to the larger population of people working within crisis pregnancy centers in the outreach branch of the antiabortion movement.

PRIMARY SOURCE TEXTUAL ANALYSIS

We used an inductive and interactive approach to conduct a textual analysis of 19th-century medical journals and two books written by David C. Reardon—*Aborted Women: Silent No More* (1987) and *Making Abortion Rare: A Healing Strategy for a Divided Nation* (1996). We initially engaged in a close reading of these primary sources to begin to identify the dominant and frequent themes emerging from the texts, which in turn, were used to refine subthemes, identify other concepts, and compare themes within and across the primary sources. With regard to the analysis of court cases, we engaged classic methods of legal analysis which, among other steps, requires a careful identification of the precise legal issue before the court, a precise articulation of the court's holding (the statement of law that answers the presented issue), and an analysis of the reasoning it deployed to get from the issue to the holding, with a focus on the precedent cases it relied upon. Legal analysis also requires a critical engagement with the court's approach to and resolution of the dispute before it.

CONTENT ANALYSIS: LEGISLATION

Using an inductive content analysis, we examined the scope and implicit meaning of antiabortion legislation passed in at least one chamber of a state's legislature from 2010 through 2015. This six-year period helped us gauge the intensity of a state's attention and willingness to expand antiabortion policies as well as to preview potential future trends.

The content analysis allowed us to establish manifest coding schemes that were generated directly from observable data—in this case, legislation passed in either a state's house or senate chamber—without imposing preconceived categories.[8] Content analysis treats each data point equally, ensuring that the first and last piece of data is coded and counted the same to systematically categorize the legislation and analyze general patterns.

Using a more nuanced latent analysis, we investigated the social constructions underlying the legislation, focusing on the meaning (unobservable dimension) of the data within a specific cultural context.[9] Latent content analysis "goes outside the immediately observable physical vehicles of communication and relies on their symbolic qualities . . . thus rendering the (unobserved) context of data analyzable," which can illuminate the meaning and consequences of the data even if they are unobvious to casual observers.[10]

A catalog of the legislation was created using search terms for *abortion, health, unborn,* and *women* from each state's legislative website, where online versions of bills are readily available. Within these subject categories, full text versions of bills were searched to identify potentially relevant legislation. The eventual data set had 299 pieces of legislation, representing 40 states. Among the antiabortion bills, 49 percent (147) were stand-alone antiabortion bills, whereas 30 percent (89) were embedded in legislation created for a different, typically broader purpose. Conversely, 3 percent (8) of the abortion rights bills were stand-alone, and 1 percent (4) were embedded in broader pieces of legislation. Seventeen percent (51) of bills were neutral.

Each piece of legislation was coded for 32 variables that included basic information about the bill, such as the state and date, to more substantive variables that included the primary content of the bill. In the analysis presented in Chapter Five, we focus on the content variable of the legislation, which was coded in vivo to reflect the main topic being discussed in the bill. Several bills contained multiple provisions resulting in overlapping categories. In these instances, the bill was counted once and coded according to the dominant abortion-related content. The following 21 categories were originally identified for the content variable: (1) fetal pain, (2) limiting a power of attorney to make abortion decision, (3) prohibiting taxes for supporting abortion (and related) services, (4) informed consent/mandatory ultrasounds, (5) fetal homicide laws, (6) regulations specific to clinics/providers (i.e., additional reporting requirements or building codes), (7) conscience refusal, (8) insurance ban/limits on abortion services, (9) waiting periods, (10) requiring determination of postfertilization age of fetus, (11) juvenile waivers, (12) parental notification/consent, (13) Choose Life license plates, (14) general regulation, (15) prohibiting sex/race selection abortions, (16) state appropriations, (17) public safety concerns, (18) declarations supporting crisis pregnancy centers, (19) declaration opposing Freedom of Choice Act (FOCA), (20) repeal *Roe*/legality of abortion, (21) protect women from coercion to have abortion.

We clustered the original 21 categories in the content variable into 10 primary themes. Our two primary themes of interest were the "protect women" and "regulate providers" categories, which were drawn from Defending *Life*, a publication of Americans United for Life, which offers a legal blueprint for a two-tiered woman-protective legal strategy. Our first theme, "protect women," includes the following categories: (1) fetal pain, (4) informed consent/mandatory ultrasounds, (5) fetal homicide laws, (9) waiting periods, (19) declaration opposing Freedom of Choice Act (FOCA), (20) repeal *Roe*/legality of abortion.

Our second primary theme of interest, "regulate providers" includes the following categories from the content variable in accordance with *Defending Life*'s legal blueprint: (6) regulations specific to clinics/providers, (10) requiring determination of postfertilization age of fetus, (15) prohibiting sex/race selection abortions, (18) declaration supporting crisis pregnancy centers, (21) protect women from coercion to have abortion.

Except for the category for minors, the remaining categories in the content variable followed their original coding and were not combined with other categories: (14) general regulation, (8) insurance, (11 & 12) minors, (3) taxes, (7) conscience, (17) public safety, (2) power of attorney, (13) license plates.

CONTENT ANALYSIS: AMICUS CURIAE BRIEF, APPENDIX B: EXCERPTS OF POSTABORTIVE WOMEN, SUBMITTED BY THE JUSTICE FOUNDATION IN SUPPORT OF PETITIONER IN *GONZALES v. CARHART*

We conducted a content analysis on the 180 testimonies included in Appendix B of the Justice Foundation's amicus curiae brief, using an inductive, interactive approach. We used an open-coded, in vivo format (using the words in the testimonies) to catalog dominant and frequent themes. These themes were then used to continually compare across testimonies to support themes, refine subthemes, and identify additional themes that surfaced in them. Our primary interest was documenting the explicit and implicit religiosity of the testimonies. Each testimony was based on that woman's experiential knowledge of abortion. We coded each testimony according to the following categories: (1) woman discussed having emotional regret, (2) woman discussed feeling shame, (3) woman discussed physical ailments she attributed to her abortion, (4) woman discussed experiencing sexual dysfunction resulting from her abortion, (5) woman discussed her abortion experience as traumatic, (6) woman discussed being coerced/pressured into abortion, (7) woman discussed her lack of knowledge about abortion, (8) woman discussed aborted fetus as her unborn/child, (9) woman discussed God.

Each testimony was coded according to the theme(s) that surfaced. In other words, one testimony may have spanned multiple categories, which we captured in the coding. Based on the findings from the content analysis, the frequencies of the nine categories in the testimonies were: emotional regret 91 percent (164 testimonies); shame 53 percent (95 testimonies); physical ailments 31 percent (55 testimonies); sexual dysfunction 14 percent (26 testimonies); trauma 51 percent (91 testimonies); coerced 10 percent (18 testimonies); lack of knowledge 8 percent (14 testimonies); unborn/child 27 percent (48 testimonies); God/Jesus 22 percent (39 testimonies).

Notes

CHAPTER ONE

1. Hugh Lenox Hodge, *Fœticide, Or Criminal Abortion: A Lecture Introductory in the Course on Obstetrics and Diseases of Women and Children, University of Pennsylvania, Session 1854–5* (Philadelphia, PA: Lindsay and Blakiston, 1854), 7. Emphasis in original.

2. Hodge, 9. Emphasis in original.

3. Hodge, 20.

4. David Humphreys Storer, "Two Causes of Uterine Diseases," *The Journal of the Gynaecological Society of Boston* 6 (1872): 196–99. Emphasis in original.

5. Storer, 201.

6. Hodge, *Fœticide, Or Criminal Abortion*, 17.

7. Storer, "Two Causes of Uterine Diseases," 200.

8. Storer, 197–98.

9. Hodge, *Fœticide, Or Criminal Abortion*, 8.

10. Hodge, 8.

11. Horatio Robinson Storer, *Why Not? A Book for Every Woman* (Boston, MA: Lee and Shepard, 1866), 81.

12. Reva Siegel, "Reasoning from the Body: A Historical Perspective on Abortion Regulation and Questions of Equal Protection," *Stanford Law Review* 44, no. 2 (1992): 279.

13. James C. Mohr, *Abortion in America: The Origins and Evolution of National Policy* (New York: Oxford University Press, 1978), 20–21.

14. Mohr, *Abortion in America*, 20–21.

15. Mohr, 42.

16. Mohr, 43–44.

17. Horatio Storer, "On Criminal Abortion in America," *The American Journal of the Medical Sciences,* no. 78 (April 1860): 5. Emphasis in original.

18. Storer, 9.

19. Hodge, *Fœticide, Or Criminal Abortion,* 18.

20. Mohr, *Abortion in America,* 44.

21. "American Medical Association Report on Criminal Abortion," *Transactions of the American Medical Association* 12 (1859): 75.

22. Andrew Nebinger, *Criminal Abortion, Its Extent and Prevention: Read Before the Philadelphia County Medical Society, February 9, 1870* (Philadelphia: Collins, 1870), 4–5.

23. Henry Gibbons, "Annual Address before the San Francisco Medical Society," *The American Journal of the Medical Sciences (1827–1924); Philadelphia,* no. 70 (April 1858): 12.

24. Augustus K. Gardner, *Conjugal Sins against the Laws of Life and Health, Sex, Marriage, and Society* (New York: Arno Press, 1974), 112.

25. Mohr, *Abortion in America,* 46.

26. Mohr, 167.

27. "American Medical Association Report on Criminal Abortion," 76.

28. "American Medical Association Report on Criminal Abortion."

29. "American Medical Association Report on Criminal Abortion," 76–78.

30. Mohr, *Abortion in America,* 157; Kristin Luker, *Abortion and the Politics of Motherhood* (Berkeley: University of California Press, 1985), 15–16.

31. Paul Starr, *The Social Transformation of American Medicine,* updated edition (New York: Basic Books, 2017), 47.

32. Starr, 58.

33. Mohr, *Abortion in America,* 163.

34. Mohr, 147.

35. Luker, *Abortion and the Politics of Motherhood,* 28.

36. "American Medical Association Report on Criminal Abortion," 76.

37. Montrose A. Pallen, "Fœticide, or Criminal Abortion," ed. James C. Whitehall, *The Medical Archives: A Monthly Journal of Medical Sciences* 3 (1869): 195.

38. Luker, *Abortion and the Politics of Motherhood,* 31. Emphasis in original.

39. Mohr, *Abortion in America,* 164.

40. Mohr, 168.

41. Mohr, 167.

42. Storer, *Why Not?*, 18.

43. Storer, 14.

44. William B. Atkinson, Philadelphia Medical Society, "Abortion: Its Causes, Dangers, and Treatment," *Medical and Surgical Reporter* 4, no. 26 (1860): 542.

45. Henry Campbell Black, *Black's Law Dictionary,* 6th ed., by the publisher's editorial staff; contributing authors, Joseph R. Nolan . . . [et al.] (St. Paul, MN: West PubCo, 1990).

46. Storer, *Why Not?*, 74–75.

47. Siegel, "Reasoning from the Body."

48. Storer, "Two Causes of Uterine Diseases," 195–97.

49. Storer, "On Criminal Abortion in America," 102.

50. Storer, 104.

51. A. E. Small, "Criminal Abortion: A Lecture before the Hahnemann Medical College, Dec. 1864," *Medical Investigator* 2, no. 2 (1865): 38–39.

52. Hodge, *Fœticide, Or Criminal Abortion,* 8.

53. G. Maxwell Christine, "The Medical Profession vs. Criminal Abortion," *Transactions of the 25th Session of the Homoeopathic Society of the State of Philadelphia,* 1889, 70–71.

54. Nebinger, *Criminal Abortion, Its Extent and Prevention,* 32.

55. Hodge, *Fœticide, Or Criminal Abortion,* 18. Emphasis in original.

56. Storer, *Why Not?*, 29.

57. "American Medical Association Report on Criminal Abortion," 76–77.

58. American Medical Association, "Report of the AMA Committee on Criminal Abortion," *Transactions of the American Medical Association,* 1871, 239–58.

59. Nebinger, *Criminal Abortion, Its Extent and Prevention,* 14.

60. Luker, *Abortion and the Politics of Motherhood,* 22. Emphasis in original.

61. Henry Miller, "Address to the Gentlemen of the American Medical Association," in *The Transactions of the American Medical Association* 13, (1860): 57.

62. "American Medical Association Report on Criminal Abortion," 76.

63. Nebinger, *Criminal Abortion, Its Extent and Prevention,* 12–13.

64. Storer, *Why Not?*, 69–70.

65. Miller, "Address to the Gentlemen of the American Medical Association," 57–58.

66. Storer, *Why Not?*, 70.

67. Reese D. Meredith, "Testimony before the Senate of the State of New York, Report of the Committee Appointed to Investigate the Health Department of the City of New York 82nd Session," *Documents of the Senate of the State of New York* 2 (February 3, 1859): 95.

68. William M. Pritchett, "Criminal Abortion," ed. I. N. Love, *The Medical Mirror: A Monthly Reflection of the Medical Profession and Its Progress* 7 (1896): 471–73.

69. John Bell, *Report of the Committee on the Relations of Alcohol to Medicine* (Philadelphia, PA: Collins, 1869), 316–17.

70. Storer, *Why Not?*, 69–70.

71. Pritchett, "Criminal Abortion," 471.

72. Gardner, *Conjugal Sins against the Laws of Life and Health*, 223–26.

73. Siegel, "Reasoning from the Body," 304.

74. Storer, *Why Not?*, 15.

75. Storer, 75–76.

76. Storer, 80–81.

77. Storer, 81.

78. Pritchett, "Criminal Abortion," 471.

79. Nathan Allen, *Population: Its Law of Increase* (Stone & Huse, 1870), 16.

80. H. S. Pomeroy, *The Ethics of Marriage* (New York, London: Funk & Wagnalls, 1888), 97.

81. Siegel, "Reasoning from the Body," 295.

82. Siegel, 296.

83. American Medical Association, "Report of the AMA Committee on Criminal Abortion," 241.

84. American Medical Association, "Report of the AMA Committee on Criminal Abortion."

85. Gibbons, "Annual Address before the San Francisco Medical Society," 11.

86. Pritchett, "Criminal Abortion," 473.

87. "Infantiphobia and Infanticide," *Medical and Surgical Reporter* 14 (1866): 212. Emphasis in original.

88. "Infantiphobia and Infanticide."

89. J. M. Toner, "Abortion in Its Medical and Moral Aspects," *Medical and Surgical Reporter* 5 (1861): 443.

90. John Davies, "Observations of Abortion," *Medical Investigator* 2, no. 10 (1873): 345.

91. Edwin M. Hale, *The Great Crime of the Nineteenth Century: Why Is It Committed? Who Are the Criminals? How Shall They Be Detected? How Shall They Be Punished?* (Chicago: C. S. Halsey, 1867), 9.

92. "Declaration of Sentiments and Resolutions 1848," *Hera,* Binghamton, August 31, 1998.

93. "Declaration of Sentiments and Resolutions 1848."

94. "Declaration of Sentiments and Resolutions 1848."

95. Horatio Storer, *Is It I?: A Book for Every Man: A Companion to "Why Not? A Book for Every Woman"* (Boston: MA: Lee and Shepard, 1868), 112.

96. George Frederick Shrady and Thomas Lathrop Stedman, eds., "Criminal Abortion," *Medical Record,* 1897, 32.

97. Hale, *The Great Crime of the Nineteenth Century,* 12–13.

98. Correspondence (editor), *The Medical Mirror* 13 (1902): 203.

99. Storer, "Two Causes of Uterine Diseases," 198.

100. Pallen, "Fœticide, or Criminal Abortion," 205.

101. Pallen, "Fœticide, or Criminal Abortion."

102. Pallen.

103. Pomeroy, *The Ethics of Marriage,* 95.

104. Pomeroy, 150–51.

105. Gardner, *Conjugal Sins against the Laws of Life and Health,* 235.

106. Gardner, *Conjugal Sins against the Laws of Life and Health.*

107. Pomeroy, *The Ethics of Marriage,* 137–38.

108. Pomeroy, 139.

109. Siegel, "Reasoning from the Body," 305 (see note 175).

110. Linda Gordon, *Woman's Body, Woman's Right: A Social History of Birth Control in America* (New York: Grossman, 1976), 66–67.

111. Gordon, 59.

112. Mohr, *Abortion in America,* 112.

113. Tracy A. Thomas, *Elizabeth Cady Stanton and the Feminist Foundations of Family Law* (NYU Press, 2016), 163.

114. Gordon, *Woman's Body, Woman's Right;* Thomas, *Elizabeth Cady Stanton and the Feminist Foundations of Family Law.*

115. Storer, *Why Not?,* 99.

116. Storer, 27–28.

117. Storer, "Two Causes of Uterine Diseases," 200.

118. Christine, "The Medical Profession vs. Criminal Abortion," 73.

119. Hale, *The Great Crime of the Nineteenth Century,* 5.

120. Christine, "The Medical Profession vs. Criminal Abortion," 73.

121. Hale, *The Great Crime of the Nineteenth Century,* 10.

122. Christine, "The Medical Profession vs. Criminal Abortion," 73.

123. Storer, *Why Not?,* 48.

124. Storer, 59.

125. Storer, 60.

126. Hale, *The Great Crime of the Nineteenth Century,* 10.

127. Storer, *Why Not?,* 43.

128. Storer, 37.

129. Storer, 49.

130. Storer, 49.

131. G. F. Shrady, ed., "Abortion as a Cause for Insanity," *The Medical Record: A Semi-Monthly Journal of Medicine and Surgery* 3 (1869): 320.

132. George F. Shrady, ed., "Abortion and Insanity, Annual Report of State Report Asylum," *The Medical Record: A Semi-Monthly Journal of Medicine and Surgery* 2 (1867): 240.

133. Judith Walzer Leavitt, *Brought to Bed: Childbearing in America, 1750–1950* (New York: Oxford University Press, 1988), 14.

134. Carroll Smith-Rosenberg and Charles Rosenberg, "The Female Animal: Medical and Biological Views of Woman and Her Role in Nineteenth-Century America," *The Journal of American History* 60, no. 2 (1973): 345.

135. Leavitt, *Brought to Bed,* 20.

136. Leavitt, 20–28.

137. Leavitt, 28.

138. Charlotte Brown, "Rest Therapy in Gynaecology," in *The Medical Standard,* vol. 17 (Chicago: G.P. Engelhard & Co., 1895), 170.

139. W. W. Johnson, "Chronic Anemia and Wasting in Newly Married Women. Some of the Causes of Their Persistence and Incurability," in *Transactions of the Washington Obstetrical and Gynecological Society,* 1887, 162.

140. Johnson, 163.

141. George M. Beard, *American Nervousness, Its Causes and Consequences: A Supplement to Nervous Exhaustion (Neurasthenia)* (New York: G.P. Putnam's Sons, [c1881]), 77.

142. Nancy Theriot, "Diagnosing Unnatural Motherhood: Nineteenth-Century Physicians and 'Puerperal Insanity,'" *American Studies* 30, no. 2 (1989): 70.

143. William Fetherston Montgomery, "An Exposition of the Signs and Symptoms of Pregnancy, with Some Other Papers on Subjects Connected with Midwifery," *The American Journal of the Medical Sciences* 65, no. 1 (January 1857): 42.

144. Montgomery, "An Exposition of the Signs and Symptoms of Pregnancy, with Some Other Papers on Subjects Connected with Midwifery."

145. Montgomery, 42–43.

146. Miriam Rich, "The Curse of Civilised Woman: Race, Gender and the Pain of Childbirth in Nineteenth-Century American Medicine," *Gender & History* 28, no. 1 (March 2016): 64.

147. Laura Briggs, "The Race of Hysteria: 'Overcivilization' and the 'Savage' Woman in Late Nineteenth-Century Obstetrics and Gynecology," *American Quarterly* 52, no. 2 (June 1, 2000): 261.

148. Rich, "The Curse of Civilised Woman," 58; Briggs, "The Race of Hysteria," 258–59.

149. Rich, "The Curse of Civilised Woman," 57–58.

150. Rich, 65.

151. W. W. McFarlane, "Proceedings of Societies," *Pacific Medical Journal* 35 (1892): 308.

152. Pallen, "Fœticide, or Criminal Abortion," 205–6.

153. Nicola Beisel and Tamara Kay, "Abortion, Race, and Gender in Nineteenth-Century America," *American Sociological Review* 69, no. 4 (August 2004): 499.

154. Beisel and Kay, "Abortion, Race, and Gender in Nineteenth-Century America."

155. Beisel and Kay, 500.

156. Beisel and Kay, 501.

157. Beisel and Kay, 499.

158. Storer, *Why Not?*, 13–14.

159. Allen, *Population*, 6.

160. Nebinger, *Criminal Abortion, Its Extent and Prevention*, 7.

161. Storer, *Why Not?*, 63.

162. Allen, *Population*, 5–6.

163. James S. Whitmore, "Criminal Abortion, A Paper Read before the Woodford County Medical Society, October 21, 1873," *The Chicago Medical Journal* 31 (1874): 392.

164. Nebinger, *Criminal Abortion, Its Extent and Prevention*, 8.

165. Joseph Taber Johnson, "Abortion and Its Effects," *Maryland Medical Journal: Medicine and Surgery* 25 (1890): 22.

166. Allen, *Population,* 31.

167. D. G. Brinton, ed., "On So-Called Enlightened Sexology," *The Medical and Surgical Reporter: A Weekly Journal* 34 (1876): 305.

168. Hale, *The Great Crime of the Nineteenth Century,* 4.

169. Storer, *Why Not?,* 63–64.

170. Storer, 85.

171. J. T. Cook, *A Book for Every Woman and Every Home!: A Book for Everybody! Startling Disclosures! Woman's Great Crime! The Slaughter of the Innocents! The Indictment and the Remedy!* (Cedar Rapids, IA, 1868), 36.

CHAPTER TWO

1. Leslie J. Reagan, *When Abortion Was a Crime: Women, Medicine, and Law in the United States, 1867–1973* (Berkeley: University of California Press, 1997), 7.

2. Reagan, 62.

3. Reagan, 138–45.

4. Reagan, 148.

5. Reagan, 204–07.

6. Rachel Gold, "Lessons from before *Roe:* Will Past Be Prologue? (Special Analysis)," *The Guttmacher Report on Public Policy* 6, no. 1 (March 2003): 8.

7. Gold.

8. Roe v. Wade, 410 U.S. 113 (1973).

9. Christopher Z. Mooney and Mei-Hsien Lee, "Legislative Morality in the American States: The Case of Pre-*Roe* Abortion Regulation Reform," *American Journal of Political Science* 39, no. 3 (1995): 599–627.

10. Reagan, *When Abortion Was a Crime,* 217–19.

11. J. Shoshanna Ehrlich, *Who Decides? The Abortion Rights of Teens* (Reproductive Rights and Policy [series]; Westport, CT: Praeger, 2006), 14–16; Eva R. Rubin, *Abortion, Politics, and the Courts: Roe v. Wade and Its Aftermath* (Contributions in American Studies), No. 57 (Westport, CT: Greenwood Press, 1982), 18.

12. "Offenses against the Family Part II: Definition of Specific Crimes—Offenses against the Family—Article 230," *American Law Institute Model Penal Code,* May 4, 1962, 187–93.

13. Reagan, *When Abortion Was a Crime,* 219–22.

14. Linda Greenhouse and Reva Siegel, "Before (and After) *Roe v. Wade:* New Questions about Backlash," *Yale Law Journal* 120, no. 8 (June 2011): 2042–44.

15. Greenhouse and Siegel, 2045–46; Reagan, *When Abortion Was a Crime,* 234–44.

16. *Roe,* 410 U.S. at 152–53.

17. *Roe,* 410 U.S. at 153.

18. *Roe,* 410 U.S.

19. *Roe,* 410 U.S. at 166.

20. Linda Greenhouse, "How the Supreme Court Talks about Abortion: The Implications of a Shifting Discourse," *Suffolk University Law Review* 42, no. 1 (January 1, 2008): 45.

21. Greenhouse, 45–47.

22. Greenhouse, 47.

23. Greenhouse, 47–48.

24. Greenhouse, 48.

25. *Roe,* 410 U.S. at 154.

26. *Roe,* 410 U.S. at 162–65.

27. *Roe,* 410 U.S. at 116.

28. *Roe,* 410 U.S. at 117.

29. Kristin Luker, *Abortion and the Politics of Motherhood* (Berkeley, CA: University of California Press, 1985), 126.

30. *Roe,* 410 U.S. at 129.

31. *Roe,* 410 U.S. at 140.

32. *Roe,* 410 U.S. at 141.

33. *Roe,* 410 U.S. at 141–42.

34. *Roe,* 410 U.S. at 117.

35. American Medical Association, "Report of the AMA Committee on Criminal Abortion," *Transactions of the American Medical Association,* 1871, 240–41.

36. American Medical Association, 241.

37. American Medical Association, 242.

38. American Medical Association, 242–44.

39. American Medical Association, 242.

40. American Medical Association, 243–44.

41. American Medical Association, 244.

42. American Medical Association, 244.

43. Greenhouse, "How the Supreme Court Talks about Abortion: The Implications of a Shifting Discourse," 46–47.

44. Luker, *Abortion and the Politics of Motherhood,* 140–41.

45. Luker, 205.

46. Alesha E. Doan, *Opposition and Intimidation: The Abortion Wars and Strategies of Political Harassment* (Ann Arbor, MI: University of Michigan Press, 2007), 72.

47. Margaret Hartshorn, "Pregnancy Help Centers: Prevention, Crisis Intervention, Healing: Putting It All Together," Heartbeat International, 2006, www.heartbeatservices.org/pdf/Putting_It_All_Together.pdf.

48. Hartshorn.

49. Greenhouse, "How the Supreme Court Talks about Abortion: The Implications of a Shifting Discourse," 2048–51.

50. Greenhouse, 2051.

51. Faye D. Ginsburg, *Contested Lives: The Abortion Debate in an American Community* (Berkeley, CA: University of California Press, 1989), 43.

52. Paul Saurette and Kelly Gordon, *The Changing Voice of the Anti-Abortion Movement: The Rise of "pro-Woman" Rhetoric in Canada and the United States* (Toronto: University of Toronto Press, 2015), 69–70.

53. Doan, *Opposition and Intimidation,* 89.

54. Scott H. Ainsworth, *Abortion Politics in Congress: Strategic Incrementalism and Policy Change* (New York: Cambridge University Press, 2011); Deborah R. McFarlane and Kenneth J. Meier, *The Politics of Fertility Control: Family Planning and Abortion Policies in the American States* (New York: Chatham House Publishers, 2001); Melody Rose, *Safe, Legal, and Unavailable?: Abortion Politics in the United States* (Washington, D.C.: CQ Press, 2007).

55. David C. Reardon, *Making Abortion Rare: A Healing Strategy for a Divided Nation* (Springfield, IL: Acorn Books, 1996), 12–13.

56. Ainsworth, *Abortion Politics in Congress,* 100–03.

57. Henry Hyde, "Departments of Labor and Health Education, and Welfare, and Related Agencies Appropriation Bill," (1976), 20410.

58. Doan, *Opposition and Intimidation,* 92–104; McFarlane and Meier, *The Politics of Fertility Control;* Rose, *Safe, Legal, and Unavailable?*

59. Duane M. Oldfield, *The Right and the Righteous: The Christian Right Confronts the Republican Party* (Lanham, MD: Rowman & Littlefield Publishers, 1996), 68.

60. Doan, *Opposition and Intimidation,* 81; Carol Mason, *Killing for Life: The Apocalyptic Narrative of Pro-Life Politics* (Ithaca, NY: Cornell University Press, 2002).

61. Doan, *Opposition and Intimidation,* 89.

62. Faye D. Ginsburg, "Rescuing the Nation: Operation Rescue and the Rise of Anti-Abortion Militance," In *Abortion Wars: A Half Century of Struggle, 1950–2000,* by Rickie Solinger (Berkeley, CA: University of California Press, 1998), 228.

63. James Risen and Judy L. Thomas, *Wrath of Angels: The American Abortion War,* 1st ed. (New York: Basic Books, 1998), 220.

64. Doan, *Opposition and Intimidation,* 88–114.

65. "Rescuing the Nation: Operation Rescue and the Rise of Anti-Abortion Militance," 229.

66. Francis J. Beckwith, "Taking Abortion Seriously: A Philosophical Critique of the New Anti-Abortion Rhetorical Shift," *Ethics & Medicine* 17, no. 3 (2001): 119.

67. Susan Faludi, *Backlash: The Undeclared War against American Women* (New York: Three Rivers Press, 2006), 402.

68. Faludi, *Backlash.*

69. Vincent Rue, "Abortion and Family Relations," § Subcommittee on the Constitution, Committee on the Judiciary (1981), 331.

70. George F. Gilder, *Men and Marriage* (Gretna, LA: Pelican Publishing, 1986), 106–07.

71. Akron v. Akron Center for Reproductive Health, 462 U.S. 416 (1983).

72. *Akron,* 462 U.S. at 714.

73. *Akron,* 462 U.S. at 713.

74. *Akron,* 462 U.S. at 709.

75. Maher v. Roe, 432 U.S. 464 (1977).

76. *Maher,* 432 U.S. at 495–96.

77. Harris v. McRae, 448 U.S. 297 (1980).

78. *Maher,* 432 U.S. at 488.

79. Ann M. Starrs, "40 Years Is Enough: Let's End the Harmful and Unjust Hyde Amendment," Guttmacher Institute, September 28, 2016, www.guttmacher.org/article/2016/09/40-years-enough-lets-end-harmful -and-unjust-hyde-amendment.

80. Bellotti v. Baird, 443 U.S. 622 (1979).

81. *Bellotti,* 443 U.S. at 643.

82. *Bellotti,* 443 U.S. at 813.

83. Ehrlich, *Who Decides?*; Helena Silverstein, *Girls on the Stand: How Courts Fail Pregnant Minors* (New York: NYU Press, 2007).

84. Planned Parenthood of Southeastern Pennsylvania v. Casey, 505 U.S. 833 (1992) at 855.

85. *Planned Parenthood*, 505 U.S. at 853–57.

86. *Planned Parenthood*, 505 U.S. at 876.

87. *Planned Parenthood*, 505 U.S. at 877.

88. *Planned Parenthood*, 505 U.S. at 879.

89. *Planned Parenthood*, 505 U.S. at 886.

90. *Planned Parenthood*, 505 U.S. at 883.

CHAPTER THREE

1. "Maternal Mortality Exceeds U.S. Goal; Age and Racial Differences Are Marked," *Guttmacher Policy Review* 35, no. 4 (September 8, 2005): 189–90.

2. Rachel K. Jones and Jenna Jerman, "Population Group Abortion Rates and Lifetime Incidence of Abortion: United States, 2008–2014," *American Journal of Public Health* 107, no. 12 (December 2017): 1904–9.

3. Sistersong, *Policy Report, Race, Gender and Abortion: How Reproductive Justice Activists Won in Georgia* (2010), www.trustblack women.org/SisterSong_Policy_Report.pdf.

4. Jennifer M. Denbow, "Abortion as Genocide: Race, Agency, and Nation in Prenatal Nondiscrimination Bans," *Signs: Journal of Women in Culture and Society* 41, no. 3 (February 16, 2016): 613.

5. Denbow, "Abortion as Genocide."

6. Willie Parker, *Life's Work: A Moral Argument for Choice* (New York: Atria Press, 2017), 163–164.

7. "Discover Birthright," Birthright International, accessed March 1, 2017, birthright.org/learn.

8. "Discover Birthright."

9. "Discover Birthright."

10. Karissa Haugeberg, *Women against Abortion: Inside the Largest Moral Reform Movement of the Twentieth Century* (Champaign, IL: University of Illinois Press, 2017), 17.

11. Margaret Hartshorn, "Pregnancy Help Centers: Prevention, Crisis Intervention, Healing: Putting It All Together," Heartbeat International, 2006, www.heartbeatservices.org/pdf/Putting_It_All_Together.pdf.

12. Hartshorn, 4.

13. Laura S. Hussey, "Political Action versus Personal Action: Understanding Social Movements' Pursuit of Change through Nongovernmental Channels," *American Politics Research* 42, no. 3 (May 1, 2014): 409–40.

14. Rory McVeigh, Bryant Crubaugh, and Kevin Estep, "Plausibility Structures, Status Threats, and the Establishment of Anti-Abortion Pregnancy Centers," *American Journal of Sociology* 122, no. 5 (March 1, 2017): 1533–71.

15. "About Care Net," Care Net, 2017, www.care-net.org/about.

16. Hartshorn, "Pregnancy Help Centers: Prevention, Crisis Intervention, Healing: Putting It All Together."

17. Kimberly Kelly, "Evangelical Underdogs: Intrinsic Success, Organizational Solidarity, and Marginalized Identities as Religious Movement Resources," *Journal of Contemporary Ethnography* 43, no. 4 (August 1, 2014): 419–55; Hussey, "Political Action versus Personal Action"; Ziad W. Munson, *Abortion Politics* (Social Movements Series; Medford, MA: Polity, 2018).

18. Hartshorn, "Pregnancy Help Centers: Prevention, Crisis Intervention, Healing: Putting It All Together."

19. "Pregnancy Resource Center Service Report, Second Edition: A Passion to Serve: How Pregnancy Centers Empower Women, Help Families, and Strengthen Communities," Family Research Council, 2010, down loads.frc.org/EF/EF12A47.pdf.

20. Munson, *Abortion Politics.*

21. Munson, 52.

22. Munson, *Abortion Politics;* Alesha E. Doan, Carolina Costa Candal, and Steven Sylvester, "'We Are the Visible Proof': Legitimizing Abortion Regret Misinformation through Activists' Experiential Knowledge," *Law & Policy* 40, no. 1 (January 2018): 33–56; "'Crisis Pregnancy Centers': Their Deceptive Tactics and Misleading Information Harm Women," National Women's Law Center, 2013, nwlc.org/resources/crisis -pregnancy-centers-their-deceptive-tactics-and-misleading-information -harm-women/.

23. Amy G. Bryant and Jonas J. Swartz, "Why Crisis Pregnancy Centers Are Legal but Unethical," *AMA Journal of Ethics* 20, no. 3 (March 1, 2018): 269–77.

24. Bryant and Swartz, 270.

25. Bryant and Swartz, 271.

26. McVeigh, Crubaugh, and Estep, "Plausibility Structures, Status Threats, and the Establishment of Anti-Abortion Pregnancy Centers."

27. Ryan, interview with Alesha E. Doan, 2007 (audio).

28. Ryan interview.

29. "What We Do," Project Ultrasound, 2017, www.projectultrasound .org/what-we-do.

30. "PRC Statistics," eKYROS.com, Inc., accessed March 27, 2018, ekyros.com/Pub/Default.aspx?tabid=16&tabindex=3.

31. Mary Gatter et al., "Relationship between Ultrasound Viewing and Proceeding to Abortion," *Obstetrics & Gynecology* 123, no. 1 (January 2014): 81–87.

32. Tracy A. Weitz, Katrina Kimport, and Diana Greene Foster, "Beyond Political Claims: Women's Interest in and Emotional Response to Viewing Their Ultrasound Image in Abortion Care," *Perspectives on Sexual and Reproductive Health* 46, no. 4 (December 2014): 185–91.

33. Weitz, Kimport, and Foster, "Beyond Political Claims: Women's Interest in and Emotional Response to Viewing Their Ultrasound Image in Abortion Care."

34. Munson, *Abortion Politics.*

35. Katherine, interview with Alesha E. Doan, 2010 (audio).

36. Kelly, "Evangelical Underdogs"; Hartshorn, "Pregnancy Help Centers: Prevention, Crisis Intervention, Healing: Putting It All Together."

37. Marsha, interview with Alesha E. Doan, 2007 (audio).

38. Kimberly Kelly, "In the Name of the Mother: Renegotiating Conservative Women's Authority in the Crisis Pregnancy Center Movement," *Signs: Journal of Women in Culture and Society* 38, no. 1 (September 1, 2012): 203–30; Kelly, "Evangelical Underdogs"; Hussey, "Political Action versus Personal Action."

39. Kelly, "In the Name of the Mother"; Kelly, "Evangelical Underdogs"; Munson, *Abortion Politics.*

40. Kelly, "In the Name of the Mother"; Kelly, "Evangelical Underdogs"; Hussey, "Political Action versus Personal Action."

41. Kelly, "Evangelical Underdogs," 204.

42. Munson, *Abortion Politics;* Kelly, "Evangelical Underdogs"; Pamela Herd and Madonna Harrington Meyer, "Care Work: Invisible Civic Engagement," *Gender & Society* 16, no. 5 (October 1, 2002): 665–88; Paula England, "Emerging Theories of Care Work," *Annual Review of Sociology* 31, no. 1 (July 11, 2005): 381–99; F. Ellen Netting, "Bridging Critical Feminist Gerontology and Social Work to Interrogate the Narrative on Civic Engagement," *Affilia* 26, no. 3 (August 1, 2011): 239–49.

43. Terry Ianora, *Crisis Pregnancy Centers: The Birth of a Grass-roots Movement* (AuthorHouse, 2009); Amy Blackstone, "'It's Just about Being Fair': Activism and the Politics of Volunteering in the Breast Cancer Movement," *Gender & Society* 18, no. 3 (June 1, 2004): 350.

44. McVeigh, Crubaugh, and Estep, "Plausibility Structures, Status Threats, and the Establishment of Anti-Abortion Pregnancy Centers"; Munson, *Abortion Politics;* Hussey, "Political Action versus Personal Action."

45. Ianora, *Crisis Pregnancy Centers.*

46. Claire, interview with Alesha E. Doan, 2010 (audio).

47. Kristin Luker, *Abortion and the Politics of Motherhood* (Berkeley, CA: University of California Press, 1985), 205.

48. Blackstone, "'It's Just about Being Fair'"; Kelly, "In the Name of the Mother."

49. Kelly, "In the Name of the Mother"; Kelly, "Evangelical Underdogs"; Ianora, *Crisis Pregnancy Centers*, 209; Munson, *Abortion Politics.*

50. Hussey, "Political Action versus Personal Action."

51. Jennifer, interview with Alesha E. Doan, 2007 (audio).

52. Jennifer interview.

53. Donald, interview with Alesha E. Doan, 2012 (audio).

54. Sandra, interview with Alesha E. Doan, 2010 (audio).

55. Lindsey, interview with Alesha E. Doan, 2007 (audio).

56. Kelly, "In the Name of the Mother," 204–17.

57. Felicity, interview with Alesha E. Doan, 2012 (audio).

58. Kelly, "In the Name of the Mother"; Orit Avishai, "'Doing Religion' in a Secular World: Women in Conservative Religions and the Question of Agency," *Gender & Society* 22, no. 4 (August 1, 2008): 409–33; Kelly H. Chong, "Negotiating Patriarchy: South Korean Evangelical Women and the Politics of Gender," *Gender & Society* 20, no. 6 (December 1, 2006): 697–724.

59. Kelly, "In the Name of the Mother," 204.

60. Brittney, interview with Alesha E. Doan, 2012 (audio).

61. Brittney interview.

62. Kelly, "In the Name of the Mother," 204–17.

63. Evelyn, interview with Alesha E. Doan, 2012 (audio).

64. Kelly, "In the Name of the Mother," 223.

65. Avishai, "'Doing Religion' in a Secular World"; Chong, "Negotiating Patriarchy, Negotiating Patriarchy."

66. Mike, interview with Alesha E. Doan, 2012 (audio).

67. Montrose Pallen, "Fœticide, or Criminal Abortion," ed. James C. Whitehall, *The Medical Archives: A Monthly Journal of Medical Sciences* 3 (1869): 208.

68. Ryan interview.

69. George F. Gilder, *Men and Marriage* (Gretna, LA: Pelican Publishing, 1986) 106–107.

70. Steven, interview with Alesha E. Doan, 2012 (audio).

71. Anonymous male activist, interview with Alesha E. Doan, 2007.

72. Paul, interview with Alesha E. Doan, 2012 (audio).

73. Mike interview.

74. Steven interview.

75. Jane, interview with Alesha E. Doan, 2012 (audio).

76. Paul interview.

77. Mike interview.

78. Katherine interview.

79. Evelyn interview.

80. Haley, interview with Alesha E. Doan, 2010 (audio).

81. Brittney interview, 2012.

82. Jane interview.

83. "Infantiphobia and Infanticide," *Medical and Surgical Reporter* 14 (1866): 212.

84. Steven interview.

85. Steven interview.

86. Donald interview.

87. Steven interview.

88. Kelly, "Evangelical Underdogs"; Hartshorn, "Pregnancy Help Centers: Prevention, Crisis Intervention, Healing: Putting It All Together."

89. Hussey, "Political Action versus Personal Action."

90. Marsha interview.

91. Sandra interview.

92. Katherine interview.

93. Mike interview.

94. Steven interview.

95. American Medical Association, "Report of the AMA Committee on Criminal Abortion," *Transactions of the American Medical Association,* 1871, 256.

96. Patricia, interview with Alesha E. Doan, 2012 (audio).

97. Jane interview.

98. Hugh Lenox Hodge, *Fœticide, Or Criminal Abortion: A Lecture Introductory in the Course on Obstetrics and Diseases of Women and Children, University of Pennsylvania, Session 1854–5* (Philadelphia, PA: Lindsay and Blakiston, 1854), 17.

99. Evelyn interview.

100. Claire interview.

101. Claire, interview.

102. Patricia interview.

103. Haley interview.

104. Donald interview.

105. American Medical Association, "Report of the AMA Committee on Criminal Abortion," 240–41.

106. Lindsey interview.

107. Patricia interview.

108. Felicity interview.

109. Jane interview.

110. Donald interview.

111. Lauren Casey and Hilary McGregor, "A Critical Examination of Experiential Knowledge in Illicit Substance Use Research and Policy," *Journal of Addiction Research & Therapy* 3, no. 5 (2012); Emily K. Abel and C. H. Browner, "Selective Compliance with Biomedical Authority and the Uses of Experiential Knowledge," in *Pragmatic Women and Body Politics*, ed. Margaret Lock and Patricia A. Kaufert (Cambridge University Press, 1998); C. H. Browner and Nancy Press, "The Production of Authoritative Knowledge in American Prenatal Care," *Medical Anthropology Quarterly* 10, no. 2 (June 1, 1996): 141–56.

112. Lori d'Agincourt-Canning, "The Effect of Experiential Knowledge on Construction of Risk Perception in Hereditary Breast/Ovarian Cancer," *Journal of Genetic Counseling* 14, no. 1 (February 2005): 55–69.

113. Horatio Robinson Storer, *Why Not? A Book for Every Woman* (Boston, MA: Lee and Shepard, 1866), 14.

114. Judith Stacey, "Can There Be a Feminist Ethnography?," *Women's Studies International Forum* 11, no. 1 (1988): 21–27.

115. Felicity K. Boardman, "Knowledge Is Power? The Role of Experiential Knowledge in Genetically 'Risky' Reproductive Decisions," *Sociology of Health & Illness* 36, no. 1 (January 1, 2014): 137–50; Emma F. France et al., "How Personal Experiences Feature in Women's Accounts

of Use of Information for Decisions about Antenatal Diagnostic Testing for Foetal Abnormality," *Social Science & Medicine* 72, no. 5 (March 1, 2011): 755–62; Beth K. Potter et al., "Exploring Informed Choice in the Context of Prenatal Testing: Findings from a Qualitative Study," *Health Expectations* 11, no. 4 (December 1, 2008): 355–65.

116. Thomasina Borkman, "Experiential Knowledge: A New Concept for the Analysis of Self-Help Groups," *Social Service Review* 50, no. 3 (1976): 445–56.

117. Hussey, "Political Action versus Personal Action"; Kelly, "In the Name of the Mother."

118. Rachel, interview with Alesha E. Doan, 2010 (audio).

119. April, interview with Alesha E. Doan, 2010 (audio).

120. Lindsey interview.

121. Casey and McGregor, "A Critical Examination of Experiential Knowledge in Illicit Substance Use Research and Policy"; Potter et al., "Exploring Informed Choice in the Context of Prenatal Testing"; d'Agincourt-Canning, "The Effect of Experiential Knowledge on Construction of Risk Perception in Hereditary Breast/Ovarian Cancer."

122. April interview.

123. Patricia interview.

124. Patricia interview.

125. Patricia interview.

126. Paul interview.

127. Deborah, interview with Alesha E. Doan, 2010 (audio).

128. Lauren Casey and Hilary McGregor, 2012.

129. Peter Conrad and Kristin K. Barker, "The Social Construction of Illness: Key Insights and Policy Implications," *Journal of Health and Social Behavior* 51, no. 1 suppl. (March 1, 2010): S67–79; d'Agincourt-Canning, "The Effect of Experiential Knowledge on Construction of Risk Perception in Hereditary Breast/Ovarian Cancer"; Kristin K. Barker, "Electronic Support Groups, Patient-Consumers, and Medicalization: The Case of Contested Illness," *Journal of Health and Social Behavior* 49, no. 1 (March 1, 2008): 20–36.

130. Paul interview.

131. Mike interview.

132. Mike interview.

133. Carl, interview with Alesha E. Doan, 2010 (audio).

134. American Medical Association, "Report of the AMA Committee on Criminal Abortion," 241.

135. Storer, *Why Not?*, 43.

136. Doan, Costa Candal, and Sylvester, "'We Are the Visible Proof': Legitimizing Abortion Regret Misinformation through Activists' Experiential Knowledge."

137. G. Maxwell Christine, "The Medical Profession vs. Criminal Abortion," *Transactions of the 25th Session of the Homoeopathic Society of the State of Philadelphia* (1889), 73.

138. Paul interview.

139. Paul interview.

140. The American Cancer Society medical and editorial content team, "Abortion and Cancer Risk," American Cancer Society, June 19, 2014, www.cancer.org/cancer/cancer-causes/medical-treatments/abortion-and -breast-cancer-risk.html.

141. Mike interview.

142. Alessandro Bessi et al., "Science vs. Conspiracy: Collective Narratives in the Age of Misinformation," *PLoS ONE* 10, no. 2 (n.d.): e0118093; Anna Kata, "A Postmodern Pandora's Box: Anti-Vaccination Misinformation on the Internet," *Vaccine* 28, no. 7 (February 17, 2010): 1709–16.

143. Conrad and Barker, "The Social Construction of Illness."

144. Nor Athiyah Abdullah et al., "User's Action and Decision Making of Retweet Messages towards Reducing Misinformation Spread during Disaster," *Journal of Information Processing* 23, no. 1 (2015): 31–40; Fang Jin et al., "Misinformation Propagation in the Age of Twitter," *Computer* 47, no. 12 (December 2014): 90–94; Bessi et al., "Science vs. Conspiracy"; Kata, "A Postmodern Pandora's Box."

145. "Rachel's Vineyard—Our Story," Rachel's Vineyard, 2018, www .rachelsvineyard.org/aboutus/ourstory.htm.

146. "Rachel's Vineyard—Our Story."

147. "Rachel's Vineyard—Our Story."

148. "Abortion Affecting You?" Abortion Recovery InterNational, 2017, www.abortionrecovery.org/afterabortion/abortionaffectingyou/tabid /218/Default.aspx.

149. Hartshorn, "Pregnancy Help Centers: Prevention, Crisis Intervention, Healing: Putting It All Together," 4.

150. "About Care Net," Care Net, 2015, www.care-net.org/about.

151. "Abortion Affecting You?"

152. Men & Abortion Network (MAN), 2018, www.menandabortion.net.

153. Czarina Ong, "Pastor Still Regrets Going along with Girlfriend's Abortion 23 Years Later," *Christian Today,* January 23, 2015, www.chris

tiantoday.com/article/pastor-still-regrets-going-along-with-girlfriends
-abortion-23-years-later/46568.htm.

154. Henry Waxman, "False and Misleading Health Information Provided by Federally Funded Pregnancy Resource Centers," Congressional Investigative Report (Committee on Government Reform, House of Representatives, United States Congress, 2006).

155. Michelle D'Almeida et al., "Perinatal Hospice: Family-Centered Care of the Fetus with a Lethal Condition," *Journal of American Physicians and Surgeons* 11, no. 2 (2006): 52–55; Eugene W. J. Pearce and Patti Lewis, "A Hospice for the Pre-Born and Newborn," *Health Progress* 87, no. 5 (2006): 56–61.

156. Amber, interview with Alesha E. Doan, 2010 (audio); Katherine interview; Deborah interview; Pearce and Lewis, "A Hospice for the Pre-Born and Newborn"; D'Almeida et al., "Perinatal Hospice: Family-Centered Care of the Fetus with a Lethal Condition."

157. Claire interview.

158. Borkman, "Experiential Knowledge"; Boardman, "Knowledge Is Power?"

159. Ryan interview.

160. Sandra interview.

161. Haley interview.

162. Katherine interview.

163. Carl interview.

164. Judith Butler, *Undoing Gender* (London: Routledge, 2004), 8.

CHAPTER FOUR

1. Francis X. Clines, "Reagan Appeal on Abortion Is Made to Fundamentalists," *New York Times,* January 31, 1984, sec. A, 16.

2. "Ronald Reagan: Remarks at the Annual Convention of the National Religious Broadcasters," The American Presidency Project, January 30, 1984, www.presidency.ucsb.edu/ws/index.php?pid=40394.

3. Dallas A. Blanchard, *The Anti-Abortion Movement and the Rise of the Religious Right: From Polite to Fiery Protest* (Social Movements Past and Present [series]; New York: Twayne Publishers, Maxwell Macmillan International, 1994), 55; Paul Saurette and Kelly Gordon, *The Changing Voice of the Anti-Abortion Movement: The Rise of "Pro-Woman" Rhetoric in Canada and the United States* (Toronto: University of Toronto Press, 2015), 77–78.

4. Saurette, *The Changing Voice of the Anti-Abortion Movement,* 77–78.

5. Alesha E. Doan, *Opposition and Intimidation: The Abortion Wars and Strategies of Political Harassment* (Ann Arbor, MI:, United States: University of Michigan Press, 2007), 83.

6. Doan, *Opposition and Intimidation.*

7. Webster v. Reproductive Health Services, 492 U.S. 490 (1989).

8. *Webster,* 492 U.S. 490 at 538.

9. Planned Parenthood of Southeastern Pennsylvania v. Casey, 505 U.S. 833 (1992).

10. Doan, *Opposition and Intimidation,* 89.

11. Doan, 106–12.

12. Doan.

13. Doan, 158.

14. James Risen and Judy L. Thomas, *Wrath of Angels: The American Abortion War,* 1st ed. (New York: Basic Books, 1998), 220.

15. John C. Willke, "Life Issues Institute Is Celebrating Ten Years with a New Home," *Life Issues* (blog), February 1, 2001, www.lifeissues.org /2001/02/life-issues-institute-celebrating-ten-years-new-home.

16. Willke, "Life Issues."

17. Paul F. Swope, "Abortion: A Failure to Communicate," *First Things,* April 1998, www.firstthings.com/article/1998/04/004-abortion-a -failure-to-communicate.

18. Swope, "Abortion."

19. Reardon, *Making Abortion Rare: A Healing Strategy for a Divided Nation* (Springfield, IL: Acorn Books, 1996), 4.

20. Reardon, *Making Abortion Rare,* 29–30.

21. Reardon, 6–8. Emphasis in original.

22. Reardon, 21. Emphasis in original.

23. Reardon.

24. Reardon.

25. Reardon, 33.

26. Reardon. Emphasis in original.

27. Reva Siegel, "The Right's Reasons: Constitutional Conflict and the Spread of Woman-Protective Antiabortion Argument," *Duke Law Journal* 57 (2008): 1679–80.

28. Frederica Mathewes-Green, "Seeking Abortion's Middle Ground: Why My Pro-Life Allies Should Revise Their Self-Defeating Rhetoric," *The Washington Post,* July 28, 1996.

29. Reardon, *Making Abortion Rare,* ix. Emphasis in original.

30. Reardon, 25.

31. Reardon, 26.

32. John C. Willke and Barbara H. Willke, *Why Can't We Love Them Both: Questions and Answers about Abortion* (Hayes Publishing Company, 1997), 17.

33. Reardon, *Making Abortion Rare,* 33.

34. Willke and Willke, *Why Can't We Love Them Both,* 17.

35. Reardon, *Making Abortion Rare,* 11.

36. Reardon, 11.

37. Reardon.

38. "After Abortion," Elliot Institute, 2018, www.afterabortion.org.

39. Reardon, *Making Abortion Rare,* 10.

40. Sandra Cano, Brief of Sandra Cano and 180 Women Injured by Abortion as Amicus Curiae in Support of Petitioner, No. 05–380 (United States Supreme Court 2006).

41. Chris Mooney, "Research and Destroy," *Washington Monthly,* October 1, 2004, 34, washingtonmonthly.com/2004/10/01/research-and-destroy.

42. Reardon, *Making Abortion Rare,* 3.

43. Reardon, vii.

44. Reardon, 1.

45. Reardon.

46. C. Everett Koop, "Letter from Attorney General Koop to Ronald Reagan on the Health Effects of Abortion on Women," January 9, 1989, www.justfacts.com/abortion.koop.asp.

47. Reardon, *Making Abortion Rare.*

48. Francis J. Beckwith, "Taking Abortion Seriously: A Philosophical Critique of the New Anti-Abortion Rhetorical Shift," *Ethics & Medicine; Highland Park* 17, no. 3 (2001): 119.

49. Beckwith, "Taking Abortion Seriously," 131.

50. David C. Reardon, "A Defense of the Neglected Rhetorical Strategy (NRS)," *Ethics & Medicine,* no. 2 (Summer 2002): 23–32.

51. Reardon, *Making Abortion Rare,* 3.

52. Reardon, 1–4.

53. Reardon, 4.

54. Reardon, 5.

55. Reardon, 10.

56. Reardon, 108.

57. Michelle, interview with Alesha E. Doan, 2012.

58. Reardon, *Making Abortion Rare,* 110–11.

59. Marsha, interview with Alesha E. Doan, 2007 (audio).

60. Reardon, *Making Abortion Rare,* 11–109.

61. Reardon, 108–9.

62. Ryan, interview with Alesha E. Doan, 2007 (audio).

63. Reardon, *Making Abortion Rare,* 109.

64. Reardon, 109–12.

65. Reardon, 9.

66. Reardon, 14.

67. Karissa Haugeberg, *Women against Abortion: Inside the Largest Moral Reform Movement of the Twentieth Century* (Champaign, IL: University of Illinois Press, 2017), 40.

68. Haugeberg, *Women against Abortion,* 40–41.

69. Orrin Hatch, "Abortion and Family Relations," § Subcommittee on the Constitution, Committee on the Judiciary (1981).

70. Vincent Rue, "Abortion and Family Relations," § Subcommittee on the Constitution, Committee on the Judiciary (1981), 331.

71. Rue, "Abortion and Family Relations," 332.

72. Rue, 331.

73. Anne C. Speckhard and Vincent Rue, "Postabortion Syndrome: An Emerging Public Health Concern," *Journal of Social Science,* no. 48 (1992): 105.

74. Olivia Gans, "When the Mothers Found Their Voice," National Right to Life Committee, 1998, www.nrlc.org/archive/news/1998/NRL1 .98/oliva.html.

75. Siegel, "The Right's Reasons: Constitutional Conflict and the Spread of Woman-Protective Antiabortion Argument," 1659.

76. David C. Reardon, *Aborted Women: Silent No More* (Ridgefield, CT: Acorn Books, 1987), 8.

77. Reardon, *Aborted Women,* xi.

78. Reardon, 7 & 25.

79. Reardon, 26.

80. Siegel, "The Right's Reasons: Constitutional Conflict and the Spread of Woman-Protective Antiabortion Argument," 1647.

81. Leslie King and Ginna Husting, "Anti-Abortion Activism in the U.S. and France: Comparing Opportunity Environments of Rescue Tactics," *Mobilization: An International Quarterly* 8, no. 3 (October 1, 2003): 298.

82. Carol Tobias, "NRLC Endorses George W. Bush for President," National Right to Life Committee, 2000, www.nrlc.org/archive/news/2000 /NRL02/endorse.html.

83. "Transcript of George W. Bush's Acceptance Speech," ABC News, August 3, 2000, abcnews.go.com/Politics/story?id=123214&page=1.

84. "Transcript of George W. Bush's Acceptance Speech."

85. Wayne Slater, "Interview with Wayne Slater," *Frontline,* "The Jesus Factor," Public Broadcast System, April 29, 2004, www.pbs.org/wgbh/pages/frontline/shows/jesus/interviews/slater.html.

86. "George W. Bush: Proclamation 7639—National Sanctity of Human Life Day, 2003," The American Presidency Project, January 14, 2003, www.presidency.ucsb.edu/ws/index.php?pid=61930.

87. "George W. Bush: Proclamation 7639—National Sanctity of Human Life Day, 2003."

88. "Ronald Reagan: Remarks at the Annual Convention of the National Religious Broadcasters."

89. "Ronald Reagan: Remarks to Participants in the March for Life Rally," The American Presidency Project, January 22, 1988, www.presidency.ucsb.edu/ws/?pid=35957.

90. Office of the Press Secretary, "Fact Sheet: Compassionate Conservatism," The White House: President George W. Bush, April 30, 2002, georgewbush-whitehouse.archives.gov/news/releases/2002/04/20020430.html.

91. Office of the Press Secretary, "Fact Sheet: Compassionate Conservatism."

92. Henry Waxman, "False and Misleading Health Information Provided by Federally Funded Pregnancy Resource Centers," Congressional Investigative Report (Committee on Government Reform, House of Representatives, United States Congress, 2006).

93. Alesha E. Doan and Jean Calterone Williams, *The Politics of Virginity: Abstinence in Sex Education* (Reproductive Rights and Policy [series]; Westport, CT: Praeger, 2008).

94. Waxman, "False and Misleading Health Information Provided by Federally Funded Pregnancy Resource Centers," 3.

95. Thomas B. Edsall, "Grants Flow to Bush Allies on Social Issues," *Washington Post,* March 22, 2006, www.washingtonpost.com/wp-dyn/content/article/2006/03/21/AR2006032101723.html; Waxman, "False and Misleading Health Information Provided by Federally Funded Pregnancy Resource Centers."

96. Bryce Covert and Josh Israel, "The States that Siphon Welfare Money to Stop Abortion," ThinkProgress, October 3, 2016, thinkprogress.org/tanf-cpcs-ec002305dd18/#.inu1bnlxj.

97. Jenn Stanley, "'Pro-Life' Pence Transfers Money Intended for Vulnerable Households to Anti-Choice Crisis Pregnancy Centers," Rewire. News, July 21, 2016, rewire.news/article/2016/07/21/pro-life-pence-shifts-funding-needy-indiana-residents-anti-choice-crisis-pregnancy-cen ters/.

98. Edsall, "Grants Flow to Bush Allies on Social Issues."

99. "Choose Life America—Choose-Life.Org. Choose Life Specialty License Plates and Promotional Items to Give Women an Option of Adoption by Supplying Funding to Pro-Adoption/Pro-Life Pregnancy Centers around the Country," accessed July 23, 2018, www.choose-life.org.

100. "Choose Life—Florida," accessed August 18, 2018, www.flchoose -life.org.

101. "Choose Life America—Choose-Life.Org."

102. Walker v. Texas Division, Sons of Confederate Veterans, Inc., 576 U.S. ___ (2015).

103. *Walker,* 576 U.S. ___ at 2249.

104. *Walker,* 576 U.S. ___ at 2250.

105. "Choose Life America—Choose-Life.Org."

106. "Operation Outcry," The Justice Foundation, 2018, thejusticefoun dation.org/cases/operation-outcry.

107. Operation Outcry, 2018, www.operationoutcry.org.

108. "Who We Are," Operation Outcry, 2018, www.operationoutcry .org/about/who-we-are.

109. Allan Parker, "News from Supreme Court and Operation Outcry," November 16, 2015.

110. Reardon, *Making Abortion Rare,* 5.

111. Reardon, 11.

112. South Dakota Task Force to Study Abortion, *Report of the South Dakota Task Force to Study Abortion,* December 2005.

113. South Dakota Task Force to Study Abortion.

114. South Dakota Task Force to Study Abortion, 7.

115. South Dakota Task Force to Study Abortion, *Report of the South Dakota Task Force to Study Abortion;* Beth Jordan and Elisa S. Wells, "A 21st-Century Trojan Horse: The 'Abortion Harms Women' Anti-Choice Argument Disguises a Harmful Movement," *Contraception Journal* 1 (March 2009); Reva Siegel and Sarah Blustain, "Mommy Dearest?" *The American Prospect,* September 17, 2006, http://prospect.org/article/mommy -dearest; Reva Siegel, "The New Politics of Abortion: An Equality Analysis of Woman-Protective Abortion Restrictions," *University of Illinois Law*

Review, no. 3 (2007): 991–1053; Siegel, "The Right's Reasons: Constitutional Conflict and the Spread of Woman-Protective Antiabortion Argument."

116. "Operation Outcry."

117. South Dakota Task Force to Study Abortion, *Report of the South Dakota Task Force to Study Abortion,* 33.

118. South Dakota Task Force to Study Abortion, 7.

119. South Dakota Task Force to Study Abortion, 38.

120. South Dakota Task Force to Study Abortion, 37–38.

121. Reardon, *Making Abortion Rare,* 5.

122. South Dakota Task Force to Study Abortion, *Report of the South Dakota Task Force to Study Abortion,* 47–48.

123. South Dakota Task Force to Study Abortion, 20.

124. South Dakota Task Force to Study Abortion.

125. South Dakota Task Force to Study Abortion, 20.

126. Lawrence B. Finer et al., "Reasons U.S. Women Have Abortions: Quantitative and Qualitative Perspectives," *Perspectives on Sexual and Reproductive Health* 37, no. 3 (September 1, 2005): 110–18, https://doi.org /10.1111/j.1931-2393.2005.tb00045.x.

127. "Mandatory Counseling for Abortion," Guttmacher Institute, February 2018, www.guttmacher.org/evidence-you-can-use/mandatory-counseling -abortion.

128. "Mandatory Counseling for Abortion."

129. South Dakota Task Force to Study Abortion, *Report of the South Dakota Task Force to Study Abortion,* 37–38.

130. South Dakota Task Force to Study Abortion, 56.

131. Caitlin E. Borgmann, "Judicial Evasion and Disingenuous Legislative Appeals to Science in the Abortion Controversy," *Journal of Law and Policy* 17, no. 1 (March 22, 2009): 15–56; Siegel, "The New Politics of Abortion: An Equality Analysis of Woman-Protective Abortion Restrictions"; Reva B. Siegel, "The Right's Reasons: Constitutional Conflict and the Spread of Woman-Protective Antiabortion Argument," 1641–92; Siegel and Blustain, "Mommy Dearest?"; Susan A. Cohen, "Abortion and Mental Health: Myths and Realities," *Guttmacher Policy Review* 9, no. 3 (August 1, 2006): 1–9; "State Facts about Abortion: South Dakota," Guttmacher Institute, May 2018, www.guttmacher.org/fact-sheet/state-facts -about-abortion-south-dakota.

132. Jordan and Wells, "A 21st-Century Trojan Horse"; Siegel, "The Right's Reasons: Constitutional Conflict and the Spread of Woman-Protective Antiabortion Argument."

133. Borgmann, "Judicial Evasion and Disingenuous Legislative Appeals to Science in the Abortion Controversy," 35–40.

134. Hugh Lenox Hodge, *Fœticide, Or Criminal Abortion: A Lecture Introductory in the Course on Obstetrics and Diseases of Women and Children, University of Pennsylvania, Session 1854–5* (Lindsay and Blakiston, 1854), 18.

135. South Dakota Task Force to Study Abortion, *Report of the South Dakota Task Force to Study Abortion,* 56.

136. South Dakota Task Force to Study Abortion, 67.

137. South Dakota Task Force to Study Abortion, 69.

138. South Dakota Task Force to Study Abortion, 69.

CHAPTER FIVE

1. Gonzales v. Carhart 550 U.S. 127 (2007).

2. *Gonzales,* 550 U.S. 127 at 158.

3. *Gonzales,* 550 U.S. at 158–59.

4. *Gonzales,* 550 U.S. at 159.

5. *Gonzales,* 550 U.S. at 159–60.

6. *Gonzales,* 550 U.S. at 188.

7. *Gonzales,* 550 U.S. at 159.

8. David C. Reardon, *Making Abortion Rare: A Healing Strategy for a Divided Nation* (Springfield, IL: Acorn Books, 1996), 4–5.

9. Terry A. Maroney, "Emotional Common Sense as Constitutional Law," *Vanderbilt Law Review* 62, no. 3 (April 2009): 894.

10. Maroney, "Emotional Common Sense as Constitutional Law," 894–99.

11. "Who We Are," Operation Outcry, 2016, www.operationoutcry.org/about/who-we-are.

12. Terry A. Maroney.

13. Allan Parker, *News from the Supreme Court and Operation Outcry,* email communication sent to Justice Foundation subscribers on November 16, 2015 (on file with authors).

14. Parker, *News from the Supreme Court and Operation Outcry.*

15. Parker.

16. "Operation Outcry," The Justice Foundation, 2018, thejusticefoundation.org/cases/operation-outcry.

17. Cano, Brief of Sandra Cano.

18. Cano.

19. Cano.

20. Cano.

21. Cano.

22. Reardon, *Making Abortion Rare,* 11.

23. Reardon.

24. "Mission Statement," The Justice Foundation, 2011, thejusticefoundation.org/mission-statement.

25. "Mission Statement."

26. OperationOutcry, *Army of Justice,* accessed August 31, 2018, www.youtube.com/watch?list=UU-LQlckdvYeJO1v7jkhPfiQ&v =wgiXlQ4E-ZA.

27. "Press Release: Supreme Court Commits Crimes Against Humanity and Invites Judgment," The Justice Foundation, June 27, 2016, www.txjf.org.

28. Allan Parker, "Supreme Court Strikes Out 3 Times," email communication sent to Justice Foundation subscribers, June 27, 2016.

29. Allan Parker, "Help Us End Legal Abortion," email communication, January 4, 2018.

30. Parker, "Help Us End Legal Abortion."

31. Parker.

32. Planned Parenthood of Southeastern Pennsylvania v. Casey, 505 U.S. 833 (1992).

33. Linda Greenhouse, "How the Supreme Court Talks about Abortion: The Implications of a Shifting Discourse," *Suffolk University Law Review* 42, no. 1 (January 1, 2008): 41.

34. Greenhouse, "How the Supreme Court Talks about Abortion."

35. Greenhouse.

36. Cano, Brief of Sandra Cano and 180 Women Injured by Abortion as Amicus Curiae in Support of Petitioner at 22.

37. Greenhouse, "How the Supreme Court Talks about Abortion," 11–16.

38. Allison Orr Larsen, "The Trouble with Amicus Facts," *Virginia Law Review* 100, no. 8 (December 2014): 1762.

39. Larsen, "The Trouble with Amicus Facts," 1789; Michael Rustad, "The Supreme Court and Junk Social Science: Selective Distortion in Amicus Briefs," *North Carolina Law Review* 72, no. 1 (November 1, 1993): 91–162.

40. Larsen, "The Trouble with Amicus Facts," 1779.

41. Larsen, 1782–95.

42. Brianne J. Gorod, "The Adversarial Myth: Appellate Court Extra-Record Factfinding," *Duke Law Journal* 61, no. 1 (October 2011): 63;

Caitlin E. Borgmann, "Appellate Review of Social Facts in Constitutional Rights Cases," *California Law Review* 101, no. 5 (October 2013): 1216–18.

43. Planned Parenthood v. Rounds, 530 F.3d 724 (8th Cir. 2008); Planned Parenthood v. Rounds, 686 F.3d 889 (8th Cir. 2012).

44. Steven Puro, "The Amicus Curiae in the United States Supreme Court: 1920–1966" (unpublished dissertation, 1971), 247.

45. Joseph D. Kearney and Thomas W. Merrill, "The Influence of Amicus Curiae Briefs on the Supreme Court," *University of Pennsylvania Law Review* 148, no. 3 (January 2000): 824–25; Puro, "The Amicus Curiae in the United States Supreme Court: 1920–1966," 2417.

46. "The Supreme Court Is Listening," Operation Outcry, accessed August 15, 2018, www.operationoutcry.org/2012/10/11/the-supreme-court-is-listening.

47. "Operation Outcry Testimony Influences 2nd Victory!," accessed August 15, 2018, www.operationoutcry.com/pdf/courtInfluenced.pdf.

48. "Who We Are," Operation Outcry, 2016, www.operationoutcry.org/about/who-we-are.

49. "Touching Hearts, Changing Lives, Restoring Justice: Declaration Introductory Letter," Operation Outcry, accessed August 15, 2018, www.operationoutcry.org/pdf/declaration_intro_letter.pdf.

50. Whole Woman's Health v. Hellerstedt, 597 U.S. ___ (2016).

51. Brief of Amicus Curiae of 3,348 Women Injured by Abortion and the Justice Foundation in Support of Respondents, Whole Woman's Health v. Hellerstedt, 597 U.S. ___ (2016).

52. Brief of Amicus Curiae of 3,348 Women Injured by Abortion and the Justice Foundation in Support of Respondents, *Whole Woman's Health,* 597 U.S. at 2.

53. Allan Parker, "Supreme Court Strikes Out 3 Times," email communication sent to Justice Foundation subscribers, June 27, 2016.

54. Michael J. New, "Analyzing the Effect of Anti-Abortion U.S. State Legislation in the Post-Casey Era," *State Politics & Policy Quarterly* 11, no. 1 (March 1, 2011): 28–47.

55. Donald T. Critchlow, *The Conservative Ascendancy: How the GOP Right Made Political History* (Cambridge, MA: Harvard University Press, 2007), 1.

56. Critchlow, *The Conservative Ascendancy,* 131.

57. Critchlow, 132.

58. Critchlow.

59. Theda Skocpol, *The Tea Party and the Remaking of Republican Conservatism* (Oxford: Oxford University Press, 2012), 34–35.

60. Joseph Borelli, "Beyond Enthusiasm, the 'Resistance' of 2018 Is Not the Tea Party of 2010," TheHill, July 8, 2018, thehill.com/opinion/campaign/395522-beyond-enthusiasm-the-resistance-of-2018-is-not-the-tea-party-of-2010.

61. Tom Cohen, "5 Years Later, Here's How the Tea Party Changed Politics," CNNPolitics, February 28, 2014, www.cnn.com/2014/02/27/politics/tea-party-greatest-hits/index.html.

62. "State Partisan Composition," National Conference of State Legislatures, 2017, www.ncsl.org/research/about-state-legislatures/partisan-composition.aspx.

63. Alan Abramowitz, "Partisan Polarization and the Rise of the Tea Party Movement," SSRN Scholarly Paper (Rochester, NY: Social Science Research Network, 2011).

64. American National Election Studies, *User Guide and Codebook for the ANES 2012 Time Series Study* (The University of Michigan and Stanford University, May 28, 2015), 505, www.electionstudies.org/wp-content/uploads/2012/02/anes_timeseries_2012_userguidecodebook.pdf.

65. Leigh A. Bradberry and Gary C. Jacobson, "The Tea Party and the 2012 Presidential Election," *Electoral Studies* 40 (December 1, 2015): 500–508, https://doi.org/10.1016/j.electstud.2014.09.006.

66. Bradberry and Jacobson, "The Tea Party and the 2012 Presidential Election."

67. Elizabeth Nash et al., "Policy Trends in the States, 2017," *Guttmacher Policy Review*, January 2018, www.guttmacher.org/article/2018/01/policy-trends-states-2017.

68. Anne L. Schneider, Helen M. Ingram, and Peter DeLeon, "Democratic Policy Design: Social Construction of Target Populations," in *Theories of the Policy Process*, ed. Paul Sabatier and Christopher Weible (Emeryville, CA: Avalon Publishing, 2014), 108.

69. Anne L. Schneider and Helen M. Ingram, *Deserving and Entitled: Social Constructions and Public Policy*, SUNY Series in Public Policy (Albany, NY: State University of New York, 2005); Anne Schneider and Mara Sidney, "What Is Next for Policy Design and Social Construction Theory?," *Policy Studies Journal* 37, no. 1 (February 1, 2009): 103–19.

70. Judith Butler, *Gender Trouble: Feminism and the Subversion of Identity*, Thinking Gender (New York: Routledge, 1990); Candace West

and Don H. Zimmerman, "Doing Gender," *Gender and Society* 1, no. 2 (1987): 125–51; bell hooks, *Feminist Theory from Margin to Center* (Boston, MA: South End Press, 1984).

71. Bree Kessler, "Recruiting Wombs: Surrogates as the New Security Moms," *Women's Studies Quarterly* 37, no. 1/2 (2009): 167–82.

72. Kessler, "Recruiting Wombs"; Dorothy E. Roberts, *Killing the Black Body: Race, Reproduction, and the Meaning of Liberty,* 1st ed. (New York: Pantheon Books, 1997).

73. Roberts, *Killing the Black Body.*

74. Rickie Solinger, *Reproductive Politics: What Everyone Needs to Know* (New York: Oxford University Press, 2013); Rickie Solinger, *Abortion Wars: A Half Century of Struggle, 1950–2000* (Berkeley: University of California Press, 1998); Roberts, *Killing the Black Body.*

75. Barbara Gurr, "Mothering in the Borderlands: Policing Native American Women's Reproductive Healthcare," *International Journal of Sociology of the Family* 37, no. 1 (2011): 71.

76. Gurr, "Mothering in the Borderlands," 71.

77. Gurr, 71.

78. Americans United for Life, *Defending Life 2018,* 2018, www.aul .org/wp-content/uploads/2018/01/Defending-Life-2018.pdf.

79. Americans United for Life, *Defending Life 2017,* 2017, 1, www.aul .org/wp-content/uploads/2017/03/AULDefendingLife2017Overview.pdf.

80. Americans United for Life, *Defending Life 2018,* 18.

81. Americans United for Life, *Defending Life 2017,* 1.

82. Reardon, *Making Abortion Rare,* 5.

83. Americans United for Life, *Defending Life 2018,* 18.

84. Americans United for Life, 9.

85. Americans United for Life, 7.

86. Americans United for Life, 359; Americans United for Life, "Fetal Pain Legislation: Women Deserve to Know," 2018, www.aul.org/blog/fetal -pain-legislation-women-deserve-to-know.

87. Americans United for Life, *Defending Life 2018,* 20.

88. Americans United for Life, 9.

89. Americans United for Life, 13.

90. Americans United for Life, 9.

91. Americans United for Life, *Unsafe: America's Abortion Clinics Endangers Women,* Unsafe Report, 2016, 7, www.unsafereport.org.

92. Americans United for Life, *Unsafe,* 108.

93. Americans United for Life, "Fetal Pain Legislation," 359.

94. Americans United for Life, *Defending Life 2018,* 301.

95. Americans United for Life, 358–59.

96. Schneider and Ingram, *Deserving and Entitled.*

97. Hsiu-Fang Hsieh and Sarah E. Shannon, "Three Approaches to Qualitative Content Analysis," *Qualitative Health Research* 15, no. 9 (November 1, 2005): 1277–88.

98. Klaus Krippendorff, "Content Analysis," *International Encyclopedia of Communication,* January 1, 1989, 403–07; Hsieh and Shannon, "Three Approaches to Qualitative Content Analysis."

99. Dan Newberry et al., "An Act Relating to Abortion; Creating the Heartbeat Informed Consent Act; Providing Short Title; Providing Legislative Findings; Defining Terms; Requiring Certain Compliance; Requiring Certain Providers to Make the Embryonic or Fetal Heartbeat Audible in Certain Circumstances; Providing for Exceptions; Prohibiting Certain Interpretation; Requiring Certification; Providing for Penalties; Permitting Certain Actions; Permitting Certain Causes of Action for Injunctive Relief; Directing Payment of Attorney Fees in Certain Circumstances; Prohibiting the Assessment of Certain Damages and Attorney Fees; Providing for Certain Anonymity; Specifying Construction of Act; Providing for Severability; Providing for Codification; Providing for Noncodification; and Providing an Effective Date," Pub. L. No. 1274 (2012), legiscan.com/OK/drafts/SB1274 /2012.

100. Newberry et al., 2.

101. Americans United for Life, *Defending Life 2018,* 7.

102. Newberry et al., "An Act Relating to Abortion," 2.

103. Storer, *Why Not?,* 70.

104. Americans United for Life, *Defending Life 2018,* 2.

105. Newberry et al., An Act Relating to Abortion," 2–3.

106. Newberry et al., 5.

107. "An Act to Amend the Indiana Code Concerning Health," Pub. L. No. 329, 1 113 829 (2015), 837, http://iga.in.gov/legislative/laws/acts /#document-2015.

108. "An Act to Amend the Indiana Code Concerning Health," 837.

109. South Dakota Task Force to Study Abortion, *Report of the South Dakota Task Force to Study Abortion,* 37–38.

110. Lance Kinzer et al., "An Act Concerning Abortion; Regarding Certain Prohibitions on Late-term and Partial Birth Abortion; Amending K.S.A. 65-445, 65-6701, 65-6703, 65-6705 and 65-6721 and K.S.A.

2010 Supp. 65-6709 and 65-6710 and Repealing the Existing Sections; Also Repealing K.S.A. 65-6713," Pub. L. No. 2035 (2011), kslegislature.org/li _2012/b2011_12/measures/documents/hb2035_enrolled.pdf.

111. Kinzer et al., "An Act Concerning Abortion," 18–19.

112. Kinzer et al., 16.

113. South Dakota Task Force to Study Abortion, *Report of the South Dakota Task Force to Study Abortion,* 38.

114. South Dakota Task Force to Study Abortion, 56.

115. Americans United for Life, *Defending Life 2018,* 19–358.

116. Carl Wimmer and J. Stuart Adams, "Abortion Clinic Licensing," Pub. L. No. 171 (2011), le.utah.gov/~2011/bills/hbillenr/HB0171.pdf.

117. Wimmer and Adams, "Abortion Clinic Licensing," 22.

118. "State Facts about Abortion: South Dakota," Guttmacher Institute, May 2018, 21, www.guttmacher.org/fact-sheet/state-facts-about-abortion -south-dakota.

119. South Dakota Task Force to Study Abortion, *Report of the South Dakota Task Force to Study Abortion,* 56.

120. Americans United for Life, *Defending Life 2018,* 359.

121. Frank Hoffman, "Provides for the Forced Abortion Prevention Sign and Woman's Right to Know Law," Pub. L. No. 586 (2011), legiscan .com/LA/text/HB586/2011.

122. Hoffman, "Provides for the Forced Abortion Prevention Sign and Woman's Right to Know Law," 2.

123. Hoffman.

124. "Life Defense Act of 2012," Pub. L. No. 3808, 1008 (2012), legiscan .com/TN/bill/HB3808/2011.

125. Sofia Resnick, "Health Experts Challenge 'Coerced-Abortion' Laws," *Rewire,* August 30, 2012, rewire.news/article/2012/08/30/health -experts-challenge-coerced-abortion-laws/.

126. Americans United for Life, *Defending Life 2018.*

127. Bette Grande et al., "An Act to Create and Enact a New Section to Chapter 14-02.1 of the North Dakota Century Code, Relating to the Prohibition on Abortions for Sex Selection or Genetic Abnormalities; to Amend and Reenact Section 14-02.1-02 of the North Dakota Century Code, Relating to Definitions; and to Provide a Penalty," Pub. L. No. 1305 (2013), legiscan.com/ND/text/1305/2013.

128. Grande et al., 1.

129. Schneider and Ingram, *Deserving and Entitled.*

130. Kathryn Conrad, "Surveillance, Gender, and the Virtual Body in the Information Age," *Surveillance & Society* 6 (2009): 380–87.

131. South Dakota Task Force to Study Abortion, *Report of the South Dakota Task Force to Study Abortion,* 40.

132. Jody Lyneé Madeira, "Aborted Emotions: Regret, Relationality, and Regulation," *Michigan Journal of Gender & Law; Ann Arbor* 21, no. 1 (2014): 1–66; Tracy A. Weitz et al., "You Say 'Regret' and I Say 'Relief': A Need to Break the Polemic about Abortion," *Contraception* 78, no. 2 (August 2008): 87–89.

133. Madeira, "Aborted Emotions," 11.

134. Weitz et al., "You Say 'Regret' and I Say 'Relief,'" 87.

135. Rachel Benson Gold and Elizabeth Nash, "Flouting the Facts: State Abortion Restrictions Flying in the Face of Science," *Guttmacher Policy Review* 20 (May 9, 2017), www.guttmacher.org/gpr/2017/05/flouting -facts-state-abortion-restrictions-flying-face-science; Caitlin E. Borgmann, "Judicial Evasion and Disingenuous Legislative Appeals to Science in the Abortion Controversy," *Journal of Law and Policy* 17, no. 1 (March 22, 2009): 15–56; Cynthia R. Daniels et al., "Informed or Misinformed Consent? Abortion Policy in the United States," *Journal of Health Politics, Policy and Law* 41, no. 2 (April 1, 2016): 181–209; "251 Anti-Abortion Restrictions Introduced in 37 States Based on Lies," National Partnership for Women and Families, 2016, www.liesintolaws.org/assets/docs/lies-memo-on-anti -abortion-restrictions.pdf.

136. Reardon, *Making Abortion Rare,* 11.

137. "After Abortion," Elliot Institute, 2018, www.afterabortion.org.

138. Chris Mooney, "Research and Destroy," *Washington Monthly,* October 1, 2004, 34, washingtonmonthly.com/2004/10/01/research-and -destroy.

139. "David C. Reardon, Biographical Sketch," Elliot Institute, 2018, afterabortion.org/1999/david-c-reardon-biographical-sketch.

140. Daniels et al., "Informed or Misinformed Consent?"; Julia R. Steinberg and Lawrence B. Finer, "Examining the Association of Abortion History and Current Mental Health: A Reanalysis of the National Comorbidity Survey Using a Common-Risk-Factors Model," *Social Science & Medicine* 72, no. 1 (January 1, 2011): 72–82; Trine Munk-Olsen et al., "Induced First-Trimester Abortion and Risk of Mental Disorder," *The New England Journal of Medicine* 364, no. 4 (January 27, 2011): 332–39; Corinne H. Rocca et al., "Decision Rightness and Emotional Responses to Abortion in the United States: A Longitudinal Study," *PLoS One* 10, no. 7

(July 2015); Sharon Cameron, "Induced Abortion and Psychological Sequelae," *Best Practice & Research Clinical Obstetrics & Gynaecology* 24, no. 5 (October 2010): 657–65; Ellie Lee, *Abortion, Motherhood, and Mental Health: Medicalizing Reproduction in the United States and Great Britain*; New York: Aldine de Gruyter, 2003).

141. Gail Erlick Robinson et al., "Is There an 'Abortion Trauma Syndrome'? Critiquing the Evidence," *Harvard Review of Psychiatry* 17, no. 4 (August 7, 2009): 268–90.

142. Brenda Major et al., "Abortion and Mental Health: Evaluating the Evidence," *American Psychologist* 64, no. 9 (December 2009): 875–80; Cameron, "Induced Abortion and Psychological Sequelae"; Susan A. Cohen, "Abortion and Mental Health: Myths and Realities," *Guttmacher Policy Review* 9, no. 3 (August 14, 2006): 1–9.

143. Priscilla K. Coleman, "Abortion and Mental Health: Quantitative Synthesis and Analysis of Research Published 1995–2009," *British Journal of Psychiatry* 199, no. 3 (2011): 770.

144. Julia R. Steinberg et al., "Fatal Flaws in a Recent Meta-Analysis on Abortion and Mental Health," *Contraception* 86, no. 5 (November 2012): 430–37; Steinberg and Finer, "Examining the Association of Abortion History and Current Mental Health."

145. Steinberg et al., "Fatal Flaws in a Recent Meta-Analysis on Abortion and Mental Health"; Tim Kendall et al., "To Meta-Analyse or Not to Meta-Analyse: Abortion, Birth and Mental Health," *British Journal of Psychiatry* 200, no. 1 (January 2012): 12–14; Toine Lagro-Janssen, Chris van Weel, and Sylvie Lo Fo Wong, "Abortion and Mental Health: Guidelines for Proper Scientific Conduct Ignored," *The British Journal of Psychiatry* 200, no. 1 (2012): 78.

146. Lagro-Janssen, van Weel, and Lo Fo Wong, "Abortion and Mental Health"; Steinberg et al., "Fatal Flaws in a Recent Meta-Analysis on Abortion and Mental Health."

147. Steinberg et al., "Fatal Flaws in a Recent Meta-Analysis on Abortion and Mental Health," 431.

148. "After Abortion," Elliot Institute.

149. Kathryn J. LaRoche and Angel Foster, "'I Kind of Feel like Sometimes I Am Shoving It under the Carpet': Documenting Women's Experiences with Post-Abortion Support in Ontario," *Facets*, (October 2017), 755.

150. Corinne H. Rocca et al., "Women's Emotions One Week after Receiving or Being Denied an Abortion in the United States," *Perspectives on Sexual and Reproductive Health* 45, no. 3 (September 1, 2013): 122.

151. Ardee Coolidge, "Researchers Uncover Hidden Risk Factor for Breast Cancer," Care Net, June 28, 2016, www.care-net.org/abundant-life -blog/researchers-uncover-a-hidden-cause-of-breast-cancer. Emphasis in original.

152. Jun Guo et al., "Association between Abortion and Breast Cancer: An Updated Systematic Review and Meta-Analysis Based on Prospective Studies," *Cancer Causes & Control* 26, no. 6 (June 2015): 811–19.

153. "BCPI Publications," Breast Cancer Prevention Institute, 2018, www.bcpinstitute.org/resources—publications.html.

154. Chinué Turner Richardson and Elizabeth Nash, "Misinformed Consent: The Medical Accuracy of State-Developed Abortion Counseling Materials," *Guttmacher Policy Review* 9, no. 4 (October 23, 2006): 8, www.guttmacher.org/gpr/2006/10/misinformed-consent-medical -accuracy-state-developed-abortion-counseling-materials.

155. "Reproductive History and Cancer Risk," National Cancer Institute, November 30, 2016, www.cancer.gov/about-cancer/causes-prevention/risk /hormones/reproductive-history-fact-sheet; Richardson and Nash, "Misinformed Consent."

156. "Reproductive History and Cancer Risk."

157. American College of Obstetricians and Gynecologists, "Induced Abortion and Breast Cancer Risk: ACOG Committee Opinion No. 434," The American College of Obstetricians and Gynecologists, June 2009, www.acog.org/Clinical-Guidance-and-Publications/Committee-Opinions /Committee-on-Gynecologic-Practice/Induced-Abortion-and-Breast -Cancer-Risk.

158. "Mandatory Counseling for Abortion," Guttmacher Institute, February 2018, www.guttmacher.org/evidence-you-can-use/mandatory-counseling -abortion.

159. Americans United for Life, *Defending Life 2018,* 34; "Medication Abortion," Guttmacher Institute, July 2018, www.guttmacher.org/evidence -you-can-use/medication-abortion.

160. Gold and Nash, "Flouting the Facts."

161. Americans United for Life, *Defending Life 2018,* 381; Gold and Nash, "Flouting the Facts"; "Medication Abortion."

162. Gold and Nash, "Flouting the Facts."

163. Americans United for Life, "Fetal Pain Legislation: Women Deserve to Know."

164. Americans United for Life, *Defending Life 2018,* 380.

165. Stuart W. G. Derbyshire, "Controversy: Can Fetuses Feel Pain?" *BMJ: British Medical Journal* 332, no. 7546 (2006): 909–12; Susan J. Lee

et al., "Fetal Pain: A Systematic Multidisciplinary Review of the Evidence," *JAMA* 294, no. 8 (August 24, 2005): 947–54; Ashley A. Wenger, "Fetal Pain Legislation," *Journal of Legal Medicine* 27, no. 4 (December 2006): 459–76; Richardson and Nash, "Misinformed Consent"; Pam Belluck, "Complex Science at Issue in Politics of Fetal Pain," *The New York Times,* September 16, 2013 (Health section), www.nytimes.com/2013/09/17 /health/complex-science-at-issue-in-politics-of-fetal-pain.html.

166. American College of Obstetricians and Gynecologists, "Facts Are Important: Fetal Pain," The American College of Obstetricians and Gynecologists, July 2013, www.acog.org/-/media/Departments/Government -Relations-and-Outreach/FactAreImportFetalPain.pdf?dmc=1&ts=2018 0715T2235193530.

167. Nash et al., "Policy Trends in the States, 2017."

168. Reardon, *Making Abortion Rare,* 4–5.

METHODS APPENDIX

1. Joseph Alex Maxwell, *Qualitative Research Design: An Interactive Approach,* 2nd ed., Applied Social Research Methods Series, v. 41 (Thousand Oaks, CA: Sage Publications, 2005).

2. Maxwell, *Qualitative Research Design.*

3. Maxwell; David R. Thomas, "A General Inductive Approach for Analyzing Qualitative Evaluation Data," *American Journal of Evaluation* 27, no. 2 (June 1, 2006): 237–46.

4. Maxwell, *Qualitative Research Design;* Thomas, "A General Inductive Approach for Analyzing Qualitative Evaluation Data."

5. Maxwell, *Qualitative Research Design.*

6. Joshua C. Wilson, *The New States of Abortion Politics* (Stanford, CA: Stanford Briefs, an imprint of Stanford University Press, 2016); Ziad W. Munson, *The Making of Pro-Life Activists: How Social Movement Mobilization Works* (Chicago, IL: University of Chicago Press, 2008).

7. Laura S. Hussey, "Political Action versus Personal Action: Understanding Social Movements' Pursuit of Change through Nongovernmental Channels," *American Politics Research* 42, no. 3 (May 1, 2014): 409–40; Ziad W. Munson, *Abortion Politics* (Social Movements Series [series]; Medford, MA: Polity, 2018); Kimberly Kelly, "In the Name of the Mother: Renegotiating Conservative Women's Authority in the Crisis Pregnancy Center Movement," *Signs: Journal of Women in Culture and Society* 38, no. 1 (September 1, 2012): 203–30.

8. Hsiu-Fang Hsieh and Sarah E. Shannon, "Three Approaches to Qualitative Content Analysis," *Qualitative Health Research* 15, no. 9 (November 1, 2005): 1277–88.

9. Hsieh and Shannon, "Three Approaches to Qualitative Content Analysis"; Klaus Krippendorff, "Content Analysis," in *International Encyclopedia of Communication*, ed. E. Barnouw et al., vol. 1 (New York: Oxford University Press, 1989), 403–7, repository.upenn.edu/asc _papers/226.

10. Krippendorff, "Content Analysis," 403.

Bibliography

CHAPTER ONE

Briggs, Laura. "The Race of Hysteria: 'Overcivilization' and the 'Savage' Woman in Late Nineteenth-Century Obstetrics and Gynecology." *American Quarterly* 52, no. 2 (2000).

Dyer, Frederick N., *The Physicians' Crusade against Abortion*. Sagamore Beach, MA: Science History Publications, 2005.

Luker, Kristin, *Abortion and the Politics of Motherhood*. Berkeley, CA: University of California Press, 1985.

CHAPTER TWO

Blanchard, Dallas A. *The Anti-Abortion Movement and the Rise of the Religious Right: From Polite to Fiery Protest*. Washington, DC: Twayne Publishers, 1994.

Doan, Alesha E. *Opposition and Intimidation: The Abortion Wars and Strategies of Political Harassment*. Ann Arbor, MI: University of Michigan Press, 2007.

Mason, Carol. *Killing for Life: The Apocalyptic Narrative of Pro-Life Politics*. Ithaca, NY: Cornell University Press, 2002.

Munson, Ziad W. *The Making of Pro-Life Activists*. Chicago, IL: University of Chicago Press, 2008.

Reagan, Leslie J. *Dangerous Pregnancies: Mothers, Disabilities, and Abortion in Modern America*. Los Angeles: University of California Press, 2010.

Risen, James, and Thomas, Judy L. *Wrath of Angels: The American Abortion War*. New York: Basic Books, 1998.

Steiner, Mark, *The Rhetoric of Operation Rescue*. New York: T & T International, 2006.

CHAPTER THREE

Denbow, Jennifer M. "Abortion as Genocide: Race, Agency, and Nation in Prenatal Nondiscrimination Bans." *Signs: Journal of Women in Culture and Society* 41, no. 3 (2016).

Doan, Alesha E. *Opposition and Intimidation: The Abortion Wars and Strategies of Political Harassment.* Ann Arbor, MI: University of Michigan Press, 2007.

Felicity, Interview with Alesha E. Doan, 2012 (audio).

Hussey, Laura S. "Political Action versus Personal Action: Understanding Social Movement's Pursuit of Change through Nongovernmental Channels." *American Politics Research* 42, no. 3 (2014).

Kelly, Kimberly. "In the Name of the Mother: Renegotiating Conservative Women's Authority in the Crisis Pregnancy Center Movement." *Signs* 38, no. 1 (2012).

Munson, Ziad. *Abortion Politics.* Medford, MA: Polity Press, 2018.

National Institute of Family and Life Advocates. "Medical Clinic Conversion." nifla.org/medical-clinic-conversion (accessed April 25, 2018).

CHAPTER FOUR

Calvert, Clay. "The Government Speech Doctrine in Walker's Wake: Early Rifts and Reverberations on Free Speech, Viewpoint Discrimination, and Offensive Expression." *William and Mary Bill of Rights Journal* 1239 25, no. 4 (2017).

Covert, Bryce. "The States that Siphon Welfare Money to Stop Abortion." *Think Progress,* 2016. thinkprogress.org/tanf-cpcs-ec002305dd18#.inu1bnlxj.

Doan, Alesha E. *Opposition and Intimidation: The Abortion Wars and Strategies of Political Harassment.* Ann Arbor, MI: University of Michigan Press, 2007.

Doan, Alesha E., and Jean C. Williams. *The Politics of Virginity: Abstinence in Sex Education.* Westport, CT: Praeger Press, 2008.

Saurette, Paul, and Kelly Gordon. *The Changing Voice of the Anti-Abortion Movement: The Rise of "Pro-Woman" Rhetoric in Canada and the United States.* Toronto: University of Toronto Press, 2015.

Stanley, Jenn. "'Pro-Life' Pence Transfers Money Intended for Vulnerable Households to Anti-Choice Crisis Pregnancy Centers." *Rewire,* July 21, 2016. rewire.news/article/2016/07/21/pro-life-pence-shifts-funding-needy-indiana-residents-anti-choice-crisis-pregnancy-centers/.

CHAPTER FIVE

Advancing New Standards in Reproductive Health. "Impact of State-Level Alcohol & Pregnancy Policy." *Issue Brief* (June 2018), www.ansirh .org/sites/default/files/publications/files/dapps_fact_sheet_final .pdf.

Americans United for Life (AUL). www.aul.org/about, accessed August 16, 2018.

Critchlow, Donald T. *The Conservative Ascendancy.* Lawrence, KS: University Press of Kansas, 2011.

Dailard, Cynthia, and Elizabeth Nash. "State Responses to Substance Abuse among Pregnant Women." *Guttmacher Policy Review* 3, no. 6 (2000), www.guttmacher.org/gpr/2000/12/state-responses-substance -abuse-among-pregnant-women.

Gold, Rachel Benson, and Elizabeth Nash. "Troubling Trend: More States Hostile to Abortion Rights as Middle Ground Shrinks." *Guttmacher Policy Review* Winter 15, no. 1 (2012).

Kolbert, Kathryn. "Texas Used Junk Science to Restrict Abortion." *SLATE,* 2015, slate.com/news-and-politics/2015/01/texas-abortion-restrict ions-experts-lied-about-research-and-vincent-rue.html.

Moore, Ann M. et al. "Male Reproductive Control of Women Who Have Experienced Intimate Partner Violence in the United States." *Social Science and Medicine* 70, no. 11, 1737–1744 (2010).

Nash, Elizabeth, and Rachel Benson Gold. "In Just the Last Four Years, States Have Enacted 231 Abortion Restrictions." *Guttmacher Institute News in Context,* 2015, www.guttmacher.org/article/2015/01 /just-last-four-years-states-have-enacted-231-abortion-restrictions.

Nash, Elizabeth, Rachel Benson Gold, Lizamarie Mohammed, Zohra Ansari-Thomas, and Olivia Cappello. "Policy Trends in the States, 2017." *Guttmacher Institute Policy Analysis,* 2018, www.guttmacher .org/article/2018/01/policy-trends-states-2017.

Planned Parenthood Federation of American. *Intimate Partner Violence and Reproductive Control.* Fact Sheet, 2012, www.plannedpar-enthood.org/files/3613/9611/7697/IPV_and_Reproductive_Coercion _Fact_Sheet_2012_FINAL.pdf.

Williamson, Vanessa, Theda Skocpol, and John Coggin. "The Tea Party and the Remaking of Republican Conservatism." *Perspectives on Politics* 9, no. 1 (2011).

Index

About the Authors

J. Shoshanna Ehrlich is a professor in the Women's, Gender, and Sexuality Studies Department at the University of Massachusetts Boston. She is the author of *Regulating Desire: From the Virtuous Maiden to the Purity Princess* (SUNY, 2014) and *Who Decides? The Abortion Rights of Teens* (Praeger, 2006), as well as a family law textbook for paralegal students. She is also the author of many law journal articles focusing on the regulation of women's and adolescents' sexuality and reproduction, including a recent article in the *Women's Law Journal* entitled "Turning Women into Girls: Abortion Regret and Decisional Incapacity."

Alesha E. Doan is an associate professor at the University of Kansas and holds a joint appointment in the School of Public Affairs & Administration and the Women, Gender & Sexuality Studies Department. Professor Doan's interdisciplinary research is guided by her broader interests in public policy, organizations, and gender/social equity, with a more specialized focus on the development, adoption, and implementation of reproductive policies. Her publications include articles in a variety of journals as well as two books: *Opposition and Intimidation: The Abortion Wars and Strategies of Political Harassment* (University of Michigan Press, 2007) and *The Politics of Virginity: Abstinence in Sex Education* (coauthored, Praeger, 2008).

DATE DUE